OBSESSION

The Bizarre Relationship
Between a Prominent
Harvard Psychiatrist
and Her Suicidal Patient

By GARY S. CHAFETZ AND
MORRIS E. CHAFETZ, M.D.

Crown Publishers, Inc.
New York

Published by Crown Publishers, Inc., 201 East 50th
Street, New York, New York, 10022.

CROWN is a trademark of Crown Publishers, Inc.

Manufactured in the United States of America

Library of Congress Cataloging-in-Publication
Data
Chafetz, Gary S.
    Obsession : the bizarre relationship between a
prominent Harvard psychiatrist and her suicidal
patient / Gary S. Chafetz and Morris E. Chafetz.—
1st ed.
        p. cm.
    1. Sex between psychotherapist and patient—
Case studies.
2. Psychotherapist and patient—Case studies. 3. Psychotherapists—Malpractice—Case
studies. 4. Bean-Bayog, Margaret. 5. Lozano,
Paul, 1962–1991. I. Chafetz, Morris E. II. Title.
RC489.S47C48 1994   93-42175
616.89′023—dc20   CIP
ISBN 0-517-59558-3

10 9 8 7 6 5 4 3 2 1
First Edition

DEDICATION

To the immediate members of our family (in order of their appearance): Marion, Marc, Adam, Andrea, Drew, Lynda, Maria, Benjamin, Deanne, Robin, Daniel, and Alexander.

EPIGRAPH

The most intense conflicts, if overcome, leave behind a sense of security and calm which is not easily disturbed . . . It is just these intense conflicts and their conflagrations which are needed in order to produce valuable and lasting results.

—Carl Jung

CONTENTS

CONTENTS

PREFACE

Numerous coincidences concerning the Paul Lozano/Margaret Bean-Bayog saga touch our lives. Let me note the obvious ones that operate here.

When Gary was 3-years-old, his mother, he, and I lived in Mexico City for a year. Instead of residing in an American enclave, we chose in our own youthful exuberance to live among Mexicans in a neighborhood, we understood, where no "gringo" had ever chosen to live before.

In short order, Gary spoke Mexican-Spanish as his first language and gave up conversing in English (except when he needed to give special instructions to his parents). Therefore, the innate identification with the Lozano family lives in the three of us, especially in Gary, since the age from birth to age five or six is so formative.

Several months after we left Mexico, in late 1952, I became a member of the Harvard Medical School community at the Massachusetts General Hospital where I remained for eighteen years. I was a psychiatrist in the Department of Psychiatry. In 1954, my professional association with alcoholism began. In 1970, I left the Harvard Medical School Department of Psychiatry and the alcoholism clinic I headed to become the founding director of the National Institute on Alcohol Abuse and Alcoholism in Washington. My coincidental connections to Margaret Bean-Bayog are: I am a psychiatrist, I worked for a long time in the Harvard medical community, and I have some history and prominence in the field of alcoholism.

I also worked closely with neurologists in Parkinsonism, epilepsy, and electro-encephalography so I have a coincidental connection to Paul McHugh, who served as the sole expert witness for the Massachusetts Board of Registration in Medicine.

I also, coincidentally, have experience with the legal profession serving from time to time as an expert witness.

Finally, by coincidence, Drew Meyer's family and our family lived in the same neighborhood, several blocks apart. Gary and Drew, who is two years younger than Gary, attended the same high school. Our families patronized the same neighborhood convenience store. But neither Gary nor Drew remembers the other.

My prefatory note would be unnecessary except for one fact: the book is written in the first person—as it should be. I acted as chief consultant, adviser, and devil's advocate. I also provided Gary with a road map of the Balkanlike wars in psychiatry. He tenaciously searched out and measured facts and evidence and interviewed most of the players and people who could provide alternative perspectives. For stylistic reasons, it also made sense for only one of us to write the manuscript and the other to review it. Gary did the former; I, the latter.

—Morris E. Chafetz, M.D.

ACKNOWLEDGMENTS

We want especially to thank our tireless research assistant D. Lopes, who made it possible for this book to be completed, more or less, on deadline. And very special thanks to Professor Albert Divver for his sage insights and contributions. We also want to thank members of our family who provided invaluable assistance, support, and advice: Marion Donovan Chafetz for her editorial assistance, attorney Marc Chafetz for his legal insights, Adam Chafetz for his computer assistance, and Deanne Chafetz for her love, support, and editorial assistance. El Paso public information officer, Sgt. William R. Pfeil, not only provided invaluable assistance but also showed us around town on both sides of the border. We also want to thank the staff of the Board of Registration in Medicine, especially Barbara Rose, who cheerfully put up with our many visits and requests. And sincere thanks go to Rhomey Moreland, Michael Blau's secretary, for responding graciously to our endless phone calls and requests. We want to thank attorney Jeff Baker for his kind assistance. In the field of forensic medicine, we are grateful to Dr. Stanton C. Kessler, associate chief medical examiner for Massachusetts, for his valuable assistance. We would like to thank private investigator James George for his kind assistance. We are grateful to Peggy Malougney, who transcribed most of the seemingly endless hours of taped interviews and shared with us her helpful insights. We thank Libby Cowles for her transcriptional assistance as well. We are very grateful to our agents Jill Kneerim and Art Horan, who got us started and held our collective hand on the bumpy road of writing a book on a controversial subject under a severe deadline. Also, we are grateful to the *Boston Globe* and to members of the staff for their invaluable assistance. Finally, we interviewed and consulted with many psychiatrists, including psychodynamically and biologically oriented ones. Even though some were willing to be acknowledged, others were fearful that the damage the Bean-Bayog/Lozano case has done to psychiatry might spread to them as well. We have decided to play it safe and omit the names of all of the many mental health professionals who assisted us. We are extremely grateful for their help.

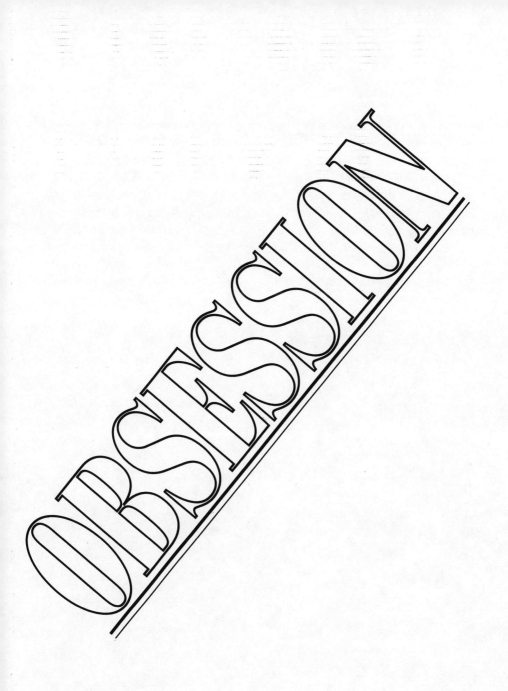

THE KEY PLAYERS

All ages at time of Paul Lozano's death

DR. MARGARET HARVEY BEAN-BAYOG, 47, Harvard psychiatrist, prominent expert in alcoholism, recovering alcoholic, accused of sexually abusing and causing the suicide of patient, Paul Lozano.

PAUL ANTHONY LOZANO, 28, promising, but suicidal Mexican-American Harvard Medical School student, Bean-Bayog's patient for four years, died from self-injected cocaine overdose on April 2, 1991, in El Paso, Texas.

MARIA DEL PILAR LOZANO WILLIAMS, 36, Paul's sister, administratrix of Paul's estate, nurse, articulate family spokeswoman.

THOMAS F. O'HARE, 46, Lozanos' first attorney, launched malpractice and wrongful death lawsuit against Bean-Bayog, married to psychiatrist also being sued.

ANDREW "DREW" C. MEYER, JR., 42, graduate C. W. Post College and Suffolk Law School, controversial personal injury lawyer, replaced O'Hare, filed 3,000-page document in court, igniting publicity in case.

WILLIAM BARRY GAULT, M.D., 52, Harvard-trained psychiatrist, son of prolific mystery writer, treated Paul Lozano with electric shock therapy, filed initial complaint against Bean-Bayog with state medical board, was last person to speak to Lozano.

AMY STROMSTEN, 48, social worker, acquainted with Paul Lozano and Bean-Bayog, crusaded on behalf of Lozano family to bring Bean-Bayog to justice for his death.

HARRISON "SKIP" G. POPE, M.D., 43, prominent Harvard psychiatrist, one of Lozano's psychopharmacologists, briefly Lozano's business partner, sold Meyer the estate in which Meyer currently resides.

MICHAEL L. BLAU, 35, Bean-Bayog's Harvard-educated personal attorney, son of a psychiatrist, hired to defend her medical license before state medical board and to assist in her defense in civil complaint brought by Lozano family.

JOHN G. FABIANO, 45, Harvard-educated lawyer, chairman of Hale and Dorr's litigation department, selected as unpaid special prosecutor by medical board to prove charges against Bean-Bayog.

PAUL R. MCHUGH, M.D., 59, Harvard-educated chairman of Johns Hopkins' department of psychiatry and behavioral sciences, distinguished biological psychiatrist, hired as Fabiano's sole expert witness.

EPIFANIA LOZANO, 70, Paul Lozano's mother, "sees things in dreams and visions," is alleged by Lozano to have sexually molested him, a charge he later recanted.

1

MARCH 26, 1992:
THE DAM BURSTS

I am a 44-year-old newspaper reporter who has two children, a girl and boy, both in diapers. My wife and I both work. We are often exhausted and rarely have time to watch the local news.

However, in the early evening of Thursday, March 26, 1992, I flicked on the TV. It was tuned to WCVB-TV5, just as an acquaintance of mine, reporter Jorge Quiroga, began a bizarre tale of sex, scandal, suicide, and psychiatry run amok.

The story was so mesmerizing I called in my wife, Deanne, to watch.

"Tonight our investigative unit," anchorwoman Natalie Jacobson began, "has a disturbing story about a Harvard Medical student who committed suicide and a Lexington psychiatrist who treated the young man before his death."

"The student's family today offered evidence," her co-anchor and husband Chet Curtis continued, "in a lawsuit against the psychiatrist, charging that she lured the young man into an active sexual relationship and used therapy that was totally unethical and inappropriate. I want to caution you that this story by Jorge Quiroga contains some very explicit material."

A photograph of a blond, smiling woman appeared on the screen. She was seated in a brown vinyl chair, playfully holding a small stuffed teddy bear, wearing a surgical mask and gown. Her demeanor seemed playful, not professional. Yet she was identified as a psychiatrist photographed by her patient during a therapy session.

"This photograph of psychiatrist Margaret Bean-Bayog,"

Quiroga said, "was taken by her patient, Paul Lozano." A photograph of a smiling, handsome young man wearing glasses appeared on camera. ". . . a Harvard Medical student, a young man who went to her for help." Quiroga continued narrating with footage of the Lozano family, dressed in their Sunday best, huddled on a couch in a middle-class home in El Paso, Texas, reviewing a scrap book of the many scholastic and athletic achievements of Paul Lozano. "That treatment, his family now claims, became so bizarre and so unorthodox . . ." The camera zoomed in on the face of Marcos Lozano, Lozano's father, and Pilar Williams, Lozano's sister. ". . . that it aggravated the anguish of his depression." A framed photo of Paul Lozano in jacket and tie appeared on camera. ". . . and eventually caused the 28-year-old Lozano to kill himself."

Williams, who was seated next to a framed photograph of her dead brother, said to the off-camera interviewer, "She's still functioning, she's still practicing medicine, she is still seeing patients, and my brother's dead."

The camera followed Williams retrieving letters from her mailbox outside her small ranch-style home and walking toward the front door. Quiroga said, "From her home in El Paso, Texas, Lozano's sister, Pilar, a nurse, relates an account of his years in Boston, where he came to study in a joint M.D./Ph.D. program, a disturbing story told by a brilliant and disturbed young man. He told his sister, another psychiatrist, and a lawyer that his four years of therapy included a sexual relationship." The close-up photo of the blond woman, presumably Dr. Bean-Bayog, holding the teddy bear in doctor garb reappeared on the TV screen. ". . . with Dr. Bean-Bayog."

Williams, back on camera, said, "[Paul] said that by the time they had their second session, [Bean-Bayog] was very seductive and very sexual, and she had sat in front of him with no panties on, and had masturbated herself."

I was stunned. A Harvard psychiatrist sexually abusing a patient? It seemed impossible.

Quiroga kept narrating as the cover page of the Plaintiff's Offer of Proof appeared on camera.

"The Lozanos today filed evidence to support their lawsuit against Dr. Bean-Bayog, charging that she coerced Paul into vivid sadomasochistic sexual fantasies and sexual conduct. The therapy, the lawsuit charges, had Lozano playing the role of a 3-year-old with Dr. Bean-Bayog playing the role of mother. This treatment is not standard medical practice. Most traditional psychiatrists shun the approach."

The camera returned to Williams. She spoke calmly but persuasively. "He had gone from a strong, independent young man to suddenly being unable to make the simplest of decisions."

The camera zeroed in on several children's books, including *Goodnight Moon, Owl At Home,* and *Just So Stories,* arranged on a table. "Before he died," Quiroga continued, "Paul showed his family dozens of children's books his therapist used in his sessions." Several other children's books, including *Where the Wild Things Are, A House is a House for Me, Sarah Plain and Tall,* appeared on screen. "The sessions were . . ." The camera focused on an index finger pushing the PLAY button of a cassette tape recorder. ". . . recorded, as she would read to him like a mother to a child."

As a woman's recorded voice was heard, the camera was filming over the shoulder of someone who had opened to the first page of *Goodnight Moon.* "Okay, is it on?," said a soft female voice, presumably that of Bean-Bayog, on cassette tape.

What was evidently Lozano's voice responded, "Yeah."

"OK, *Goodnight Moon,"* began the voice of Dr. Bean-Bayog. "In the great green room there is a telephone and a red balloon . . ."

Williams's voice broke in saying, "The children's books are Dr. Seuss books, *Velveteen Rabbit."* Williams appeared on camera. "I mean we're talking a large volume of children's books that were signed by her to him." The camera focused on a handwritten and clearly legible inscription: THIS ONE IS FOR THE BABY. LOVE DR. BEAN. ". . . to the 3-year-old, to my little boy," read Williams, shaking her head sadly. Some of these books, Williams would later tell me were the same ones Lozano used to teach himself to read when he was 3-years-old.

My wife and I then watched the carefully choreographed investigative report reach the first in a series of progressively explosive revelations.

Reporter Quiroga, a balding, round-faced, serious man, finally appeared on camera. He was holding several 3″ x 5″ cards. "Paul also showed his family flashcards in Dr. Bean-Bayog's handwriting. He was to study these in times of crisis or when she was out of town," he said. "On one side, a question Paul might ask. On the other, the doctor's answer. These too were recorded." Quiroga pushed the PLAY button on the tape recorder next to him. The same female voice was heard again. There was a small photo of Bean-Bayog superimposed in the upper right-hand corner of the screen over a blown-up photo of her handwritten flash card. "We'll do the flash cards again," the female voice said. "Do I love you? Yes, absolutely. Lots. I'm keeping you in my heart all the time I'm away and afterwards." Another flash card appeared on screen. "I think you're my mom." "Right, you are. I'm your mom and I love you and you love me very very much. Say that 10 times: You're my mom and I love you very very much."

"Say that 10 times: You're my mom . . ." I felt indignation beginning to boil within me. It was becoming clear that this female Harvard psychiatrist had essentially murdered an innocent, vulnerable working-class Mexican-American kid, who was gifted enough to escape from the barrio by gaining acceptance to one of the world's finest medical schools.

Quiroga's voice was dubbed over a shot of two children's books, *Goodnight Moon* and *Just So Stories,* "The stories, and the sex stopped . . ." The camera returned to a snapshot of Bean-Bayog seated in her office . . . "Bean-Bayog, they claim, ended this doctor-patient, mother-son, two-lovers relationship. Three months [actually, it was ten months] later, despondent . . ." A photo appeared on camera of a smiling, handsome Paul Lozano. ". . . Lozano killed himself, overdosing on cocaine."

The scene changed to Bean-Bayog's home in an affluent suburb, which boasts a circular drive, white columns reminiscent of a southern mansion, and a large swimming pool in the backyard. ". . . Dr. Margaret Bean-Bayog practices psychiatry at an office in her home in Lexington." The camera panned the quadrangle of the Harvard Medical School campus. ". . . She's an assistant professor at the Harvard Medical School and a recognized expert in the field of substance abuse." Quiroga was standing in front of the campus quadrangle. "The last psychiatrist to treat Paul says that the story Lozano told him about his years of therapy was unlike any he had heard before. It was so troubling he took the unusual step of filing a complaint with the Board of Registration in Medicine." A photo of the doctor's typed letter appeared on screen. "Newton psychiatrist William Barry Gault wrote that Dr. Bean-Bayog 'has done this patient great harm.' His opinion was based in part on Dr. Gault's belief that Dr. Bean-Bayog had seduced Paul into a sexual relationship." Another flash card appeared on camera, with Bean-Bayog's photo in the upper right-hand corner of the screen; the words are superimposed as they are read. "The family alleges that this flash card, written in Bean-Bayog's handwriting, confirms the claim. It read, 'I worry about you spending so much time with me. You're going to resent me.' And on the flip side: 'I love spending time with you. I'm going to miss so many things about you, the closeness, and the need, and the *phenomenal* sex, and being so appreciated.' "

Up to that point, I had retained a measure of a reporter's skepticism. Now, there was none. The only remaining doubt was that the flash card was a forgery.

Williams, on camera again, said, "The very warped part about this is that she speaks to him as if she is his mother. 'I am your ma, I love you, I am your mother, I am your mother.' And then at the same time is having a sexual relationship with him."

Quiroga continued to narrate over a photo of Bean-Bayog seated in her home office, "Dr. Bean-Bayog refused to talk to us about Paul Lozano." Then a puzzling and damning piece of evidence appeared on camera—a photo of Bean-Bayog's hand-written letter denying the allegations.

I wondered why she had submitted a handwritten denial. It seemed bizarre. If she were going to bother denying the irrefutable, why didn't she at least type it? Why didn't her lawyers respond on her behalf? My impression was that this woman was stupid, insane, or both.

"But she did send us a handwritten statement," continued Quiroga, "denying she 'had any sexual relations with Paul Lozano or that she exceeded the proper bounds of psychotherapy.' But if the case goes to trial, Dr. Bean-Bayog will undoubtedly be asked to explain these: fifty-five pages of lurid sexual fantasies, all in Dr. Bean-Bayog's own hand." Photos of several pages of lined notebook paper filled with her handwriting appeared.

"Paul told his family she read them to him in therapy: 'You tell me to take off all my clothes. I'm startled and ashamed but I begin to undress,' she writes. The fantasies depict graphic depictions of sex, bondage, and beatings."

There was no mistake about it. The handwriting in Bean-Bayog's letter of denial was identical to the handwriting of the phenomenal sex flash card and the sexual fantasies.

Williams, again on camera, said, "I think he felt very ashamed of himself. I know he did. He told me. He was very ashamed and very humiliated." Williams would later say that her brother felt obligated to sleep with Bean-Bayog because he was on scholarship and could not afford to pay for psychotherapy. Lozano's brother, Abel, would later tell investigators that Lozano told him that the psychotherapy—and a nearly $26,000 unpaid bill—was a "sham" to cover their sexual relationship. The family would also claim that Bean-Bayog terminated therapy with Lozano, whom she had reduced to the state of a dependent 3-year-old, because she was about to adopt a child of her own.

A photo of Lozano wearing glasses appeared, as Quiroga said, "Three months short of graduation, Lozano overdosed while working in a Texas hospital." Another framed photo of Lozano in jacket and tie appeared. ". . . [His] death, the family charges, is the result of sexual misconduct and malpractice Dr. Bean-Bayog must answer for."

Again, Williams was on camera, saying, "A promising career. He had everything in the world to live for. And he died at 28, broken."

Quiroga, now seated at the anchor desk next to Jacobson and Curtis, said, "The complaint against Dr. Bean-Bayog was filed with the Board of Registration in Medicine one year ago. As with all such cases, the board does not acknowledge the status of any of its investigations until the cases are formally closed. As for the Lozano lawsuit, a pretrial hearing is scheduled next week."

Jacobson, who seemed visibly indignant, asked, "I gather that the family didn't know very much about, if anything, about the so-called therapy during these four years."

Quiroga replied, "The family says that by the time that they were well aware of their brother's troubles with depression and suicidal thoughts that he was well into his therapy with Dr. Bean-Bayog. And he was unwilling—very, very reticent—to talk about her at all and their relationship. And then they say, they charge, that they tried to reach her and call her, and she also apparently refused to tell the family about Paul or the therapy."

"So when did he talk with his sister?" asked Jacobson.

"He talked with his sister, and made the confession, as it were, in his last hospitalization [actually, his second to last hospitalization]. He had been hospitalized five times under Dr. Bean-Bayog's care. Apparently, there is documentation in the filing that some of the doctors who had also treated Paul Lozano for his depression had expressed concern and documented that concern of, and I quote, 'overinvolvement.' And Dr. Bean-Bayog was aware of that concern. And obviously the question, the critical question in this case is whether or not the warning was heeded. But he reluctantly told his sister, she says, and the last psychiatrist about the alleged relationship and the intimacy of the relationship in his last hospitalization. And then they say he somewhat got better and he went down to Texas, he was in his last turn of working in a hospital, shortly before . . ." Quiroga stumbled.

Jacobson finished the sentence, ". . . when he committed suicide and the hearing's next week."

Quiroga had scored a remarkable coup. I felt a reporter's envy.

One thing that struck my wife and me were the photographs of Paul Lozano. He seemed so young, innocent, and vulnerable.

I flicked off the TV, called the city desk, and asked for Bill Doherty, the night editor at the *Boston Globe*[1] where I work as

---

1. THE *GLOBE* WAS PURCHASED BY THE *NEW YORK TIMES* IN 1993.

a freelance reporter. In addition to dredging up scandal, I also cover the city of Cambridge. Harvard University is headquartered in Cambridge, though the medical school campus is located in Boston. Technically, I could argue that this was a Cambridge story and I should cover it. However, I was worried that the *Globe* would not run the story at all, simply because a competitor broke it first.

When Doherty came to the phone, he said he had already assigned it to a reporter. We agreed that this was a terrific "man bites dog" story (because it is invariably male therapists who are accused of seducing female patients) with an unusually rich blend of themes: a deranged shrink, an endearing but troubled victim, Oedipal sex, adultery, suicide, sadomasochism, an older WASP seducing her much younger minority male patient. We figured the story would run for several days at the most. The psychiatrist's license would be quickly revoked, her medical malpractice insurer would settle out-of-court with the grief-stricken family, and Bean-Bayog and her odd, alliterative name would disappear from the news.

The paper's deadline was looming. This would not be an easy story for any reporter to cover in an hour or two. The Lozanos—a common Hispanic name—lived in El Paso and their phone might not be listed. Bean-Bayog would refuse comment. The lawyers involved, as well as the appropriate state officials, would be difficult to reach because by now they had all gone home.

I told Doherty that I knew Quiroga and WCVB-TV5's news director, Emily Rooney.[2] I'd call them and pass along whatever they shared with me.

I reached Rooney at home and congratulated her on her coup.

She called it "a story of a lifetime" but told me it was not an exclusive. WBZ-TV4, a local competitor, had run the story too. Rooney shared some details that had not been aired. The Lozano family claimed that Bean-Bayog had given her explicit sexual fantasies to Lozano, and they had discussed and acted them out

---

2. THE DAUGHTER OF ANDY ROONEY, SHE BECAME THE EXECUTIVE DIRECTOR OF ABC'S "WORLD NEWS TONIGHT," BUT LEFT IN EARLY 1994.

in therapy. However, Bean-Bayog's lawyer, Michael L. Blau, had confided privately to Rooney that Lozano had, in fact, broken into Bean-Bayog's office and stolen the fantasies.

Also, Rooney revealed that Quiroga had had the story since last November (1991), but had promised Andrew "Drew" Meyer, the lawyer representing the Lozano family, not to run it until Meyer filed the documents in open court. So it was a story that had been prepared and fine-tuned well in advance. But Rooney was vexed when she learned that Meyer had not kept his end of the bargain. He had also tipped Channel 4.

Meyer later told me that Joe Bergantino, the investigative reporter for WBZ-TV4, had "gotten wind" of the story and approached him. What could he do?[3]

Another allegedly broken bargain involved Dr. William Barry Gault, the psychiatrist who had triggered both the civil lawsuit and the action by the medical board against Bean-Bayog. Both TV stations had promised not to mention his name. Nevertheless, despite a last-minute protesting phone call from Williams in El Paso to Rooney, Gault's name was used on the air by WCVB-TV5. Rooney had been led to believe that Gault's name would not become a matter of public record. When it was included in the Plaintiff's Offer of Proof, she felt it could not be omitted.[4]

I called Quiroga at home, then passed what I had learned to the *Globe*.

Both Rooney and Quiroga were dismayed that the state medical board, which had received the initial complaint against Bean-Bayog four months *before* Paul Lozano committed suicide on April 2, 1991, still had not revoked this woman's medical license nearly a year *after* his death. In fact, the board apparently had no immediate plans to take any disciplinary action against her at all until forced to by the pressure from the media. It appeared that the board had no stomach to act against a well-to-do, well-

---

3. ROONEY'S TOP ASSISTANT, CANDY ALTMAN, IS MARRIED TO BERGANTINO. IN THE MEANTIME, ALTMAN HAS SINCE REPLACED ROONEY AS THE STATION'S NEWS DIRECTOR.

4. PILAR BITTERLY RECALLED THIS ''BROKEN PROMISE'' NEARLY A YEAR LATER WHEN I MET WITH HER.

connected Harvard psychiatrist on behalf of a mentally ill Mexican-American student from El Paso. We were all disgusted with the incompetence and, perhaps, cowardice of the board.

I went to bed wondering how Bean-Bayog and her husband had felt watching the local news that evening. Did they tape it? Did friends call to console them? Would they be able to sleep at all?

"We didn't watch," Bean-Bayog later told me. "I've never watched any of it since this nightmare began."

2
MARCH 27, 1992

THERAPIST ACCUSED IN PATIENT'S SUICIDE, ran the story's headline
on page seventeen of the March 27 edition of the *Boston Globe*.

Although the *Globe*'s reporter had referred to Bean-Bayog as
a psychologist, not psychiatrist,[1] she had managed to interview
Lozano's sister, Pilar, in El Paso and compose a hundred-line
story under severe deadline duress:

> The behavior of a Lexington psychologist who
> tried to convince a patient that he was her child
> and then engaged in sex with him, led to the
> Harvard Medical School student's suicide, ac-
> cording to allegations filed in Middlesex Supe-
> rior Court in Cambridge yesterday.

The *Boston Herald*[2] ran a similar story on page five: FAMILY
SAYS HARVARD DOC SEX ABUSE KILLS SON:

> A Lexington psychiatrist allegedly had sex with
> a Harvard Medical School student she was
> treating for depression, forced him to regress
> and call her 'Mommy,' gave him sadomaso-
> chistic pornography and eventually drove him
> to suicide, according to court papers filed yes-
> terday.

But in the news business, a reporter moves quickly to the next
crisis, and I was no exception. My tangential involvement with

---

1. A CORRECTION RAN THE NEXT DAY.
2. THE *HERALD* IS OWNED BY AUSTRALIAN MEDIA MOGUL RUPERT MURDOCH.

the story was over, regardless of the public's subsequent interest. If additional stories were to be written, the task would probably fall to a health-and-science reporter. What's more, I was saddled with too much work. I was pursuing an investigation of a Cambridge city councilor suspected of massive bank fraud in a real estate scheme involving thousands of condo conversions. It had me crisscrossing the state copying unit deeds and mortgages. Meanwhile, I had to churn out the usual topical stuff: puff pieces, features, fires, crime reports, protest marches and candlelight vigils, political squabbles, and news briefs.

At 1 P.M. I was at home working the phones on a rent-control story. I had promised to deliver it later that day to my immediate editor, Joanne Ball, when the phone rang. It was Ellen Clegg, the *Globe*'s city editor. Clegg told me to drop what I was doing, hurry over to the Middlesex Superior Courthouse, and review all the documents attached to the lawsuit.

"What lawsuit?" I asked.

"You know, the one you helped out on last night, the Beanbag [sic] one."

I asked where Patty Nealon was, the reporter specifically assigned to the Middlesex Superior Court.

"She's working on something else."

"Is there anything in particular you want me to look out for?"

"Just extract the nuggets. You're a public records sleuth. Use your judgment. Ship it in by five. Gotta go."

I figured I had about four hours to cull and glean about fifty pages of legalese, so, armed with a laptop computer, I jumped into my car and sped to the courthouse in East Cambridge. To my surprise, I found the place filled with reporters from local and national periodicals, jostling one another for the Plaintiff's Offer of Proof.

I realized immediately how enormous my task was. The Plaintiff's Offer of Proof was encyclopedic. It was divided into three volumes, about 3,000 pages in all. Meyer had filed only one copy. Other reporters were reading the volumes. Eventually when my turn came, I would have a couple of hours to read, digest, judge, type, and transmit key excerpts to the *Globe*.

I also realized that the actual lawsuit, called the complaint, had not been filed yesterday but last September by the Lozano's first attorney, Thomas F. O'Hare. What's more, in the original complaint there was no mention of sex or suicide.

An Offer of Proof in Massachusetts is a threshold that a civil suit against a physician must pass before it can go to trial. The civil suit was a totally discrete legal action from the administrative complaint before the medical board. In the former, the plaintiff must submit to a medical claims tribunal a summary of the evidence, twenty to fifty pages long, including portions of the medical records and the statement of an expert witness. The tribunal, which consists of an independently selected lawyer, doctor, and judge, reviews the evidence and weeds out frivolous cases. About 60 percent of the time, the tribunal votes to allow the plaintiff to proceed to trial. If not, there is no trial unless the plaintiff posts a $6,000 bond to defray the defendant's legal costs. If the plaintiff loses at trial, the bond is forfeited to the defendant.

The tribunal in the Lozano suit was scheduled for April 2, 1992. The actual trial, assuming the case got that far, had been scheduled for the summer of 1994, two-and-a-half years away. The action before the medical board would be heard much sooner.

Meyer's 3,000-page Offer of Proof, which included the records of Lozano's numerous hospitalizations, angered the judge, because of its exceptional length, believed to be the longest ever filed in Massachusetts. Meyer could have submitted only fifty carefully selected pages. Clearly, he was using the sensational evidence in the civil suit to arouse public outrage through the media and, in turn, force the medical board to take administrative action against Bean-Bayog. If the medical board revoked her license, it might, in turn, force a settlement in the civil suit.

I picked up volume one. It contained Bean-Bayog's contemporaneous and often shorthand notes, hurriedly jotted down during or immediately after the psychotherapy sessions. They are officially called the Process Notes.

The chronological notes began with two consultations in September 1984. In July 1986, Lozano returned and began psychotherapy with Bean-Bayog, which continued without interruption until June 1990 when she ended his sessions.

I needed to review the basic facts of the case, which I still did not fully grasp. Volume one had a table of contents, describing the items contained in the other volumes. These included, "[the] flashcards . . . used in conjunction with therapy;" "children's books and . . . stories authored by Dr. Bean-Bayog . . . as part of therapy;" letters and cards from doctor to patient and from patient to doctor; "articles on sadomasochistic sexual torture, incest, sexual abuse of children . . . discussed . . . during therapy;" "sexual fantasies authored by Margaret Bean-Bayog, M.D. read and discussed . . . during therapy;" the complete records of Lozano's twelve hospitalizations; Lozano's death certificate and autopsy report; the affidavit of Lozano's sister, Pilar Williams; and expert testimony from Drs. William Barry Gault and Larry H. Strasburger on the quality of Bean-Bayog's care.

In volume one, I discovered the introduction to the Offer of Proof, written and signed by Andrew C. Meyer, Jr., the Lozano's attorney. It was exactly what I was looking for, an impressive thirty-page summary of the case against Bean-Bayog.

Meyer wrote that the lawsuit sought to recover damages for an unspecified sum.[3] The damages consisted of personal injuries, conscious pain and suffering, and the wrongful death of Paul Lozano because of negligent, unacceptable and unethical medical care and treatment by his psychiatrist, Margaret H. Bean-Bayog.

More specifically, the suit claimed that when Lozano sought psychiatric help, Bean-Bayog:

> (M)anipulat(ed) him into a dangerous cycle of regression and transference wherein the patient was caused to become completely de-

---

3. THE REGULATIONS GOVERNING PERSONAL-INJURY LAW WERE CHANGED RECENTLY TO PREVENT A PLAINTIFF'S ATTORNEY FROM SUING FOR A SENSATIONAL SUM IN ORDER TO PREJUDICE THE JURY AND ATTRACT PRESS ATTENTION. THE AMOUNT IS DETERMINED BY THE JURY IF IT FINDS THE DEFENDANT LIABLE.

pendent, as a three year old child, on Dr.
Bean-Bayog as his mother, all the while simultaneously coercing him to participate in vivid
sadomasochistic sexual fantasies and sexual
conduct, thereby creating and encouraging
an inappropriate morbid emotional bond . . .
As a direct and proximate result of Dr. Bean-
Bayog's negligent and unacceptable care
and treatment, Paul Lozano was caused to
suffer severe mental anguish and emotional
trauma resulting in multiple suicide attempts,
extensive psychiatric hospitalizations, care and
treatment and ultimately, his tragic and premature death at the age of twenty eight.

Meyer had backed up his conclusions with more than ample
supporting facts and documents. He had clearly done his homework. In one example, Meyer stated, "Dr. Bean-Bayog employed an inappropriate course of treatment with Paul Lozano
that focused on regressing this young man to a little boy, three
years of age, all the while provoking him with intense sexual
stimulation and imagery." This was supported by sixty-three
individual page references to Bean-Bayog's own Process Notes!

In another instance, he wrote that,

The restraints Mr. Lozano was placed in during
this (hospital) admission would become the
subject matter for numerous discussions between Dr. Bean-Bayog and Paul Lozano during
therapy, centering around sadomasochistic
sexual fantasies involving bondage, rape, torture, degradation and humiliation.

This statement was supported by twenty-three separate citations from her notes.

Finally, he used eleven page references to support the assertion
that "there are numerous references to descriptive sexual fanta-

sies involving both Mr. Lozano and the defendant recorded throughout her notes."

Meyer also quoted directly from Bean-Bayog's Process Notes. For example:

> sexual feelings on both sides very much . . .

> clarified (the) reasons I can't touch him . . . clarified that while he's in hospital we could cool down what was happening with him and me.

> being pulled apart by her (Dr. Bean-Bayog) slowly—that the boy was clinging to her and she had no use for him . . . that she should have left him alone.

> only one of them (he or Dr. Bean-Bayog) could survive the relationship . . .

Finally, Meyer concluded:

> (Paul) sustained an irretrievable loss of dignity and selfworth, and an extreme impairment of his mental and emotional health and well-being. He was defiled, humiliated, debased and embarrassed. His ability to function as a well-adjusted human being was permanently and adversely affected. Paul Lozano's struggle to rationalize a dichotomy between the three-year-old boy and the twenty-seven-year-old man, his complete dependence on the defendant, perpetrated and encouraged during every aspect of the defendant's treatment, escalated to a point where Mr. Lozano could no longer bear life. On April 2, 1991, Paul Lozano took his life.

The evidence was abundant. Meyer had a rock-solid case, which undoubtedly would result in a multimillion-dollar judgment for his grieving clients. Quiroga had accurately reported the story.

When I finally got my hands on volume two, I went directly to the section called, "Sexual Fantasies authored by Margaret Bean-Bayog, M.D. read and discussed by her with Paul Lozano during therapy sessions." Quiroga had been permitted to quote only the mildest passages.

My eyes caught the following phrases:

> (P)ressing my clitoris into your mouth . . . kissing one of your balls, taking it into my mouth . . . I suck and suck. I love your penis, your erection. You plunge it in and out of my mouth.

I began randomly reading:

> I start stroking your balls. I am fascinated by them, exploring softly. I start kissing the inside of your legs and begin working my way up. I come up to your balls again. My head is between your legs, kissing and nibbling you. I start kissing one of your balls, taking it into my mouth, playing with it and then the other. I lick along the crack between your legs and your body. I come to the base of your penis, which is erect by now. I begin to trace over it with my fingers and mouth. I kiss the shaft, starting at the base up to the tip, working my way around it. I kiss the tip of it, working over it with my whole mouth, nibbling it, sucking lightly. The skin is velvet.
>
> When I started you were making a running commentary of editorial remarks but you have shut up, breathing fast and pushing into me. I am sucking harder now, tracing it with my

tongue, sometimes encircling it with my fingers and thumb, drawing my hand up and down. Then I cover my teeth with my lips and take your whole penis in my mouth, pressing down over the shaft and then back up, at first slowly, over and over, over and over. You are breathing hard and pushing yourself into my mouth. You'd love to get your hands free to press my head up and down. I want to swallow the whole thing . . . I move my breast against your cheek, and up to your mouth. You start sucking on it, and I start caressing your body. I discover one of your nipples, finger it, and, leaving my breast in your mouth, begin to kiss and suck it, toying with it with my tongue. I pull my breast away from you as I begin kissing my way down your chest and stomach, around your navel. My body moves along over yours as I work my way down, back to the insides of your thighs again, and then to your balls and penis, this time licking and sucking and nibbling lightly.

I kneel over you and bring my vagina down to you mouth. You kiss it hungrily. I move my clitoris into range and you go to work on it. I am still eating your penis . . . Finally, satisfied at the condition you have me in, you move next to me, rubbing your penis over the mouth of my vagina, and finally, coming into me. You begin thrusting hard. I am scared by the violence of it, but not long. You hold my hips for leverage and plunge into me over and over. I am in a frenzy, rocking under you, mad with pleasure and relief. I climax and climax. You keep on storming into me and finally exuberantly come yourself and collapse on top of me.

I turned to another page:

> I twist and haul on the restraints. You move your mouth over my pubic hair, nibbling, breathing hotly, and then begin seeking my clitoris with your tongue. Suddenly, you find it, and connect. I am flooded with intolerable, exquisite excitement and pleasure. I haul desperately against my bonds, pulling my legs in. They don't move at all. They don't budge. I stay widely open to you. You keep greedily licking and sucking, licking and sucking. You are out of your head yourself now. You massage my breasts and press on my pubis. I am completely out of adjectives to describe what you are producing inside of me. You reach your fingers inside my vagina and begin to press and stroke down along the front of it. You are still all over my clitoris. I alternately whimper and beg you to stop and pull on the restraints and whimper and shove myself into your mouth and beg you and beg you and beg you to fuck me.

Finally, I turned to the last page. Bean-Bayog wrote:

> You take off your pants and begin tantalizing me with your penis, touching my vagina and clitoris with it lightly, then bringing it near my mouth. I am wild for it, but you won't give it to me. At last, kneeling over me, you let me begin to suck on it, swallow it. It feels wonderful. I worship you. I suck and suck. I love your penis, your erection. You plunge it in and out of my mouth.
>
> Finally, you enter me, giving me a huge rush of pleasure and satisfaction. I never wanted anything so much in my life. You move inside me, deliciously, slowly. Every time I start to climax, you stop. Then, at last, not caring, you begin to move in and out fast, hard, hurling

yourself against me, harder and harder, until finally both of us explosively come and come and come.

I found the fantasies unarousing; they seemed tastelessly perverted. They were too well-written, I thought, carefully composed, rather than excited jottings. Anyone can have erotic fantasies. What troubled me is that these fantasies may have described sexual encounters between Bean-Bayog and Paul Lozano, doctor and patient. And they were found in her patient's possession!

I went on reading the encyclopedia of evidence that Meyer had cobbled together. I read through the discharge summaries of each of Lozano's twelve hospitalizations, ignoring the handwritten nurses' and physicians' notes.[4]

Lozano's first admission was from September 24 to November 19, 1986, at McLean Hospital, a private mental hospital in suburban Boston, affiliated with Harvard University. His in-house psychiatrist, Dr. Frances Frankenburg, wrote:

> We should note that Paul's depression was an extremely serious one with very lethal suicidal ideation. We are somewhat concerned that given Paul's extremely unsupportive family and the self-deprecating guilty nature of his depressions, that should depression occur again, without the immediate assistance of a psychiatrist, that this could have fatal consequences for him . . . Paul says that he has actually felt rather depressed for all of his life. He describes a childhood history of abuse by his older siblings, and perhaps by his parents, and two suicide attempts at the age of five and thirteen . . . Paul is the youngest of (six) children of immigrant Mex-

---

4. RECORDS OF LOZANO'S THIRTEENTH ADMISSION DID NOT BECOME AVAILABLE UNTIL THAT SEPTEMBER.

ican farmers . . . Apparently, his mother has been chronically and episodically extremely depressed . . . Paul did well at school and went to West Point. He hated West Point and dropped out, and felt that he was a failure to his family . . . he eventually went to the U of Texas where he dated another premedical student, Diane (Halperin).[5] His parents told him at that time that if he kept seeing her they would tell her medical school that she had once been hospitalized for depression. In anger, Paul retaliated two days later by marrying Diane. She, however, continued to be depressed and Paul felt increasingly guilty toward her and toward his family. He finally annulled the marriage to please his family and came to Harvard Medical School.

In his second McLean admission from May 3 to June 22, 1987, Frankenburg observed:

We should note that in a family meeting at least with us, Paul's mother and sister gave a slightly different version of Paul's childhood and described him as being a spoiled child whom every one adored . . . Prognosis: . . . extremely guarded. Given Mr. Lozano's previous history of suicide attempts and his ongoing preoccupation with suicide, and his drinking, suicide seems to be a very real option to him and he is impulsive enough, we feel, to be at risk for doing this. He also has a very poor support system in that he has only one friend in the Boston area, and has such a conflictual relationship with his family that he seems able only to feel burdensome expectations from them rather

5. HER NAME HAS BEEN CHANGED TO PROTECT PRIVACY.

than any thought of loving support which, at least to us, they professed to feel for him. As well, while (hospitalized) he repeatedly displayed such shame and misery about himself and conveyed, at times, an air of hopelessness about himself, that again, the possibility of suicide for him unfortunately seems a real one.

There was also an affidavit signed by his sister, Pilar Lozano Williams:

Prior to his death, my brother told me that during the course of psychotherapeutic treatment with Dr. Bean-Bayog and as part of this treatment, Dr. Bean-Bayog read her sexual fantasies to Paul, used sexually provocative language during treatment sessions, wore sexually provocative clothing, i.e. short skirts with no underwear during therapy sessions, masturbated in front of him in her office during therapy sessions, and engaged in sexual acts, including but not limited to intercourse with him.

Meyer had also found an expert witness, Dr. Larry H. Strasburger, M.D., who, like Bean-Bayog, is a graduate of and an assistant clinical professor of psychiatry at Harvard Medical School and of the same school of psychiatry as Bean-Bayog. Both are affiliated with the Boston Psychoanalytic Society and Institute. Strasburger stated that he had reviewed all of the documents available and:

Based on the information which I have reviewed, it is my opinion, to a reasonable degree of medical certainty, that Dr. Bean-Bayog employed . . . a deviant course of "therapy," erased appropriate boundaries of the psychotherapist-patient relationship and violated acceptable standards of psychiatric practice. In addition, Dr. Bean-Bayog acted in a sexually provocative manner with her patient, used sexually provocative language with him, read her sexual fantasies to him, masturbated in front of him, and engaged in sexual contact with him . . . contributed to his premature death on April 2, 1991.

The only inconsistency I noticed was Lozano's death certificate. It did not state his cause of death as suicide but as accidental cocaine intoxication. The autopsy reported:

innumerable needle marks are noted both antecubital fossae (the crooks of his elbows), both forearms and both hands, estimated to be approximately 75. They all appear fresh.

I could find r o reference to a suicide note, and I was puzzled by the death certificate. I quickly reexamined the original lawsuit, a copy of which was not included in the Offer of Proof, to see if suicide were mentioned at all. It was not.

As I electronically beamed 322 lines of excerpts to the *Globe* at 4:50 P.M., two things convinced me of Bean-Bayog's guilt. First, the allegations of her "overinvolvement" that had been noted and reported by Frankenburg, who was hardly a biased plaintiff's medical malpractice attorney, but a Harvard colleague of Bean-Bayog's. Second, the explicit fantasies about her patient found in his possession. This was the most troubling aspect of all. It seemed that Bean-Bayog had wantonly exploited a vulnerable young man while defiling the Hippocratic oath.

3

MARCH 28, 1992

With little time to prepare and less to reflect, the *Globe* ran the story that I reported and a colleague wrote based on the information available at the time:

> Four years before Harvard medical student Paul Lozano committed suicide, Harvard psychiatrists raised questions about the unusually intense, dependent relationship he had with his psychiatrist, Dr. Margaret Bean-Bayog . . .
>
> Bean-Bayog, 49, is charged in a wrongful death suit with seducing Lozano and reducing him to a childlike state of dependency—leaving him filled with feelings of shame and humiliation that led to severe depression and suicide last April 2 (1991) by a self-administered cocaine overdose.
>
> Cases of alleged seduction of a male psychotherapy patient by a female therapist are almost unheard of. But the Lozano case stands out for another reason: the voluminous evidence that is being used to support the Lozano family's allegations.
>
> Ordinarily, the difficulty in proving sexual and psychiatric abuse by therapists is precisely that there is no documentation. The truth is usually a matter of the therapist's word against the patient's. And by definition, such patients' credibility is open to question because they had psychiatric problems.

In the Lozano case, the issue is apparently what to make of the documents—the pages and pages of sexual fantasies, allegedly in Bean-Bayog's handwriting; the flash cards, again allegedly written by the psychiatrist, that illuminate the bizarre relationship she is said to have fostered with Lozano; the notes and letters with allusions to the sexual relationship between patient and doctor . . .

The *Herald* took a different tack:

The state board of medicine failed to act on a sexual and psychological manipulation complaint filed against a Harvard psychiatrist who has been charged in a lawsuit with leading a student to suicide, according to lawyers for the family.

In fact the first letters of complaint to the state Board of Registration in Medicine by two respected Wellesley physicians were apparently lost, and had to be resent.

Andrew Meyer, attorney for the student's family, charged that Dr. Margaret Bean-Bayog "regressed" former Harvard Medical School student Paul Lozano, 27, "into a 3-year-old and caused him to believe she was his mother." Bean-Bayog, who was married but had no children of her own, abruptly cut off the relationship in July 1990, claiming she no longer had time for Lozano because she was adopting a child.

Unable to cope with the end of their sexual and therapeutic relationship, Lozano committed suicide by injecting himself 75 times with cocaine on April 2, 1991, in his family's Texas home, Meyer said . . .

One social worker said yesterday Lozano said

the two had "kinky and weird" sex, but that he
was too embarrassed to talk about it.

Bean-Bayog, 48, of Lexington, called the
charges "outrageous and false" in a statement
yesterday. Much of the damning material,
which was in Lozano's possession at the time
of his death, was "stolen" from her files and
never intended for his eyes, her attorney, James
Barry, said.

The Lozano family vehemently denies Barry's
allegation . . .

Later that morning, March 28, I called my father in Washington, D.C., and asked if he knew or knew of Bean-Bayog. He had
been a professor of psychiatry at Harvard Medical School for
nearly twenty years but had departed for a high federal government position in 1970. He was also a noted pioneer in the treatment of alcoholism, Bean-Bayog's specialty. He did not know
her, had never met her, and had never heard of her.

I summarized the Bean-Bayog story. He said that the press
should proceed cautiously. The psychotherapeutic free-associa-
tive process involves the most volatile, primal, and unpredictable
ingredients of the human psyche, he told me. Anything is possible. Raw material ripped from context can be easily miscon-
strued, inadvertently or intentionally. The irrefutable may have
a plausible explanation.

However, he had not seen the "thank you for the phenomenal
sex" flash card. He had not read any of the troubling sadomasochistic sexual fantasies. He had not heard her taped voice, reading Lozano children's stories and reading the flash card, " 'I
think you're my mom?' 'Right, you are. I'm your mom and I love
you and you love me very very much. Say that 10 times. You're
my mom and I love you very very much."

Again, my minor role in this story seemed finished, and I went
back to my Cambridge beat.

Over the weekend, the *Globe* and the *Herald* ran stories about
the emergency hearing that the state medical board would hold

on Monday night.[1] Experts predicted the board would summarily suspend Bean-Bayog's license, pending a full-blown hearing before an administrative judge.

The local press had been harping on the board as one of the
worst in the nation based on the number of suspensions. Now,
charges were flying between Gloria C. Larson, the Secretary of
Consumer Affairs for Massachusetts, and Drew Meyer, the
Lozano's attorney. Larson bristled at Meyer's claim that the
board had taken too long to act on the complaints against Bean-
Bayog filed in mid-December 1990. She called the evidence startling, said that Meyer "could have fast-tracked an investigation
of this case had he provided earlier to the board all the information he holds." She did concede that the board, backlogged with
over a 1,000 pending complaints, was underfunded and under-
staffed, and called for more state funding for the medical board.
Meyer countered that Larson was trying to minimize the board's
blunders.

> **For (Larson) to claim she is startled by the evi-
> dence is absolutely an attempt to cover up the
> inadequacies of the board and her inadequa-
> cies in overseeing the board. There are doctors
> harming patients out there, and (Larson) is
> doing nothing.**

Meyer, claiming the board had had the evidence all along,
produced a "startling" document, which he faxed to the press. It

---

1. THE STATE MEDICAL BOARD, OFFICIALLY CALLED THE BOARD OF REGISTRATION IN
MEDICINE, PROTECTS THE PUBLIC FROM SUBSTANDARD PHYSICIAN CARE. IN RECENT
YEARS, THE BOARD HAS BEEN CRITICIZED FOR MOVING TOO SLOWLY ON COM-
PLAINTS AND BEING SOFT ON PHYSICIANS. THE PRESS REPORTED THAT IN 1990, THE
BOARD RANKED 49TH IN THE NATION IN DISCIPLINING ERRANT DOCTORS. IN 1991,
46TH. BUT THE STATISTICS ARE SOMEWHAT MISLEADING. DIFFERENT STATES HAVE DIF-
FERENT CRITERIA FOR DISCIPLINING PHYSICIANS. THE MEDICAL BOARD IN MASSA-
CHUSETTS NO LONGER SUSPENDS PHYSICIANS WHO HAVE BEEN SUSPENDED BY
OTHER STATES OR THOSE WITH CHEMICAL DEPENDENCIES IF TREATED AND MONI-
TORED. OTHER STATES INCLUDE THOSE TWO DISCIPLINARY CATEGORIES IN THEIR STA-
TISTICS, SKEWERING MEANINGFUL COMPARISONS.

was a handwritten memo confirming that the medical board had long had in its possession most of the "smoking gun" evidence: Bean-Bayog's Process Notes, the flash cards, her sexual fantasies, children's stories, and other material. The memo was signed by the board's chief investigative attorney, Margaret F. Holland, and dated March 8, 1991, a month *before* Lozano killed himself. After that, we didn't hear much from the Secretary of Consumer Affairs.

On Monday morning, March 30, as I was about to hurry to Cambridge City Hall to complete the rent-control story, the phone rang. It was Ben Bradlee, Jr., the *Globe*'s metro editor, and son of the former editor of the *Washington Post*. He ordered me back to the Middlesex Superior Courthouse, this time to photocopy the Offer of Proof.

"This yarn has legs," Bradlee said. He told me the *Globe* needed to study the documents more carefully.

So I spent the day tediously photocopying volumes two and three by hand at $.50 a page. I ignored the nearly indecipherable 987 pages of treatment notes. What was the point of copying a thousand pages of gibberish?

In the meantime, Michael Blau, Bean-Bayog's personal lawyer, met with her at noon in downtown Boston. The legal costs of the defense of her license before the medical board, a parallel but totally discrete action from the Lozano's civil lawsuit, were not covered by her malpractice insurance. Blau, who had not seen his client since June and had been notified of the hearing earlier that morning, pleaded for a delay so he could have time to prepare an adequate defense. The board denied his request. The defendant was essentially being given no time to prepare for a summary suspension of her license to practice medicine. The board, which had been criticized as slow and ineffective, was demonstrating it could be tough and expeditious. The emergency closed-door hearing would begin at 6 P.M. that evening. According to state law, the medical board is empowered to summarily suspend a medical license, pending a full hearing, if the physician is deemed to be "an immediate and serious threat to public health."

In anticipation of the board's decision that evening, a highly placed source in the medical board told the *Herald,* "I can't imagine that a vote (to suspend) would not be taken."

Bean-Bayog spent the afternoon obtaining affidavits from all of her current patients.

"Basically to try to maintain my license, I had to go to every single patient and ask them if they thought I treated them professionally and what I got was an extraordinary outpouring of people saying, 'We know you and this can't be true,' " she told me later. "The letters I got from my colleagues have all had two invariable sentences. One is, 'I'm terribly sorry this is happening to you,' and the other is 'If there is anything I can do to help, let me know.' None of them say, 'We know you.' I think they all were really frightened that I'm a potential abuser, something like that. There's been a terrible shunning that has taken place."

The closed-door hearing ended at 11 P.M. Aware that reporters were waiting downstairs, Bean-Bayog and her lawyers decided to linger in order to foil her appearance on the late night news. At 1 A.M., they finally rode the elevator down to the first floor.

A crowd of reporters surged forward. Squinting, Bean-Bayog looked bewildered as she plunged into a sea of bright lights that TV news people had set up in the narrow hallway. A journalist snaked her microphone close to the doctor's lips and shouted, "Margaret, how many other patients did you have sex with other than Lozano?"

Bean-Bayog ignored the assault and —shielded by two lawyers in front and Michael Blau behind—marched down a narrow hallway, out into an icy early morning rain, and into a waiting taxi.

She had, until this moment, an excellent reputation and unblemished career. No other complaint had ever been filed against her with the medical board and she had never been sued for malpractice. There weren't even any "rumors or rumors of rumors about her," said one of her colleagues. Another called her "an inspiring lecturer" who had "the highest reputation." The president of the Boston Psychoanalytic Society and Institute said, "This is a lady who is known for being completely ethical."

The director of the Massachusetts Commission on Compulsive Gambling described her as "a national figure in all areas of addiction study."

Apparently, Bean-Bayog had achieved national distinction in the treatment of alcoholics, and had pursued an ethically irreproachable, private practice for over fifteen years.

Now, her career was forever tainted.

The *Herald* reported that she stopped in the bathroom "and could be heard sobbing."

"That's simply not true," she told me later. "I stopped in the bathroom to comb my hair . . . I felt dissociated. It wasn't me walking past them, it was someone else. This was happening to someone else. Actually, I felt pretty good. Maybe a little tense, a little annoyed, but I knew I wasn't guilty and it would just be a matter of time before all of this went away once the truth came out."

Bean-Bayog left the board's emergency hearing savoring a victory: Though the board had issued a statement of allegations against her, her license to practice medicine had *not* been summarily suspended, she had not been accused of sexual misconduct, and she was being allowed to continue practicing under the supervision of another psychiatrist. According to regulations, the full hearing—essentially a trial—would not be conducted by the board itself but remanded to the State Division of Administrative Appeals. The hearing officer would be an administrative magistrate. The board, however, would act as the prosecutor. The expedited hearing was slated for July 20 before Judge Robert Tierney, who would weigh the evidence—presented by medical board prosecutor, Richard E. Waring, and by Bean-Bayog's defense attorney, Michael Blau—and render a recommendation. The unpaid seven-member medical board, consisting of five physicians and two members of the public, appointed by the governor for staggered three-year terms, would then vote to accept or reject Tierney's recommendation.

4

MARCH 30, 1992

Michael Blau, Bean-Bayog attorney, viewed the results of the March 30 emergency hearing as an unqualified victory.

"The last time I felt good was that night," he said to me a year later. "Things couldn't have gone better. It was exciting, exhilarating. We were faced with a monumental challenge to stare down a summary suspension hearing . . . purely on the basis of all this avalanche of horrible, adverse publicity. And we had stared it down. We had gotten through it. I was sitting on top of the world. It was the last time I felt unqualified enthusiasm."

Bean-Bayog had, indeed, weathered what most had predicted was an inevitable conclusion—summary suspension of her medical license. The board had been persuaded by Blau's arguments that raised doubts about Meyer's claims that Bean-Bayog had directly contributed to Lozano's death. Ten months had passed between Bean-Bayog's termination of Lozano's therapy and his death. During those ten months, Lozano had been subjected to nine shock treatments, hospitalized eight times, treated by many other psychiatrists, medicated with a cocktail of antidepressant drugs, and ultimately died two thousand miles from Boston on his parents' doorstep. In addition, Blau contended that sexual contact between doctor and patient could never be proven. Even the Lozano's first attorney, Tom O'Hare, tacitly (and later explicitly when I interviewed him) agreed. This is why O'Hare had not mentioned psychiatric sexual misconduct in the initial complaint. Blau also presented plausible explanations for the "phenomenal sex" flashcard and for the countertransference fantasies. What's more, he argued, the claims of the alleged victim, who was dead, could not be trusted because he was a pathological liar and severely mentally ill.

As a consequence, the board voted to issue a "statement of allegations" against Bean-Bayog but did not accuse her of sexual misconduct or causing Lozano's death, only of:

> substandard care . . . during the course of treatment . . . (she) wrote explicit fantasies which may have related to Paul Lozano. Her failure to terminate or otherwise address these fantasies did not conform to the standards of accepted medical practice.[1]

Blau and James Barry, Bean-Bayog's malpractice insurance attorney, advised her against speaking directly to the press, standard procedure. It was more prudent for her to speak through her lawyers, they felt, a decision that in hindsight proved controversial.

"In retrospect, I would have let her talk to the press right away," said Blau, "but only in knowing what she finally ended up doing. We had strategic reasons why we didn't want her stepping up to the cameras, but ultimately it was her decision. Frankly, it was not necessarily in her best interest to face the press at that time. We knew we had a very strong defense. We knew that defense rested in part upon the credibility of who she was and how she presented herself . . . We did not want to dissipate the full impact of that for the hearing. Also, a lot was not known about this case on March 30, 1992. And the last thing I want to do as an attorney is have a client going out there being asked questions about things which she doesn't yet know about."[2]

---

1. LATER, THE BOARD AMENDED THE CHARGES, SAYING BEAN-BAYOG "HARMED" HER PATIENT AND RESERVED THE RIGHT TO INTRODUCE EVIDENCE OF SEXUAL MISCONDUCT.
2. BLAU ALSO MENTIONED ANOTHER, MORE ARCANE, REASON, WHICH HE ESSENTIALLY DID NOT MENTION AGAIN AS THE CASE UNFOLDED. DOCTOR-PATIENT CONFIDENTIALITY SURVIVES A PATIENT'S DEATH, PASSING TO THE HEIRS. HOWEVER, WHEN THE PATIENT OR THE HEIRS FILE A LAWSUIT AGAINST THE TREATING PHYSICIAN, DOCTOR-PATIENT CONFIDENTIALITY FALLS AWAY. BUT, SOME LEGAL EXPERTS ARGUE, THE PHYSICIAN MAY ONLY DISCUSS THE PATIENT IN THE CONTEXT OF COURT DOCUMENTS OR TESTIMONY, NOT BEFORE THE PRESS. OTHERS DISAGREE, CLAIMING THAT ALL

There was also the fear that Bean-Bayog, a recovering alcoholic, would start drinking again and appear intoxicated in public. She took the precaution of putting herself on Antabuse. Her lawyers even forbade her from attending A.A. meetings because she might make a damaging revelation that would end up in an affidavit or deposition.

The day after the board voted a statement of allegations against her, Blau and Bean-Bayog crafted and released a response to the board's allegations, which contained explanations for the "mommy-baby" therapy, the sexual fantasies, and the now notorious "phenomenal sex" flash card.[3]

Bean-Bayog responded through her attorney:

> **Mr. Lozano was a severely mentally ill patient. He was chronically suicidal and reported to Dr. Bean-Bayog that he was a victim of horrendous childhood abuse. Mr. Lozano also disclosed to Dr. Bean-Bayog his problems with alcohol and drug abuse, his sociopathic symptoms, such as lying, stealing and cheating, and his overwhelming feelings of anxiety and rage. He harbored homicidal, violent and delusional thoughts; and he had periods when he was completely out of control. The patient was so severely mentally ill and difficult that many psychiatrists would not have even attempted to treat him.**

Conventional psychotherapy, which included drug therapy and hospitalizations, was not working.

CONFIDENTIALITY FALLS AWAY. APPARENTLY, THE ISSUE HAS NEVER REACHED APPELLATE COURT AND HENCE REMAINS UNRESOLVED. IT WAS HARDLY A COMPELLING REASON NOT TO ALLOW BEAN-BAYOG TO SPEAK TO THE PRESS.

3. MEYER LATER SCOFFED AT THESE ''LAWYER-GENERATED'' EXPLANATIONS. HE TOLD ME THAT A LAWYER, GIVEN ENOUGH TIME, COULD COME UP WITH AN EXPLANATION FOR ANYTHING. HE SAID THAT AS A PLAINTIFF'S ATTORNEY, HE HAD A MARKED ADVANTAGE. HE COULD SELECT THE STRONGEST CASES ONLY. BLAU DID NOT HAVE THAT LUXURY. HE HAD NO CHOICE BUT TO DEFEND HIS CLIENT, GUILTY OR NOT.

> Mr. Lozano told her that he found comforting the idea of a 'nonabusive mom'—i.e., a benevolent mother who would not abuse him . . . this concept (was used) to help calm him down when he was out of control. Dr. Bean-Bayog made it perfectly clear during therapy, and Mr. Lozano understood, that she was not his real mother, that he was not her real child, and that the therapeutic process was aimed at allowing him to relive and come to grips with his childhood memories of abuse . . . a stuffed bear, which he brought to therapy sessions . . . (and) children's books and stories also helped to stabilize and overcome his impulsive and self-destructive behavior.

Next, the seemingly incontrovertible "phenomenal sex" flash card was addressed.

> In addition, Dr. Bean-Bayog developed with Mr. Lozano a set of flash cards with messages intended to contradict his depressive and suicidal thoughts. The content of these cards principally were dictated by Mr. Lozano, including the well-publicized compliment about 'phenomenal sex,' which is a statement Mr. Lozano desired to have from, and was attributing to, his then girl-friend. Mr. Lozano would review these index cards as painful thoughts arose, and the constructive messages they contained helped to get him through the day.

Meyer belittled this explanation, pointing out that every one of the approximately sixty flash cards written by Bean-Bayog expressed a thought or suggestion coming from Bean-Bayog herself. However, she was now asserting that this "phenomenal sex" flashcard was the exception, the only one in which she did not take the persona of Lozano's "nonabusive" mother but that of Lozano's girlfriend, written down at Lozano's request.

Bean-Bayog's official public statement then turned to another troubling issue. How had her sexual fantasies ended up in Lozano's possession?

The statement read:

> Much has been made of Dr. Bean-Bayog's two (2) private sexual fantasies. These two fantasies were dreams that Dr. Bean-Bayog recorded in privacy and were never intended for Mr. Lozano's eyes. Mr. Lozano broke into Dr. Bean-Bayog's office on at least one occasion and stole a file folder of his medical records and other materials, including these fantasies, which Dr. Bean-Bayog kept locked in her office. Dr. Bean-Bayog was not even aware that these fantasies were among the documents stolen by Mr. Lozano until they surfaced in connection with the Board of Registration's investigation.

Bean-Bayog would later tell me that she had discarded the originals in summer of 1990 and she was "horrified" to learn that they had been obtained by Lozano and were now being circulated at the state medical board, her insurance company, and at Harvard Medical School.

She knew that Lozano had broken into her office in Cambridge, but believed he had stolen only his McLean Hospital records and a mother-child fantasy. About two weeks before the break-in, he had written to the hospital formally requesting that copies of his medical records be released to Bean-Bayog. He was infuriated at and was considering a lawsuit against McLean Hospital. She told him that she had received the hospital records he had requested. They began discussing the records, but she did not want him to see his entire file because some of the information might make him suicidal. So he broke into her office and stole them.

The statement continued:

In November of 1987, Paul Lozano admitted to
Dr. Bean-Bayog that he had broken into her
office and had stolen his McLean hospital records. He said that he did so because he was
seeking corroboration that he had been sexually abused by another female psychiatrist at
McLean. Dr. Bean-Bayog believes that Mr.
Lozano's allegation about this other female psychiatrist, like his allegations against her, are the
product of delusion, or a lie.

The approach Dr. Bean-Bayog used in treating Mr. Lozano was unique and somewhat unconventional. It was treatment tailored for what,
in retrospect, may have been an untreatable
patient.

Calling her treatment "unique" was unfortunate because it
suggested her treatment was unconventional and experimental,
hence not necessarily "accepted medical practice." What Blau
meant was that difficult patients demand creative therapy, often
tailored for them.

Also in her press release, Blau raised an issue that was beginning to trouble some of us: "No male therapist has ever been the
subject of such an assault."

"When this has happened to men, there was not a single occasion when newspapers flashed photographs of men across their
pages, with reporters hounding friends and colleagues for biographical details of their lives," Bean-Bayog said later.

It does appear the publicity surrounding male psychiatrists has
been less sensational. For example, as Harvard Law Professor
and psychiatrist Dr. Alan Stone noted in *Psychiatric Times*, "The
way the mass media dealt with [Bean-Bayog] is in startling contrast to the American Psychiatric Associations' former president
Jules Masserman. The sordid allegations against him . . . were
reported several years ago on the back pages of a Chicago newspaper, but the national media essentialy ignored the matter."

Later, Stone reviewed *You Must Be Dreaming,* a book by

Barbard Noel (with Kathryn Watterson), one of Masserman's patients, detailing the alleged sexual abuse and chronicling her battle for justice. Stone referred to Massermann, as "one of the most preeminent psychiatrists of the 20th century." In the book, Masserman was accused by several female patients of injecting them with Amytal, a dangerous and addictive drug, and then raping them in his office over a span of years. Twice in 1987, the charges were mentioned in "On the Law," a column in the *Chicago Tribune*. The columnist, quoting Noel's attorney, claimed ten other women had made similar complaints but were unwilling to endure a public hearing. The press paid no attention until Ann Landers announced the book's publication in 1992.

Now, in his nineties, Masserman, who vigorously denied the charges, claimed his license was suspended for five years because the medical board "differed with my integrated analytic-pharmocologic-behavior modes of therapy of Ms. Noel, but could find no evidence of any sexual transgression—hence the verdict of 'suspension,' but not 'expulsion.' " He also claimed that he considered settling Noel's suit without admitting guilt to spare his ill wife the stress of protracted litigation, but never agreed to the decision formally. He said that he learned "of the settlement only after it was concluded."

If the charges against Masserman, a gentle and likable man (according to my father who knows him well), were true, he may have fooled many of his colleagues. Perhaps Bean-Bayog, accused of only a single instance of sexual misconduct, had too. Nonetheless, the contrast between the two cases is indeed "startling."

5

THE MYSTERY WITNESS

As the medical board was acting against Bean-Bayog in Boston, there was a significant development in the civil suit across the Charles River in Cambridge at Middlesex Superior Court. Judge Thomas E. Connolly suddenly seized the 3,000-page Offer of Proof to review it for the April 2 tribunal. These documents were no longer available to the press and public.

Since the Offer of Proof was now temporarily—possibly permanently—unavailable, my job as photocopier was over. Relieved, I went back to tracking down stories on Cambridge.

However, like most of my colleagues, I carefully read both Boston dailies the next day, April 1. The interest in Bean-Bayog seemed unquenchable. The *Globe* ran three stories and the *Herald*—which had already sent two reporters to El Paso—ran four!

On Thursday, April 2, 1992, a new bomb exploded for Bean-Bayog, as well as the medical board. The day before, a mystery witness had unexpectedly filed an affidavit on behalf of the Lozano family, signaling the onset of a division between the city's two daily newspapers. From this point, the *Globe* appeared to tilt toward Bean-Bayog (though we now called our coverage "more balanced"), and the *Herald* seemed to lean toward the presumption of her guilt. Each paper, however, did continue to present damning and exculpatory evidence as it became available.

Because a psychiatrist and a patient meet alone, there are virtually never any other witnesses. It is one person's word against the other's. The emergence of a witness was a signal event, though not entirely unexpected by the medical board and the press.

Margaret Holland, the medical board's chief investigative attorney, had launched her initial investigation on February 26, 1991, about a month before Lozano died, based on the complaint lodged against Bean-Bayog by Gault. In February and March, Holland tried but was unable to contact Paul Lozano in Texas to "confirm allegations and [for him to] provide [a] statement."

Holland learned of Lozano's death the day after he died from attorney O'Hare. Although the death of one of the only two participants was a blow to the investigation, Holland decided that there was "sufficient reason to pursue investigation without [a] patient statement."

O'Hare wrote to Holland immediately urging her to "press this investigation." He cited a state law that declared in part, "In any action or other civil judicial proceeding, a declaration of a deceased person shall not be inadmissible as hearsay . . . if the court finds that it was made in good faith and upon the personal knowledge of the declarant." Such hearsay, however, is inadmissible in criminal court.

It meant that Williams's and Gault's assertions that Lozano told them he had had a sexual relationship with Bean-Bayog was admissible in an administrative hearing (the medical board) and in civil court.

In the ensuing months, Holland read Bean-Bayog's response to the charges and interviewed the Lozano family. Holland also began reviewing Lozano's copious hospital records, Bean-Bayog's Process Notes, sexual fantasies, and other materials. But Holland was having difficulty locating a local psychiatrist to serve as an expert witness, who could help evaluate the case. She contacted three local psychiatrists and each declined.

In the fall of 1991, Holland learned that an independent witness existed, who might have significant information about the case. Again, in mid-March 1992, Holland tried but failed to learn her identity.

A couple of *Herald* reporters knew the mystery witness's name but had promised not to reveal it. In fact, they had spoken to and quoted her at the end of March. For example, the *Herald* interviewed her the day after Meyer filed the Offer of Proof. In a March 28 story, the tabloid reported,

> A therapist who knows Bean-Bayog said the doctor ended the relationship because she was adopting a "real" baby and "would not have time for two of them." Lozano's family said the rejection killed him, especially after he had been assured again and again of her love. Bean-Bayog wrote (in her countertransference fantasies), "I am head over heels in love with you . . . I also know that I will never rigret (sic) it . . . and the memory will always be sunlit."

Comments from the mystery witness appeared again three days later in another *Herald* story, which reported that the tribunal for the civil suit would take place the following day, April 2, the first anniversary of Paul's death.

> Sources said . . . witnesses for the plaintiffs will say Bean-Bayog told colleagues she was experiencing a sexual attraction toward one of her patients and that she admitted to giving Lozano copies of the sexual fantasies.[1]

Deeper in the story, the mystery witness was indirectly and then directly quoted again:

> A counselor who treated Lozano at McLean and participated in (a) supervision group run by Bean-Bayog said she recalled Bean-Bayog discussing countertransference. "She (Dr. Bean-Bayog) discussed Paul and her erotic countertransference with him. There was no

---

1. THIS CLAIM WAS NEVER REPEATED IN ANY AFFIDAVIT OR INTERVIEW GIVEN BY THE MYSTERY WITNESS.

question it was Paul, it was very clearly Paul. She didn't say she had sex with him, she said she had a very strong countertransference," said the counselor who did not want her name used. Lozano later told her he was sleeping with Bean-Bayog, the counselor said.

The timing of the mystery witness's appearance was perfect. It allowed Drew Meyer to bring pressure on Bean-Bayog's defense attorneys and sour their victory over the board's decision not to suspend her license. Meyer knew that if the judge presiding over the full-blown hearing in July, recommended a sanction against Bean-Bayog, it would either help persuade a jury to award his client a titanic judgment, or her malpractice insurer would agree to a princely out-of-court settlement.

When the mystery witness filed her affidavit, Bean-Bayog's defense attorneys were caught unprepared.

"It was a punch in the gut, a rabbit punch. It made me feel sick," said Blau. "Out of the blue comes this affidavit. After that I was holding my breath to see what else was going to shake out of the woodwork. I wondered if there were any others out there who were going to take a cheap shot at Margaret."

After the affidavit was filed, James Barry, the attorney representing Bean-Bayog's malpractice insurer, the Medical Malpractice Joint Underwriting Association of Massachusetts,[2] quickly waived the tribunal scheduled for the following day. Barry was, in effect, conceding that the lawsuit would easily pass this preliminary hurdle. But he would have waived the tribunal anyway in order to deny Meyer another opportunity to stage a media event.

Only a handful of people knew, including Drew Meyer, Dr. Harrison Pope, and Pilar Williams, that the mystery witness was already one of this tragedy's most influential behind-the-scene players. She was now about to become one of its most controversial. She is a social worker and her name is Amy Stromsten.

2. THE ASSOCIATION WAS CREATED BY STATE LAW IN 1975 TO ENSURE THAT PHYSICIANS COULD OBTAIN MALPRACTICE INSURANCE. TODAY, IT INSURES ABOUT 75 PERCENT OF THE STATE'S PHYSICIANS AND DENTISTS. IN 1993, ITS NAME WAS CHANGED TO MASSACHUSETTS MEDICAL PROFESSIONAL INSURANCE ASSOCIATION.

6

DR. MARGARET HARVEY BEAN-BAYOG

Dr. Bean-Bayog was born Margaret Harvey Bean in Louisville, Kentucky, on July 9, 1943, to a privileged and cultured Protestant family of English and Scottish descent. She endured a childhood that was abusive in ways different from, though perhaps as painful as, Paul Lozano's.

Abigail Bean, Bean-Bayog's mother, was an amateur historian and genealogy buff, who had traced the family's arrival in the New World to the early seventeenth century. Later, many of her forebears fought as officers in the American Revolution. This qualified her for admission to the Colonial Dames.

"The Colonial Dames think the D.A.R. [Daughters of the American Revolution] are hoi polloi. They only have to show that their ancestors fought in the Revolution, whereas the Colonial Dames have to demonstrate that at least three-quarters of their relatives were officers. My mother did it for me, because she wanted me to meet the right people," said Bean-Bayog. "I, of course, ended up marrying, to my mother's chagrin, a Filipino psychiatrist."

Many of her ancestors were Tory sympathizers. Later, they were cotton farmers in Virginia and fought on the Confederate side of the Civil War. One of her great grandparents owned a plantation of ten thousand acres in Fairfax County, Virginia. But much of that advantage perished in the Civil War. In fact, Bean-Bayog's grandfather, Dr. Robert Bennett Bean, was so poor he had to work in coal mines for 13 cents a day to save enough to enter the University of Virginia Medical School at the age of 40. He didn't marry until after he graduated.

Robert Bennett Bean's wife, Adelaide, was orphaned at age nine. Adelaide was sent to live with relatives who treated her "like Cinderella," leaving her feeling empty and lonely. Her capacity for enormous self-sacrifice came to characterize the family's succeeding generations. When Adelaide married Dr. Robert Bennett Bean, she taught her children, including Bean-Bayog's father, frugality and self-sacrifice. However, Robert Bennett Bean was a spendthrift. While his family ate turnips and peanut butter, he bought himself a new car.

Robert Bennett Bean was hired by his alma mater as a professor of anatomy and physical anthropology, and he developed an interest in the physical characteristics of the Filipino headhunter tribes. Soon after his marriage to Adelaide, he decided to pay an extensive visit to the subjects of his research interests. From 1906 to 1910, he and his new bride lived in the Philippines, where Bean-Bayog's father, William, was born in 1909. Bean-Bayog said she grew up with stories told by her grandmother of bamboo fires and volcanoes in the Philippines. Her grandfather helped set up the University of the Philippines Medical School and wrote a stream of tracts on the physiognomy of the Filipino and the Fiji islanders. His most famous work, *The Racial Anatomy of the Filipino Islands,* correlated skin color to intelligence, a hypothesis in vogue at the time.

"I was browsing in a bookstore one day and I opened up Stephen Jay Gould's *The Mismeasure of Man.* To my surprise there was this thing about my grandfather being a terrible scientist and racist . . . Of course, Gould was absolutely right about him," she said.

Most anthropologists of that period were racist, however.

Robert Bennett Bean, his wife, and now two children returned to America from the Philippines via Tokyo and San Francisco on a six-week steamer. Dr. Bean resumed his professorial position at the University of Virginia Medical School. One of those children was Bean-Bayog's father, Dr. William Bennett Bean, who was raised in the shadow of the school's rotunda.

"I don't think they were a happy people. They were very devout and my father was supposed to be a Protestant minister. Fortunately his mother relented and made his baby brother [become a minister]. Anyway, my father went to medical school. He was put through by a cousin that everyone called 'aunt.' She was the oldest of a large family and never married because she had to go to work right away to help support the family. And so there were all of these people who had appalling standards of self-sacrifice, altruism, and righteousness. And not much joy. And when I talked to my father about this, he was truly taken aback. He said, 'Oh, it was so wonderful and we used to sing all the time, and we popped corn and we did various things.' So that my way of perceiving his family is not the way he remembers it," Bean-Bayog said.

After his graduation from medical school during World War II, William Bennett Bean was stationed at Fort Knox in Tennessee when his daughter, Margaret, was born. Her father conducted various studies of metabolism and basic survival conditions, such as food, water, and temperature minimums and maximums for human survival. Soon after her birth, he was posted to the Pacific Theater for two years.

On his return, Bean-Bayog's father devoted himself to medicine with a missionary's zeal and led a long, distinguished career as the Sir William Osler Professor of Medicine at the University of Iowa. According to his only daughter, he felt compelled to compensate his mother, Adelaide, for her years of deprivation and self-sacrifice by communing with God on her behalf. He did so not as a minister of God, but as a physician who wrote widely read homilies on the meaning of medicine. At dinner, the family would say grace[1] and then listen to their father lecture them on how to listen to and care for patients.

"I grew up knowing that a patient's welfare was more important than anybody else's, including my own. I mean, it was a fact in my family. A patient's care was everything. Nothing else mat-

---

1. BEAN-BAYOG STILL SAYS GRACE AT MEALS.

tered," Bean-Bayog said. "He was very caring and nurturing with students and patients, but with his own family, it was just too dangerous."[2]

When I asked her to elaborate on her relationship with her father, Bean-Bayog reached into her notebook and removed several typewritten pages. Shortly before he died of colon cancer in 1989, she wrote a private ode to him and to herself, which she then read to me.

---

2. LATER, SHE RECALLED THAT HER FATHER LOVED TO SING. "HE USED TO SING CONTINUOUSLY. WE HAD NO RADIO IN OUR CAR AND WE WOULD DRIVE FROM IOWA TO OHIO, WHICH WAS 500 MILES, AND BACK IN 1950. THAT TOOK A DAY AND A HALF AND HE WOULD START SINGING WHEN WE GOT IN THE CAR AND STOP WHEN WE ARRIVED AND HE WOULD NOT REPEAT HIMSELF . . . (HE SANG) MOSTLY ELIZABE-THAN BALLADS."

7

DR. AND MRS. WILLIAM BENNETT BEAN

During my last visit home, in the middle of my father dying, the hospital routine, all the doctors whom Daddy trained or worked with, the phone calls to social workers, my mother, more demented by the minute, plucking my sleeve, forgetful, dependent and fretful, my brothers turning to me—the (only) doctor of the three of us—I was doing fine, except when someone approached me to tell me solemnly how wonderful my father was, thoughtful, attentive and kind, how well he listened . . .

I'm glad for you. He's the hero, noble physician, great humanitarian, scholar, writer, and champion. Once on an airplane I sat next to a medical student whom he had taught. She was jealous, she said. "He was so wonderful and inspiring. What a great father he must be."

It wasn't kind, but I said, "You may be right, but I wouldn't know. All the time I was growing up, he was with you . . ."

He loved to write letters but he rarely wrote to me . . . He didn't send cards or buy presents, except once or twice when he'd been on long trips. Usually he gave us the airplane peanuts.

And he never telephoned me to talk to me. After all, he had mother to handle all that. He didn't know what grade we were in, who our friends were, or what was on our minds. He missed out on our childhoods and has no idea who any of us are . . .

I remember once when he was furious about some one of our transgressions, he snorted that none of us had enough drive to get through medical school. I gathered my courage and asked, "Do you mean me too, Daddy? Do you mean me too?" He was still furious. He turned on me and said, "None of you."

I chewed on that one for a long time. I was perhaps eight.

He had a study where he disappeared after dinner to work. The door was shut . . .

But family life was a threat to this enterprise. He came home tired and preoccupied, and all he wanted to do was get away into that study. As a child, I gradually grasped that the only way to be loving to him was *not* to seek contact with him. It was a paradoxical thing for a little girl to learn, but I was desperate to please him and I got it nearly perfect.

One thing I did, when he was away on trips, was to go into that study and just *be* in there. I was trying to absorb him from the books and things. One time I found a book—*Collected Papers of W.B. Bean.* Much of it was beyond me, but he wrote a lot of editorials. Those, I could read. I came to one entitled, "Women in Medicine" and sat down to read it full of pleasure. "Women," it said, "take the place of a man in the medical school class. Women, if they do make it through medical school, will only drop out anyway. And women, if they are really women, belong at home and want to be there."

I don't believe, from the time I read that paper, that I ever could read anything else my father wrote. Years after, when I was through medical school, had recovered from alcoholism, and had had a lot of analysis, it became safe, but by then I wasn't much more interested in him than he ever had been in me.

Mother wrote a poem once, after many years of marriage, about looking over the coffee cups and wondering if she'd ever find out who he was. Work protected him and when his locomotive of a career began to slow a bit he needed some other insulation. He found alcohol. He had always loved to drink but he settled into a pattern of drinking about a pint of gin a day, more on social occasions, for the next twenty years.

When each of us talked to him about it, he said he'd thought about it, knew he should stop, but had decided he didn't want to. From then on his withdrawal and irritability increased. He never did stop drinking—or, for that matter, working.

I was lucky that my own alcoholism was so rapid and virulent that I didn't have his choice.

Now I'm considered an expert on alcoholism: ironic, since I could never help my own father . . .

I always knew I wanted to be a doctor. I remember as a tiny child being taken to his office, the walls lined with books, diplomas, and signed pictures, feeling the cold linoleum floor on my legs as I sat playing with his stethoscope.

Besides, I was looking for him. I knew he was in those hospitals somewhere and if I could get into medical school I could find him . . .

He's dying now and I'll never tell him this. To grasp how I loved him, he'd have to have acknowledged the kind of father he was and where he failed us. He seemed so fragile. I never had the heart to blow his cover.

Other men, a teacher, an analyst, my husband, had time for me, listened and understood me. I'm in a family now which feels different from the one I grew up in. We sure don't accomplish as much as my father did, but we are after something else and we have it. When people need me I don't have to run, like Daddy did. When I married, I left academic medicine, though I still practice. It is hard for me not to view academic medical life as a violent enemy to simple family coziness . . .

But now I've come to a point where I can value what Daddy did for medicine . . . I'm glad he made a terrific contribution. I'm glad he was so productive. I'm glad he gave so much to so many people. Writing this digests the bitterness. So when people come to me full of gratitude and praise, I can smile. I love him too. I'm luckier than he. I don't have to do what he did to the people I love.

Soon I will go home and help him see through the dying,[1] and take care of mother. I'm not doing this as a martyr. I'm doing it because I'm whole, and free. I don't have to hate him. I don't have to be like him. I've won . . .

She put the essay down. I said nothing.

Finally, I asked, "So that was the abuse you suffered in your childhood?"

---

1. JUST BEFORE HIS DEATH, DR. WILLIAM BENNETT BEAN TOLD AN INTERVIEWER, "IN ADDITION TO CARDIOLOGY, NUTRITION, AND LIVER DISEASE, MY FAVORITE HOBBY IS DEFLATING STUFFED SHIRTS."

She didn't answer right away. Then she said that during her ten years of psychoanalysis, all she talked about was her mother.

"The abuse was more to do with my mother. Daddy was the good guy in my childhood. He was the better parent," she said.

"But he was never there," I said.

"Right," Bean-Bayog said, "but Mommy was."

"My mother," she said, pausing for several moments, "was cold, cruel, and abusive."

"Sexually abusive?" I asked.

"No, emotionally abusive. Her control was unbearable. She didn't express feelings. I never saw her in tears, except when I got into medical school, and I saw tears in her eyes when her brother died of his alcoholism and multiple sclerosis. No one ever admitted that he was alcoholic, simply [that he had] multiple sclerosis. The fact is he burned himself up in bed. He lit a cigarette and the bed caught fire."

Born in 1911, Bean-Bayog's mother, Abigail Shepard, grew up and became a slender, green-eyed beauty with black hair and thin jaw line, who graduated with honors from Sweet Briar College and was offered a position as an art professor at Mills College. Instead, she married Dr. William Bennett Bean and raised three children: Bennett[2], John[3], and Margaret. Abigail, a frustrated painter and poet, suffered bouts of depression because her artistic gifts were never allowed to flourish.

Under Abigail's regime, her children had to memorize a poem a week to be recited at Sunday dinner, were tutored in French on Saturday mornings, spent nearly every summer in Europe, and were never exposed to a home television set, because "it rotted the mind."

"[My mother] was not thrilled with me . . . And she, like her mother, was very much more interested in my brothers than she

---

2. BENNETT BEAN IS A SCULPTOR IN NEW JERSEY. "BENNETT IS A NATIONALLY KNOWN CERAMICIST, WHOSE WORKS ARE DISPLAYED IN MUSEUMS AND GALLERIES ACROSS THE COUNTRY," BEAN-BAYOG SAID.

3. JOHN BEAN IS A PROFESSOR AT THE UNIVERSITY OF INDIANA SCHOOL OF MEDICINE. "HE'S THE WORLD'S LEADING EXPERT ON COLLEGE DROPOUTS," SHE SAID.

was in me. And she was very dismayed that I was smart. She said, 'Margaret, I hope you're clever enough not to let on that you're clever.' She saw this as a very serious obstacle to my social future. But actually, she was jealous of me. She competed with me. Anything she knew I wanted, some way got screwed up. So I knew that if she found out that I was going to medical school, I wouldn't end up in it, so I didn't tell her I was premed in college until after I was accepted at medical school."

Asked what made her decide to become a doctor, she replied, "I never decided to become a doctor; I just always knew I would, but never talked about it because girls didn't. I remember when I was 13 and the family was in England and we visited with Dr. Sir Francis Walsh, and during dinner he told my father that I should become a doctor. I don't remember what my father said."

When Bean-Bayog was 13, she was sent away to Saint Katharine's School, a boarding school for girls, in Davenport, Iowa. Though she was now free of her mother's deprecations, she avoided the areas in which her mother excelled such as painting or poetry.

"I didn't do any art. And I didn't do the social marry-young-have-a-family stuff. I mean that stuff was much too dangerous," Bean-Bayog said.

Saint Katharine's was well stocked with intelligent young women. In her class of thirty, many were accepted by Radcliffe College, including Margaret Bean.

"I really had a very superb education. I really did a lot of reading and writing. When I applied to Radcliffe, they asked you to write a list of the books you'd read in the last year, and I had read 130 in my junior year in high school—that was on top of my courses. I was voracious. My brother and I would go to the paperback bookstore and buy ten books, and then go back again the next week," she said.

Bean-Bayog studied hard, kept a low profile in college, and rarely dated. She liked to dance and canoe. But she was unhappy at college.

"Being happy wasn't high priority. How you felt wasn't important. How you behaved and what you achieved is what my parents had taught me. You'd better do well, whatever it costs you. You were expected to go to the outer edges without a whimper," she said.

She also said she realized in college that a man like her father "wasn't going to look twice at a woman like me because I was not what he wanted. And I remember deciding that I was going to go to medical school anyway, because I wasn't sure that I would ever find a man who would take care of me, and I expected to have to take care of myself."

She had been raised in an environment that shunned emotional and carnal expression. Intimacy with the opposite sex had terrifying implications, and she feared that she might end up frustrated and embittered like her mother.

In 1965, Bean-Bayog graduated cum laude from Harvard College[4] in biology and was accepted at Harvard Medical School.[5]

In medical school, she suddenly came face-to-face with a personal crisis that nearly destroyed her.

"When I was a medical student, I got alcoholism and I went around to various people trying to get help for it and the care that I got was scandalous, not because they weren't well intended but because no one knew what they were doing. My father was a well-known internist. Even people in Boston had heard of him. They'd go, 'Oh, you're Dr. Bean's daughter. Oh, wow.' And they would do me the favor of not diagnosing me. And they would say things like, 'Everybody's under a lot of stress when they're an intern.'

4. IN 1963, GRADUATES OF RADCLIFFE COLLEGE BEGAN RECEIVING HARVARD DEGREES BUT JOINT COMMENCEMENTS DID NOT BEGIN UNTIL 1970.
5. IN 1990, SHE WROTE FOR HER TWENTY-FIFTH RADCLIFFE COLLEGE REUNION, "I DIDN'T EXPECT, WHEN I WAS AT RADCLIFFE, THAT I WOULD BE A HAPPY WOMAN. I CERTAINLY WASN'T THEN. I GOT INTO MEDICAL SCHOOL, AND MADE IT THROUGH IT. I DISCOVERED PSYCHIATRY, WHICH I LOVE, AND WHICH GAVE ME ACCESS TO A PERSONAL PSYCHOANALYSIS WHICH TRANSFORMED MY INNER AND OUTER OPPORTUNITIES.
"FOR NEARLY FIFTEEN YEARS I SAW PATIENTS AND TAUGHT AND WROTE AND PARTICIPATED FULLY WITH ALCOHOLIC AND ADDICTED PEOPLE. IT WAS WONDERFUL, AND I HAD TIME TO CHANGE MYSELF SO I COULD, FINALLY, TO MY FAMILY'S SURPRISE AND RELIEF, MARRY."

"But not everybody is as sick as I was. Not everybody was as terrified at how out of control they were getting. Not everybody needed some kind of intervention the way I did, but people did me the honoring unprejudiced favor of refusing to label me and keeping me out of treatment. I was sent to a lovely psychotherapist, a woman who said things like, 'We could send you to alcoholism treatment, but we understand why you drink. We remember all the things that happened to you as a child . . . so I was in a bind between what I loved and knew worked, which was psychotherapy, and what I needed and wasn't sure worked which was alcoholism treatment and I saw them as mutually exclusive. My caretakers did too and so I got very bad treatment.

"The lectures that I eventually developed that I gave to first and second year [Harvard] medical students stressed forgiving and being respectful and empathic toward the type of experience that a person whose developing alcoholism has and the way they rationalize what's going on and the way they deny it and the way they struggle to get it under control and the way they lose control and the way they hate themselves and I've had a whole lot of feedback from people who heard my lectures and went off and got into A.A. and I've had a number of people who've showed up on my doorstep and so I used to put my phone number on the board and I would say, 'I do not care who you are, I do not want to know your name, use an alias if you want, all I care about is if you have a drinking problem yourself or if you have somebody in your family who does, get some help for it.' "

After graduating from Harvard Medical School in 1969, Bean-Bayog won an internship in pediatrics at the Harvard-affiliated Massachusetts General Hospital. The following year she was accepted for a three-year psychiatric residency at the Harvard-affiliated Massachusetts Mental Health Center, several blocks from where Paul Lozano would eventually rent an apartment in Boston's Mission Hill neighborhood.

"I experienced her as being distant," said a colleague who worked with her at the time. "She came from the MGH and she was hot stuff. I know some of her supervisors thought she was the best and the brightest."

Not everyone thought so, however. A nationally known psychiatrist told me, "I was someone who supervised her and I had a lot of reservations about her. She used to wear too much makeup, which I thought was odd . . . I can't remember exactly why, but she was asked to leave Mass. Mental, or maybe she left on her own accord."

In fact, Bean-Bayog did take a one-year leave of absence from her psychiatric residency to confront her alcoholism. During the year spent in an alcohol treatment program and attending Alcoholics Anonymous meetings, she also earned a master's degree in epidemiology from the Harvard School of Public Health studying infant malformations. In 1974, she returned to Massachusetts Mental Health Center, completed her psychiatric residency, then did a two-year residency in child psychiatry, and then a four-year residency in advanced psychotherapy. In 1980, she became a candidate at the Boston Psychoanalytic Society and Institute, where she was in training off and on for another ten years as a psychoanalyst. In the meantime, she opened a private practice as a psychotherapist, and from 1976 until 1991, she was an instructor and then an assistant professor at Harvard Medical School.

At age 41, she married a widower, Dr. Rogelio "Roger" Bayog, a Philippine-born psychiatrist, on May 26, 1984, in a Newton, Massachusetts church. Future Philippine president Corazon Aquino attended the wedding.[6]

Her husband's previous wife, Antonia, also a physician, died of leukemia in 1980, leaving their two children, Franz, 10, and Ruby, 6, inconsolable.

"I mean that I'm openhanded and I'll do anything for anybody and I want people to feel better and I can't stand somebody who's depressed and when I married this man, well, they were so depressed that they couldn't move and their mother and wife had died. I just loved this guy. I thought it was a great situation and I just marched right in, they're terrific people, terrific people, and

---

6. AQUINO'S SIGNED PHOTOGRAPH "TO ROGER AND MARGARET" SITS ON A TABLE IN BEAN-BAYOG'S DEN NEAR A BABY GRAND PIANO.

I married the whole gang, and I knew I was old and I knew I might not have a baby biologically and I thought it was a made-from-heaven situation because they had exactly the kind of strength that I wanted. They had a sense of humor and they were smart, and they were gorgeous and they were charming, and they were impossible . . . and we fell in love and we really manufactured a family. At first it wasn't really a very comfortable place. There was a big culture shock on all sides. We were all stunned."

Before marriage, she bought a cookbook every month because, she said, her favorite pastime was cooking. But when she became a wife and an instant mother, her stepchildren did not readily accept her, viewing her as the usurper. She found solace in spending long periods outside the house in the yard where she took up gardening. Scattered around her one-acre plot are raised beds, built with railroad ties, in which she grows flowers, vegetables, and herbs. Also, in the summer she swims in her pool.

On June 22, less than a month after her marriage, while moving some of her belongings from her home in Brookline to her new husband's home in Lexington, Bean-Bayog was pulled over and arrested by a Newton, Massachusetts, police officer at 8:45 P.M. She was drunk. She pled guilty and was fined $15. Her license was suspended for thirty days and she was assigned to a Driver Alcohol Education Program.

Less than three months later, a first-year medical student from El Paso saw Bean-Bayog's name at the top of an alphabetical list of Harvard-approved psychotherapists on the bulletin board in the school's health center. He called her up. She told him she could see him on September 24 at 10 A.M. He said his name was Paul Lozano.

Several years after Bean-Bayog's marriage, her mother Abigail announced that she and her husband had decided to give each of their three children a $5,000 Christmas gift.

"And we got a package from mother of some little odds and ends, and I called her up and said, 'Mother, I really just called you because the check isn't in there and I wanted to let you know that you should stop payment on it and send us another one because—.' And she said, 'Oh, I forgot to tell you. You've done so well that I've decided to give it to your brothers.' Right? She had divided it up and given it to my brothers, which was her characteristic way of interacting with me. I was convinced that if she had not gotten Alzheimer's and Daddy had died, she would've cut me out of the will. And I wouldn't have had any money to pay Michael Blau with. I mean that's where all the money my father squirreled away in his careful WASP way is going."

On March 14, twelve days before Drew Meyer filed the Offer of Proof in civil court, Bean-Bayog's mother died. In her will, Abigail bequeathed about $250,000 to each of her children.

On March 21, Bean-Bayog and her siblings buried their mother in Iowa. Grieving, Bean-Bayog boarded a plane and landed in Boston the following day. When she got home, there was a message on her answering machine from Jorge Quiroga, a reporter from WCVB-TV5, asking her to call him.

8

PAUL ANTHONY LOZANO

The summer of 1962 was hot and the Mexican-American family was low on funds. The parents and their five children found themselves marooned at a cheap hotel in an airless room, the mother about to give birth. Having just crossed the Rio Grande several days before, they moved quickly northward because the father, a mason, had heard he could earn twice as much laying bricks in Ohio than Texas. Their jalopy had expired in East Sigglington, close to Upper Sandusky, Ohio, stranding them.

At least, that was Paul Lozano's version.

His sister Pilar Williams had a different one. The family, who had lived in Texas for fifteen years, drove north from San Antonio, to seek a better life. After a four-day journey, their red 1946 Ford pickup truck broke down in Findlay, Ohio. Her father heard that thirty miles away in Upper Sandusky construction work was available. They arrived in the city on May 19, 1960, more than two years before Paul Lozano was born. Her mother was not pregnant. A local farmer, Johnny Eyestone, hired her father as a farm worker. Later, he worked for Clinton Karg as a brick layer. Eventually, her father owned his own construction company.

Paul Anthony Lozano was born to Marcos and Epifania "Fanny" Lozano, on August 2, 1962, in the Wyandot Memorial Hospital on Route 4 in Upper Sandusky, the capital of Wyandot County, a county that is 85 percent rural and stocked with farmers mostly of German descent.

The town, loath to countenance minorities or surrender its

youth, has two salient features. First, it is punctuated by several white, towering—and when the heartland's summer sun is setting—shimmering grain silos. Second, no blacks reside in the city. In fact, the Lozanos were only one of two Hispanic families in Upper Sandusky, and the only black family in town at the time of their arrival has since moved on.

"This is not a town that accepts minorities well, but the Lozanos never ran into prejudice," said Bette Snyder, editor of the local daily newspaper. Lozano's father laid the foundation of Snyder's home, and her daughter and Pilar Williams's son used to walk to grammar school together.

When Paul Lozano was born, his father, a former union activist and brick mason from Monterey, Mexico, was 39. His mother, the daughter of migrant Mexican farm workers, also from Monterey, was 42. She never learned to speak English. Lozano claimed that he refused to speak Spanish to his mother until he was 12 years old. When he and his mother had to communicate, one of his siblings, usually Pilar, would translate.

In McLean Hospital, Lozano later told a nurse that he had refused to speak or respond to the family's use of a "foreign language" and that he kept it up until about age 12 when he decided they'd all "had enough of it." The Lozanos already had five bilingual children: Norma, 18; Martha, 15; Mark, 13; Pilar, 9; and Abel, 3. Paul Lozano was the baby of the family.

"We were an average family. The only thing that made us any different was that we were Mexican. After Lozano was born, my mother [Epifania] said he was a 'gift,' " said Williams.

In Upper Sandusky, Marcos's skills were in demand. He quickly found work as a mason, pointing brick, laying a patio or blocks for a new foundation. The family soon moved into a two-story, two-car garage home on the edge of town on 435 N. 4th Street. Paul Lozano and his brother Abel walked across their backyard to the East Elementary School a couple of blocks away. Lozano particularly remembered two of his teachers: Janice Schmidt and Mary Steiner.

Schmidt was Lozano's third-grade teacher. "[Paul] was an intelligent boy," she told me, "but not always with straight A's, who was always quiet and serious about what we were discussing or doing. I don't know why he remembered me in particular. Probably because we did things that were fun: puppet plays and book reports. We wrote our own puppet plays like the *Three Little Pigs*. The kids would make up their own words following the story line. We'd make the puppets out of papier-mâché or clay."

Schmidt had several other memories of Lozano. In particular, she recalled his temper and ambivalence about his Mexican roots. Lozano yearned to be the same color as everyone else; he wanted badly to blend in.

About twenty-six years later the McLean Hospital staff would note in his hospital records that Lozano "always felt like a misfit . . . described his childhood as a miserable one . . . felt responsible for mother's depression . . . felt tremendous burden from expectations from family."

He felt like a misfit at home too. He was the only one with curly hair. Lozano told Bean-Bayog that his siblings told him that he was adopted and that he "never felt too attached." He repeated these claims in most of his other hospitalizations. For example, Roberta Goldwyn, one of Lozano's social workers, noted in a phone conversation she had with his sister that:

> (Pilar) feels that much of his difficulty is related to difficulty adjusting socially to medical school, in the light of his minority background. He admires the students who are socially advantaged (the prep school graduates) and hates his disenfranchised background (as he perceives it). This dichotomy engenders an internal struggle, which permeates his relationship with most people.

Lozano's ambivalence over his heritage was not unique in his family. On his birth certificate, his parents list his race as "white." In his sundry hospitalizations, Lozano gave his race as "white" or "Caucasian," never Hispanic. He is, however, listed as a "minority—Mexican-American" on his Harvard Medical School application, where he was accepted on scholarship. And finally, Williams put "white" on his death certificate. However, Lozano's autopsy report read:

> The body is that of a well developed, well nourished, Latin male, measuring 69 inches in length and weighing an estimated 170 pounds . . . the hair is dark brown . . . The eyes are brown. The pupils are mid-dilated and equal.

Schmidt was not alone in recalling Lozano's temper. The Lozano's next door neighbor, Brian Getz[1], also spoke of Lozano's temper tantrums and said that he was "somewhat emotional." Another neighbor, Debra Amos, remembers his "short fuse." But the neighbors, including Fire Chief Nelson Dilley, who lived across the street, agreed there was no hint of abuse in the Lozano family and no sign that the mother was depressed.

Mary Steiner was Lozano's seventh-grade math teacher but declined to discuss him, saying "Because I respected Paul Lozano, all of my memories of him were buried with him and will stay there." A school official told me privately that she was surprised by Steiner's response because Steiner has strong opinions and never hesitates to express them.

However, Lozano was remembered later by Tom Harper, the other seventh-grade math teacher. Harper, who is also still teaching at the school, said that "Paul did not stand out. He was a very quiet individual, who was pleasant to speak to in the hallways, but was definitely a kid who could apply himself to schoolwork." Harper added that until the news of the lawsuit reached the town, he hadn't known that Lozano attended West Point Military Academy. "You know, we've never had anyone from Upper Sandusky successfully complete West Point. Several kids have tried. You have to wonder about that small community, what it is."

---

1. IN THE PROCESS NOTES, PAUL SAID THAT GETZ THOUGHT HE WAS "CRAZY."

As a toddler, Lozano was clearly precocious. The *Globe* reported that the Lozanos claimed he skipped kindergarten. However, his school records indicate he graduated with his age group.

Williams said that by the age of 3 or 4, Lozano had taught himself to read English and had announced that his favorite author was Dr. Seuss. During the next year, he consumed every book by that author and ordered other children's books by mail. He even tried to mail order a Mercedes Benz. Dr. Seuss books were among those that Bean-Bayog would read to Lozano and that Williams would discover in her brother's Brookline apartment twenty-one years later, inscribed "To the baby, Love Dr. B."

Lozano insisted on reading the directions on a bottle of St. Joseph's aspirin for children before taking them, Williams added. If true, then Lozano was also able to read the dosage instructions. It is ironic Williams recalled this detail. Lozano told Bean-Bayog, as well the staff of several mental hospitals, that at age 5 or 6 he tried to commit suicide by swallowing a bottle of aspirin.

While hospitalized at McLean, Lozano told Bean-Bayog: "The aspirin my sister glossed over it . . . I don't think I was treating myself for headache. Age 6, could read [the] instructions. Took whole bottle. Then I told 'em."

Bean-Bayog asked Lozano how his family had responded. He replied, "[They said] I was probably just acting out. I didn't even know what acting out was."

Bean-Bayog replied, "Who are you kidding. That was a suicide attempt."

Lozano also told a number of mental health professionals that he tried to hang himself in the family basement when he was 13. In his sixth therapy session with Bean-Bayog, he said, "[When I was] 13 [I] tried to hang [my]self in [the] basement. I never told my [family]. [It's] hard to hide rope burns, petechiae[2] eye spots. They brushed it off. She probably suspected."

---

2. MINUTE HEMORRHAGES IN THE SKIN OR EYES ARISING FROM EITHER INFECTIOUS DISEASE OR PRESSURE.

Williams later told me that Lozano must have made this up too.

When he was 4 or 5 years old, Lozano claimed that his parents took him to a psychotherapist, because he was talking to himself a lot. The Hispanic culture is generally skeptical of psychiatry and the Lozanos, like most families, were ashamed of mental illness. If true, the fact that the Lozanos sought psychotherapy for their son suggests how concerned they were about his conversing to himself.[3]

Lozano also told Bean-Bayog that when he was sick, his mother would put a few aspirin in his pocket and insist on sending him to school. When I told Williams this story, she called her brother a "liar," something she did repeatedly. Williams said that it was Lozano who insisted on going to school when sick because he wanted a perfect attendance record. His mother would stick a few aspirin in his pocket and tell him to take them if needed. On June 1, 1976, Lozano won an Award of Honor in recognition of perfect attendance at the Upper Sandusky Junior High School.

Lozano was the family's pride. McLean Hospital's Frankenburg noted that "he was identified as the intelligent child in the family . . . he felt no benefits, just expectations."

Frankenburg also stated that she believed that Lozano had made at least two suicide attempts as a child. Though in his discharge summary she mentioned his alleged childhood abuse by his older siblings, Frankenburg could not recall whether she had discussed it directly with Lozano.

Though the youngest child, Lozano was soon helping his older siblings with their homework. Williams asserted that Lozano's only problem growing up "was that he suffered from the boy-genius syndrome. We doted over him . . . We didn't even make

---

3. IN LOZANO'S ADMISSION NOTES TO THE HUMAN RESOURCE INSTITUTE, A PRIVATE MENTAL HOSPITAL IN BROOKLINE, DR. CHRISTOPHER GORDON, THE ATTENDING PHYSICIAN WROTE: "THE HISTORY IS FROM THE PATIENT HIMSELF, FROM EXTENSIVE RECORDS SENT WITH HIM FROM THE FAULKNER . . . HE HAS A HISTORY OF SEVERAL SUICIDE ATTEMPTS AS A YOUNG CHILD BELOW THE AGE OF 10 AND EXTENSIVE HISTORY OF TREATMENT DURING THAT TIME AS WELL.

him do chores." But his older siblings also called him a "nerd," "weird," and "eccentric." He told Bean-Bayog how much he hated and resented being teased and labelled. He especially loathed trying to live up to the unrealistic expectations with which his family had burdened him. When he first expressed this resentment, no one listened. He told Bean-Bayog that he was teased, mocked, and ridiculed incessantly, and locked in a closet by his older siblings. The McLean Hospital social-work intern, Amy Stromsten, noted that Lozano's Harvard Medical School roommate, Victor Gonzalez, reported to her that Lozano

> **(T)old Victor that his siblings frequently locked him in a closet and ignored his cries, and he said that this was only the tip of the iceberg.**

A nurse in the Faulkner Hospital wrote that:

> **Paul acknowledged that his difficulties began long before medical school. So just removing medical school would not end difficulties. (He) stated he feels very upset (over) childhood issues, which he is working on in therapy.**

Lozano also told Bean-Bayog that his parents beat him and yelled at him, that when his mother was angry at him she would be:

> **(F)uming for hours/days . . . (I) couldn't stand it. (I) was furious. I didn't want to get hit, but I couldn't stand it. Finally, I'd do something to make her so mad (that) she'd hit me. Sometimes she'd make me get the strap. It was better to get it over with. Later, she'd want to hug me and I wouldn't.**

Even his older siblings apparently hit him. Lozano told Bean-Bayog: "When I was little I told them at school [that] we had mice in our house. My sister Martha was so mad she slapped me. She was embarrassed."

Dr. Bean-Bayog replied, "You just told me you have mice in your house."

Paul answered, "I guess I have," and Bean-Bayog said, "And you're not sure if you want me to slap you or help you set some traps."

As a child, Lozano began repressing his resentment—and perhaps much more. He only shared his inner anguish with his "imaginary friends." The same Faulkner Hospital nurse added:

> He states he had heard voices since he was very young, ("imaginary friends,") who could talk to him and comfort him. This continued until adolescence. Voices reappeared at last hospitalization as per his memory and changed into very anxiety-provoking voices. "They say bad things about me. They call me bad names. They comment on things that I'm doing and tell me I'm stupid . . ." He described his anxiety as a pull to fall back into the "white noise" which is as per (his) description almost continual, low-level voices that create a low noise for him, but which when he is anxious became louder and more distinct. When he becomes more overwhelmed, these become separate voices . . . Admitted to hearing the voices, (they) sound like his voice but call him names (two voices both male, both his) . . . Reviewed distraction techniques and to think of peaceful thoughts. (He could recall no other peaceful thoughts than being 3 years old.)

In 1987, Bean-Bayog wrote: "When [I] first saw him [in September 1984, he was suffering from a] very severe [mental] illness."

At the time, Lozano was indignant over Bean-Bayog's conclusion that he needed psychiatric help, saying: "You told me I had

serious problems. I was mad. [What a] son of a bitch. She's only
seen me twice. What right [does she have to say that?] How does
she know? [I] just [have] a little problem here to fix."

Nonetheless, Lozano carried her card around with him for two
years, because, as Bean-Bayog pointed out, "[Paul had a] strong
cultural antagonism to [the] idea of [his] illness and psychotherapy." And when he began psychotherapy, he thought his problems could be cured in three months. When they were not, he saw
this as a failure.

Bean-Bayog continued: "[There were] huge areas of his experience he was alone with because [they were] forbidden and bad
including dependent needs, anger, and all sexual experience.
These were all major inner storms, all unacceptable, so self-hate
[was] very big."

Apparently, he could only share these travails with his imaginary friends. Other therapists reported these voices too, but only
Bean-Bayog realized they had distinct personalities representing
different stages of Lozano's development. These friends included
the "baby," the "toddler," and the (8-year-old) "boy." The only
aspect of Lozano that was at peace was the "infant." Therapy
with Bean-Bayog was apparently the first time that Lozano
dared permit someone else to make the acquaintance of these
"lost boys."

After Bean-Bayog terminated therapy, a new voice was added
to Lozano's cast of imaginary characters. Lozano's subsequent
psychotherapist was Dr. Leonard Lai, who said that Lozano was
hearing "command hallucinations . . . that he heard Dr. Bean[-
Bayog] tell him to inject himself."

The Lozanos claimed that Bean-Bayog was using "regression
therapy" to make him believe he was 3-years-old. Williams told
the *Herald:* "The most heinous crime in all of this is the way she
destroyed his mind. She converted him into a toddler in his mind.
We couldn't understand why he was reverting to this infantile
behavior."

Williams acknowledged to me that Lozano as a child did,
indeed, have conversations with imaginary friends, though earlier in a deposition, she flatly denied it.

Nonetheless, it was with these "imaginary friends," not his

family, that Lozano apparently shared his anguish. Revealing his anguish and/or dependence on these "friends" to his family would only have exposed him to additional ridicule and torment. It is not uncommon for young children to invent "friends." What is uncommon is that Lozano maintained these "friendships" well into adulthood.

In the spring of 1990, his brother Abel, told a psychiatric nurse at Faulkner Hospital that:

> **Paul's preoccupied, sealed-over (anxious state, psychotic state presentation) look was something he saw often in childhood. "Paul would get that look and just look worried and away until he would solve it, I guess, then stop and be himself again."**

In the same records, Lozano said that whenever he was "sealed over," he was conferring with his imaginary friends. Perhaps he was using what psychiatrists call "habitual defense mechanisms" or "adaptations to psychic traumata" because he could not bear to dishonor his family, himself, and especially his mother, but had no one with whom he could ventilate these feelings. On the other hand, perhaps these imaginary friends developed for completely idiopathic reasons. At the same time, his family's enormous expectations put enormous pressure on him. Lozano struggled to live up to his reputation as family genius, destined for greatness. According to Lozano, his mother would later admit her complicity. Bean-Bayog wrote:

> **This morning his mother who "sees things in dreams and visions" told him (that) last night at 3 A.M. she was speaking to him in a vision and realized they might have been putting pressure on him. They only meant to motivate him, (by her) saying (that) she needed him (to) hurry and finish school.**

There was additional anguish. When Lozano was in high school, his father's business collapsed. Lozano felt guilty that he did not quit school and get a job to help support the family. Williams told me that Lozano was the only sibling who did not have a part-time job in high school. He was never required to work for the family construction company. In medical school Lozano felt obligated—almost haunted—by the dream of buying his impoverished parents a house. They had reached retirement age but were still working in a marginal neighborhood of El Paso as managers of a run-down retirement home. In his Harvard Medical School application, he listed his father's occupation as "manager" and his mother's as "cook."

Two diametrically discrete Paul Lozanos seem to emerge. One is described by his family, friends, and neighbors as a shy but brilliant student from an exemplary Mexican-American family that was accepted, to its credit, by a conservative midwestern town that didn't particularly care for minorities. The other was an enraged, anguished, suicidal child who revealed himself not just to Bean-Bayog, but to many of the other approximately 120 highly trained Harvard-affiliated mental health professionals he encountered during his first eleven hospitalizations. Lozano, however, had successfully concealed the private, troubled version of himself from his teachers and classmates, from his friends and colleagues, and, if they can be believed, from his family.

This concealment continued after he left home. For example, Mark Burrows, who worked with Lozano from 1988 until 1990 part-time in a Brookline psychiatric hospital, reported that he appeared to be a "stable, likable guy," who was "very quiet, good-natured and hardworking . . . Nothing in his character would suggest that he was being seen (by a psychiatrist) or that he would have a psychiatric breakdown."

Evidence of his wish to conceal information from his family is found in Lozano's 1980 West Point records. He signed a form specifically forbidding "the release of my USMA [U.S. Military Academy] academic grades or other academic information to my parent(s)."

In McLean Hospital, Frankenburg observed: "[Paul] didn't, during this [first] admission, give us any permission to contact the family, which is unusual."

In his second McLean hospitalization, however, he was finally persuaded to allow his sister and mother to visit him in late May 1987, but only if he could govern what they would be told. For example, he gave strict orders to the staff not to tell his family about his earlier hospitalization. At the family meeting, the hospital's social worker, Roberta Goldwyn, noted:

> (H)e was embarrassed at his family having to see him in hospital and felt extremely guilty at putting his family through so much. Patient continues to wish total control over communication with his family.

Lozano's need to conceal and control the flow of information to his family apparently replicated his childhood experience. Williams claimed that Bean-Bayog tried to isolate and alienate Lozano from his family. Bean-Bayog claimed that Lozano specifically refused to give her permission to contact them. His medical records appear to support Bean-Bayog's contention.

During the later stages of Lozano's therapy Bean-Bayog said she began to perceive a pattern: He seemed to become more suicidal whenever he visited home. He claimed to have witnessed his mother sexually abusing her grandchildren when she was changing their diapers. He telephoned Bean-Bayog from his parents' home in El Paso and told her he was playing Russian Roulette with his father's gun. Lozano may have barred Bean-Bayog from contacting his family out of fear that she would reveal what he was saying about them. He may have also feared that his family would strip him of Bean-Bayog as they had Diane Halperin, his wife of seven days. Lozano claimed his family had pressured him into annulling the 1984 union. In the Process Notes, Bean-Bayog wrote: "[Patient] feels possessive of me. [He's] afraid if they see me they'll take me away from him, like they did Diane."

Lozano may have been replicating his childhood in other ways as well. Bean-Bayog wrote in his McLean Hospital records some observations for the staff to consider:

> (T)he patient seems to have succeeded in exactly replicating his family constellation around him in the hospital, creating a split . . . Dr. Frankenburg is cast as his mother, who physically and emotionally abused him, and whom he tortured in return. Dr. (Harrison G.) Pope may be his father. "I respect him but he's not really involved." I am Pilar, the older sister who raised him, whom he loved and who saw him positively. The staff (with exceptions) are cast as his other 4 siblings who also tormented him and whom he made to feel stupid.
>
> I suggested to him that this might be happening and I wasn't sure quite how he was generating it. He was interested: 'It certainly does feel familiar.' And he began talking about how he protected himself in his hostile family, and how he provoked them, and then parallels here: "Why should I talk to them about what's really going on with me. They don't like me. Maybe one or two, but none of the rest of them want to hear it. That's something I don't feel like doing with people who don't give a damn about me."
>
> I suggested he might try talking to staff about how angry he feels instead of just acting it out, whereupon he acknowledged that he was brewing a plan to avoid swallowing his pills. I asked about my talking to staff about this. He said, "I assumed if I told you, you'd tell them." He agreed to take them. But he also said, "I'm afraid they *will* work. I don't deserve to feel better. I should be punished!!"
>
> We discussed that he is pretty expert at ar-

> ranging to have people do that for him . . . I
> would hate to see him off the desipramine . . .
> One more thought. The split makes you look
> sadistic, Big Nurse (*One Flew Over the Cuckoo's
> Nest*) types, which you're not. It makes me look
> like a complete idiot, which I'm not. but it also
> leaves him feeling like he can destroy any help
> that is offered, and humiliate us all, and that he
> is beyond help, which I don't think he is.

Bean-Bayog told me, "If you read my notes about what went on at the second McLean, I mapped the split that he had built and I explained it, saying that he had got the staff thinking that I am an idiot and he has got me thinking that the staff are sarcastic, sadistic, uncaring, and incompetent. I mean he made no question about the fact that the staff had blown it when they had given him a few hours out and that they had played risks with his life. What he did is he set up groups of people. He would tell Pope and Frankenburg that I was saying he didn't need any medication at all, and he would tell me that Pope and Frankenburg felt that I was an idiot, but he knew that he needed me and that my psychotherapy was the only thing that was gonna keep him alive, so he was very, very slippery and very gifted and he kept his lies straight in the most amazing way. He had different ranks and levels of stories that he would manage to convey to different people at all times."

Lozano told many mental health professionals that as a child he had suffered at the hands of his siblings, but revealed the most closely held and disturbing allegation of his childhood to three people only: Drs. Bean-Bayog, Gerald Adler, and Leonard Lai.

According to Adler, Lozano told him "I have had a relationship . . . an incestuous relationship."

Lai, the psychiatrist who took over Lozano's psychotherapy from Bean-Bayog, stated that "[Patient] remembered being sexually abused by his mother when he was younger. By the time he was 12 and 13, he was able to fight her off, and he told me that he was made to suckle his mother's breasts; that he was made to masturbate in front of his mother."

In the Process Notes, Lozano told Bean-Bayog:

> "Can I suck my thumb? I get too excited. I hate this. There was a game we played. I'd crawl around and around but I can't tell you, you might do it too."
>
> "The boy is only 3. I don't touch him."
>
> "I know you don't, I know you don't, but she would. I'd crawl around and end up under her skirt, hot and moist. I got scared . . . I was her favorite. She loved me the most . . . I never knew why I needed to be 3. (I'm) understanding what is happening in here. Having a childhood is great. I always wanted one. I never thought I could. When (I was) at McLean they said you'll never get it. I'd just want it more. (I'm) longing, (I'm feeling) hopeless. When I first came to see you, I was looking for someone who'd be like a mom, but it was never safe. (It was) forbidden. (It) would always just end in something horrible."
>
> "Now we know what that was."

Later, Bean-Bayog wrote:

> (He was) able to remember her stimulating him. (His mother would say), "Let me check your diaper." "No, you don't need to. I'm dry, but she would anyway. (She would) reach in and touch me 'til I didn't want her to stop . . ." (Lozano continued to speak very hesitantly.)
>
> "(I) used to play games all around her, touch her breasts, play on her lap. I could make her stop whatever she was doing. I'd go up under her skirt when she was doing dishes, put my hands in there."

> "Wouldn't (she) stop you(?)"
> "No, she'd push my head toward it. Then we'd
> go play. My room or (the) living room sofa. We
> did it a lot. I could make her respond, move, get
> excited. I'd keep doing it. She adored me. (I
> was her) favorite. Sometimes I wouldn't want to,
> but we would anyway. (I) couldn't control my
> feelings. (It) wasn't her fault. I did it. I liked it."
> "(It's) not your fault. (The) job of (an) adult (is)
> to see that (a) child is protected."

Lozano claimed that he and his mother were alone at the time, because his father was out laying bricks and his siblings were in school. So, if Lozano's claims were true, it might explain why no one else in the family knew.

Lozano told Bean-Bayog that his father, however, suspected:

> "My father would make dirty jokes (about)
> bread basket . . . (I) don't want to tell you. (It's)
> okay (to say it) in Spanish. (I) don't want to say
> (it) in English."
> "Why not?"
> "He'd call it her bread basket and say (that)
> I like her bread basket. (I) hated that."

Lozano recalled that his mother used to wash his hair with adult shampoo forcing him to keep his eyes shut. Dr. Bean-Bayog's notes stated:

> Retrieved memories of hating to have his hair
> shampooed because his mother would touch
> him then and he had to keep his eyes shut.
> Described lurid details of her sexual play with
> him.

In the spring of 1990, Bean-Bayog met Lozano's father in Boston. Lozano also attended the meeting. It was the only time

Lozano allowed Bean-Bayog to meet a member of his family. She wrote,

> (I) reviewed . . . (the) severe nature of his son's illness . . . and (his) ongoing suicide risk. (I told his father that Paul's) illness had a chemical component and also that there may have been childhood trauma, including (questions of) physical abuse, (and questions of) sexual abuse . . . (The) father said he was relieved to know what the problem was.

Bean-Bayog added that the "patient was very rigid during meeting with father, spoke little after [the] father left.

This meeting is a typical, but important, example of the many conflicting claims between the Lozanos and Bean-Bayog. The Lozano family denied that she ever told Marcos of sexual abuse or that the father expressed relief in knowing "what the problem was."

In Williams's 1992 deposition, she was asked about the visit:

> A. I recall my father visiting my brother at the hospital at the Faulkner, and him telling me that he spoke with Dr. Bean-Bayog, and at that time she told him that my brother had an 80 percent chance of killing himself while he was sitting in the room with him.
> Q. (Did) Your father tell you anything else about that discussion with Dr. Bean-Bayog.
> A. No.

A few moments later, the lawyer asked her again:

> Q. Just so I understand, your father didn't tell you anything else about that conversation with Dr. Bean-Bayog, other than she related

to him that Paul had an 80 percent chance
of killing himself?
A. That's correct.

When Marcos was interviewed by the *Globe* in April 1992, he
said he asked Bean-Bayog the cause of his son's illness. According to him, she responded:

"No, no, no, it's not drugs or alcohol. The problem with Paul is he was born this way. It's the
result of some chemical in the blood . . . You
have a good example in your father. He never
broke the law, never asked for anything. Why
are you having these depressions?" Before
leaving, she also reportedly told the father that
Paul had "an 80 percent chance of committing
suicide" (causing Paul's face to) look different.

If Bean-Bayog's version is true, it would suggest that since the
father was relieved—but not surprised or shocked—he and possibly others in the family were aware of Lozano's incest. Argua-
bly, when Bean-Bayog wrote this down in the spring of 1990, she
could not have anticipated a lawsuit or that reporters and lawyers would scrutinize every word in the Process Notes. What is
intriguing is that if the father did indeed tell all family members
about Lozano's incest, their subsequent denials may have been
orchestrated.

Only an independent, contemporaneous source could corrob-
orate one version or other. Fortunately, one exists.

Eleven days after Marcos Lozano's visit, a Faulkner Hospital
nurse wroted in Lozano's records:

Paul met with this writer and Cheryl Izen[4] briefly
to discuss news that brother Abel (2nd youngest

---

4. IZEN WAS A SOCIAL WORKER LISTED IN LOZANO'S RECORDS AS HIS "PRIMARY
THERAPIST."

brother, Paul is youngest) will be coming into town this (weekend) to assist Paul. As per Cheryl Izen's conversation with Abel, Paul's father has told family about info from Dr. Bean-Bayog—most notably abuse info and Dr. Bean's ass-(ess)m(en)t that "Paul has an 80% chance of killing himself." Family is concerned and invested in helping out.

In his deposition, Dr. Thomas W. Watkins, the Lozano family's pediatrician, made an offhand but intriguing remark:

These people were always upbeat, nice, friendly, and no complaints, and if they were up to anything, you would have had—this would have had to be a full conspiracy, because, I mean, if the mother was doing something, the sisters would have had to know about it, the—the two sisters, the brother, the—everybody.[5]

In late May 1990, Abel visited Lozano for three days at the Faulkner Hospital. The reunion went well. A nurse recorded that: "Paul stated he had not appreciated how much he missed a sense of family around him . . . [and that] he missed his brother."

Nearly two years later, however, Abel told the medical board's special prosecutor, Jack Fabiano, a remarkable story. In an internal memorandum, summarizing his ninety-minute telephone interview with Abel, Fabiano wrote:

Abel came to Boston in May 1990 to visit Paul at the Faulkner . . . Abel says that Paul sat outside

---

5. WATKINS, WHO WAS THE LOZANO FAMILY PEDIATRICIAN FROM 1970 TO 1979, SAW PAUL "APPROXIMATELY THIRTY-EIGHT TIMES." WATKINS STATED THAT HE ONLY REMEMBERS MEETING PILAR, PAUL, AND ABEL, BUT NEVER MET WITH OR SPOKE TO THEIR PARENTS.

Faulkner on a grassy hillside and told him that "things are out of control now." Paul said that he was in love with Dr. Bean-Bayog and that she was in love with him. However, they couldn't be together. He had hoped that he would graduate, that they would get together and practice together. Paul told Abel that (Bean-Bayog) had tricked him in some ways; that he was having a sexual relationship with her; that (the) therapeutic relationship was "somewhat a charade;" that he was very much in love with her and that she was very much in love with him. Abel was aware of an outstanding bill for treatment (which he remembers as being approximately $20,000) and he asked Paul about it. Paul said that it was a cover for their relationship, that she had to charge that amount to justify their seeing one another. Abel said that sounds like "big bucks for a date." Abel told Paul that the relationship had to stop. He also called Pilar and suggested to her that perhaps Paul was having an affair with (Bean-Bayog). Paul also made very elliptical references to (Bean-Bayog) "having written things about me. They can't be taken back now." He said to Abel that "Margaret seems to think I was abused as a child." Abel reacted angrily to that suggestion.

In effect, Abel was suggesting to Fabiano that the Process Notes, Lozano's numerous suicide attempts, and nearly two thousand pages of sundry hospitalization records were a charade to cover up his sexual relationship with Bean-Bayog.

I carefully read and reread the Faulkner Hospital records, seeking a hint of the information that Abel would two years later supply to Fabiano. Nowhere in the Faulkner records did Abel express these concerns. However, Abel did express concerns of another sort. He was very worried that Lozano might move in with him.

Several days after Abel headed home, he telephoned the
Faulkner Hospital. A nurse jotted down the following:

> Patient's brother Abel called from North Caro-
> lina at 12:30 A.M. to express his concern about
> Paul. (He) said that he has had several conver-
> sations with him this past week, and that in a
> couple of those conversations, (the 1st of which
> was Wednesday 5/30) Paul said that he "was
> getting ready to just leave this place," and that
> he thought he might go down to his (brother's)
> place. Abel Lozano wanted us to be aware that
> Paul has been entertaining these thoughts. (He)
> stated that he realizes that Paul is probably not
> ready to make such a decision, and said that
> he was able to "talk him out of it each time" so
> far, but that he knows we should be aware, just
> in case. Paul is not sharing these feelings and
> ideas with us. He also would like to know ahead
> of time, if his expressed concern over these con-
> versations is going to be shared with Paul, as he
> is fearful "that Paul will never speak to me again
> when he finds out I told you!" I assured Mr.
> Lozano that I would give that message to the
> family (social) worker on Paul's team.

Abel expressed no other concerns to the hospital staff—at least
none that were recorded in the 269-page record of Lozano's
fourth admission to the Faulkner Hospital.

Bean-Bayog, who is embittered at the Lozano family and believes they are either lying or in denial, said they had both a
psychological and financial incentive to blame someone else for
the sins of the mother.

In his final Boston-area hospitalization at the Newton-Wellesley Hospital, however, Lozano told Gault that allegations of his
abuse as a child were "utterly without a basis in reality."

Despite her claims that Lozano had a "beloved" childhood,
Williams was hardly surprised when she heard Lozano tell Gault

that there was no "basis in reality" for allegations of his childhood abuse.

She had heard something similar about two years before. On May 26, 1987, Williams and her mother met in McLean Hospital with Lozano, Frankenburg, and Roberta Goldwyn, the social worker who replaced Amy Stromsten. Goldwyn wrote in Lozano's medical records:

> **(Williams) opened the meeting . . . She went on to say that she had the feeling that Paul had been telling (the) staff his childhood had been unhappy and she wanted us to know that he had always been beloved by the family and still is, and, as the youngest probably had the most attention. Contrary to what he might be assuming, the family's love for him is unconditional . . . whether or not he has a high status job. Pilar did acknowledge everyone in the family suffered from being one of two minority families in town, but she thought this reinforced family cohesiveness.**

Pilar Williams, "who opened the meeting," was undoubtedly a force to be reckoned with.

9

MARIA DEL PILAR LOZANO WILLIAMS, R.N.

Paul was not the only source of pride for the immigrant family. Pilar was the town belle.

"Pilly," as she was then called, was endowed with "movie star" beauty, according to townsfolk who remember her. This is confirmed by a photograph of her that sits on the mantle in her home in El Paso. She was indeed striking. She had long, black hair and weighed about 100 pounds. Today, she remains attractive, has cut her hair, and put on a pound or two. Lozano repeatedly characterized Williams as his mother in the Process Notes. At one point, Lozano said to Bean-Bayog: "[Pilar] felt more like my mother. [It's a] good thing she was there."

Lozano's biological mother kept to herself. She certainly had trouble communicating with the outside world, because she never learned to speak English. And Williams told me that there was no contact with the town's other Hispanic family because they had "nothing in common" with them.

In March 1969, when she was fifteen, Williams's high school sweetheart impregnated her. For a Roman Catholic Mexican-American family, abortion was not an option. The child's natural father, who still lives in the Upper Sandusky area, was "quiet, well liked, and willing to marry her, but his parents objected," said a school official who went to high school with them. Williams was still living at home. Suddenly, Lozano was no longer the baby of the family.

Williams reacted to her predicament with exceptional dignity. First, she biologically and legally established the child's paternity and required the father to pay child support, even though another man, whom she would later marry, is listed as the father on the child's birth certificate. Next, resisting pressure from school officials, she insisted on graduating from public high school with her class. At that time and in that place, this was a courageous and revolutionary act.

Three years later, Municipal Court Judge L. C. Schoenberger solemnized the marriage of Maria del Pilar Lozano, 19, occupation "case worker,"[1] and Hal Richard Williams, 23, occupation "teacher." Hal Williams legally adopted the child, Jonathan Erick, and is listed on the emended and back-dated birth certificate as the child's natural father. Williams told me that she informed Hal before they married that he would have to agree never to sire any children with her. She told him that it would be psychologically damaging to her son if she had a child by another man. It seems like a curious resolution. At 19, she made this decision and stuck to it. Seven years later, when Marcos Lozano's business failed, Williams insisted that she and her husband accompany her bankrupt parents to El Paso. Her husband complied. After twenty-one years, the marriage, having weathered many storms, was shipwrecked on the reef of Paul Lozano. Pilar Williams became consumed by the lawsuit against Bean-Bayog and the marriage dissolved in 1993.

Soon after Pilar Williams's 1972 marriage, her father built a brick ranch-style dwelling on a vacant lot that he purchased for $2,500. He then built a second house next door. Paul, Abel, Epifania, and Marcos moved into the first. Pilar, Hal, and Jonathan Erick moved into the second. Norma Grossman[2], the oldest sister, who had married a high school biology teacher, lived in a rented house behind them. Her yard was contiguous to theirs.

---

1. IT IS IRONIC—PILAR HERSELF CALLED IT THAT—THAT HER JOB WITH THE WYANDOT COUNTRY'S DEPARTMENT OF HUMAN SERVICES WAS AS AN INVESTIGATOR FOR ABUSED CHILDREN.
2. GROSSMAN HAS SINCE DIVORCED AND REMARRIED. HER NAME IS NOW KILGORE.

Fifteen hundred miles from the Mexican border, the Lozanos had established a Chicano enclave in America's heartland.

Marcos was now fairly prosperous. The Lozano Construction company constructed a number of new homes on spec and served as a masonry subcontractor. The company, manned by Mark and Abel, also built wooden crates for Chrysler Motor Corporation. The family now owned and moored two boats on Lake Erie, vacationed in Mexico, and bought new cars and snowmobiles.

Years later, as I sat on Pilar Williams's couch in El Paso, holding the Pound Puppy[3], a stuffed animal Williams claimed that Bean-Bayog had given to Lozano, and the actual "phenomenal sex" flash card, she flipped on her VCR and played a tape of home movies that had been converted to video by her mother. Spliced haphazardly and unchronologically, Lozano's life was visually scrambled the way it was scrambled in my attempts to understand his psychodynamics. First, a smiling Lozano is riding the family snowmobile as a 10-year-old, bumping across the snow of the nearly one-acre combined backyards of the three Lozano homes. Next, he is standing proudly with cap and gown, graduating from the University of Texas at El Paso, a few months before he matriculates at Harvard Medical School. It is also a few months after his mysterious seven-day marriage to Diane Halperin. Then, suddenly he is a 9-year-old child at a birthday party, 5 years old at Thanksgiving and 7 years old at a baby shower, then 13 years old at the Inca monuments in Mexico, and 10 again on the family sailboat. He certainly was not a scene stealer. Indeed, he hardly appeared on camera at all. I peered into Pilar's TV screen, freezing Paul whenever he appeared, searching for telltale signs of what was to come. The images, shimmering with static, made it impossible to see him clearly. I saw a typical boy in a normal, happy, middle-class

---

3. THE POUND PUPPY IS A WHITE-AND-BLACK BASSETT HOUND WITH LONG BLACK EARS, A BROWN NOSE, ATTIRED IN RED SHORTS HELD UP BY RAINBOW-COLORED SUSPENDERS, A PURPLE SATIN SHIRT, AND A RED COLLAR.

American family. Though something sinister apparently lurked and festered beneath the banal, I couldn't see it. Apparently, his family couldn't either.

Lozano's accomplishments were impressive. He ran cross-county in the fall and track in the spring, earning varsity letters in each. Ralph Young, his coach, told the *El Paso Herald-Post* that Lozano was "the kind of boy that if you wanted somebody to have the other kids model after, he'd be the one." Lozano worked as a photographer of the yearbook and was a crew member for the junior class play. As a straight-A student, he was a member of the school's scholarship team and of the National Honor Society in his junior and senior years.

The country, however, was in recession and his father's business was teetering. Nonetheless, the summer between Lozano's junior and senior years was busy and intoxicating. Lozano was one of two students from his junior class of 115 selected by the faculty to attend the prestigious Buckeye Boy's State, a week-long summer course in state government, the first time he was away from home alone. He completed the Minority Introduction to Engineering at Purdue University, attended a science and engineering symposium at Case Western Reserve University, and was admitted to Ohio State's Martin W. Essex School for the Gifted. He is listed in *Who's Who Among American High School Students 1978-79*. He was nominated by U.S. Representative Tennyson Guyer of Ohio to the West Point Military Academy, to which he was accepted on February 26, 1980, with a full undergraduate scholarship, including "room and board, medical and dental care, and monthly pay."

Lozano did tell a fib, however. He had been elected to the Student Council, but in his West Point and Harvard Medical School applications he listed himself as "Student Council President (Junior Year)." According to the yearbook in Lozano's junior year, the 1978-79 student council president was Pam Williams.

Lozano was not a member of the senior class of Upper Sandusky High School. As his father, "who stuck a few local people financially," prepared to file bankruptcy, the family evaporated, one by one, from town in 1979.

Suddenly, Lozano's secure world shattered. He found himself uprooted from the only hometown he'd ever known, and forced to flee in humiliation to the mean streets of El Paso. His Mexican heritage placed great weight on the sanctity of and duty to family and in Upper Sandusky his family was his community. Lozano told Bean-Bayog that his parents' wishes were sovereign: "[In] my culture . . . [it's] more important to please [one's] parents [and] do what they want. I don't understand [the] Anglo culture very well."

Earlier, he had said, "Before I didn't kill [my]self for [the sake of my] parents. [I'm] tired of living for them; [I'm] finished . . . [I] owe them something, gratitude, [but] I really don't care for them."

Lozano was alienated from his family, yet chained to it. In the fall of 1979, Marcos, Epifania, Abel, and Paul were the last of the Lozanos to leave. As they had arrived seventeen years earlier, they departed by car, strapped for cash, carrying a few belongings. They headed back to Texas, because the two oldest siblings, Mark and Norma, were already living in El Paso. Lozano described how disappointed he was in their reception: "When Dad took us to El Paso, [my] other brothers and sisters [were] out all the time. [It] would've been nice if they'd put us up, but they ignored us. [They] all had new jobs. [They were] ashamed of us."

Lozano was fortunate. He didn't have to stay in El Paso very long. In his senior year, he attended Coronado High School. On May 29, 1980, he graduated nineteenth in a class of 617. His grade point average was 93.3; the class average was 82.9. Lozano was a quiet young man, who kept to himself and was hard to get to know. According to Coronado High School principal, Burl Whatley: "[Lozano's] not even in the Coronado (High School) year book."

But Lozano did befriend Armando R. Castellanos, who is now an army captain stationed in South Korea. Castellanos was also accepted at West Point. Exactly thirty-two days after their high school graduation, Lozano and Castellanos became members of the United States Corps of Cadets and then survived ten weeks of cadet basic training. Lozano told Bean-Bayog, however, that he had serious misgivings about attending the U.S. Military

Academy. "[I] kicked [my]self [and] went to West Point. [I got an] offer from Case Western [for] one of ten slots for [a combined] undergrad-MD program . . . but [there] was some negative letter about money, so West Point offered [a full scholarship] and I accepted."

As a cadet in upstate New York, Lozano was lonely. He did not date. He loathed military regimentation and the foolishness of "attention to detail in all areas of cadet life," especially his personal appearance. Seventeen days after Lozano's arrival, Cadet Sgt. Steven Johnston warned Lozano that he needed to improve his "self confidence when speaking in a group." Lozano later told Bean-Bayog: "I hated it, really hated it . . . When I was there I got drunk a *lot* . . . [I] had reached my limit. [I got] drunk, [was] looking out [a] window, thinking about jumping. [I] did a lot of punishment tours."

In his first term, Lozano barely got a passing grade in Introduction to Computers and didn't fare much better in Military Heritage and Studies. In January 1981, he was counseled by a superior officer, Major George Durham, who determined the following: Cadet Lozano's interpersonal relationships and time-management skills were weak, he had not shown improvement, and he did not seem motivated to improve. Durham recommended that Lozano try cooperating more with his roommates and his squad leader. Lozano told Bean-Bayog that he didn't get along with his roommates, who both came from military backgrounds. "[They were] good at making beds; I wasn't . . . Once, [there was a] shoving match. [One of my roommates] shoved me across [the] room into [the] windows and cut [my] head. [I] bled all over the place."

During the summer of 1981, Lozano completed cadet field training as a platoon medic. In Lozano's second term at West Point, he fared slightly better, but performed poorly in his favorite subject, Small Unit Tactics. He slightly lifted his overall grade. But that fall, he resigned.

Major Robert Wagner, who certified Lozano's resignation, wrote: "On 2 November 1981 I contacted Mrs. Williams, sister of Cadet Lozano, who acknowledged her brother's desire to resign. Cadet Lozano's parents are not fluent in English.''

Lozano told Bean-Bayog that this was one of the bleakest moments in his life. "I left feeling a failure . . . my mother [was] crying every night . . . my mother didn't speak [to me] for two weeks."

From November 1981 until early January 1982, Lozano worked as a materials handler at Farah Slacks, Inc. in El Paso, matching fabric parts by code. "[My mother] reminded me I was a factory worker. [She] reminded me what kind of failure she thought I was. I said [I was going to be an] M.D. She said [I'd end up being a] nurse."

In January 1982, Lozano matriculated at the University of Texas at El Paso. Without taking summer breaks, he was able to graduate in May 1984, thanks to tuition loans from the West Texas Higher Education Authority and the Texas Guaranteed Student Loan corporation. He died owing them $9,500.

Once again, close to his family and his sister, Lozano, at least on the surface, thrived. He majored in microbiology and achieved a 4.0 grade-point average, was awarded a minority biomedical research grant, worked as a chemistry tutor in his junior year, and worked as a volunteer assisting the elderly.

In an application to Harvard Medical School, he wrote,

> During the last year I have worked as a volunteer for 5 hours a week at a nonprofit, sheltered residence for the elderly, Pilot Home Inc . . . (This small facility was managed by his parents and was Lozano's residence as well.) I realized the importance of maintaining an understanding, nonjudgmental attitude in dealing with others. I feel physicians must possess these skills in order to interact effectively with their patients."

The premedical committee at his university gave Lozano a score of "well above average—probably in the upper 1/4 of applicants I have known." He was accepted at Harvard Medical School.

Chemistry Professor James E. Becvar, who was Lozano's supervisor on his senior independent research project, remembered Lozano as "very quiet and a very good student academically . . . [Paul] did not make a big deal about [his grades], and when students asked specifically how he had done, he would avoid their potential resentment in the best manner he could in the particular situation."

Becvar also recalled that Lozano "kept to himself." He only had one "real relationship or association" at college, spending many hours at the chemistry lab with fellow premed student, Diane Halperin of New York. She was 27; Lozano was 21. They fell madly in love.

As with many other aspects of Lozano's life, there was a dispute over this entanglement. Amy Stromsten, the social-work intern at McLean Hospital, wrote in Lozano's records that:

> When (Paul) transferred to U. Texas he met . . . Diane . . . a woman his family vehemently disliked . . . His parents said that if he kept seeing her they would tell her medical school (she'd already been accepted at the University of Texas at Houston Medical School) that she had once been hospitalized for depression. Paul retaliated two days later by marrying Diane. She continued to be suicidal, and Paul felt guilty toward her and toward his family . . . Paul and his wife both applied to Harvard but only Paul was accepted. (She is now in medical school in Texas.) . . . The family told Paul that he had to choose between them and his wife . . . He finally annulled the marriage to please his family and came to Harvard Medical School hoping to escape.

In one of the two early evaluations with Bean-Bayog in September 1984, eight months after the marriage was annulled, Lozano said:

> (O)ne of (my) sisters called her. (I) was so upset
> with (my) family. (I) didn't want anything to do
> with them. (We) said horrible things (to one an-
> other). (I was told), "It's stupid, you don't just (go
> out and get married)." But I did. (I) decided to
> marry. Two days later, (I) moved out of (the)
> house (into) Diane's. (It was) not a game.

Lozano and Halperin were married by gospel minister David J. Lynch on January 27, 1984 in El Paso. She took Lozano's last name. Seven days later, a decree of annulment was issued by a judge in the probate court. The decree restored her maiden name.

Becvar reported that "I found it extremely curious that he would do this. This was out of character for him . . . Frankly, it was all a surprise for me that they got married and later had their marriage annulled. I don't know of any other couple who would do that."

Throughout the Process Notes and his hospital records, Lozano expressed bitterness over his family's pressure to end his marriage to Halperin.

During his stay at the Faulkner Hospital in July 1987, Lozano told Bean-Bayog that the family began to reconsider its position on Halperin:

> Why do I feel this desolation? Why do I feel this
> solitude? Is there something that gives me an
> anchoring, roots, a sense of belonging? After
> wandering around today, I finally realized why
> I decided to go into medicine! It would give me
> the sense of being needed, anchoring, roots, I
> just couldn't get plucked off this earth. My sister
> said something to me when she heard all this.
> (She said), "We wondered how much (of a)
> disservice we had done when we interfered with
> you and Diane. You looked so happy then."
> "You wondered too?"
> "Yeah, a lot, because I knew Diane really

loved me, shared so many special moments. (It's) not hard to do because till that time I hadn't shared special moments (with anyone). (My) sister said "(I) guess she wasn't that screwed up after all. (She's) finishing up med (ical) school." Our words and acts come back to haunt. Now it's her crazy brother (who is) embarrassing her.

Williams, however, denied the family was opposed to Lozano's marriage to Halperin or pressured him in any way. To the *Herald* and the *New York Times,* Williams claimed that the marriage was a ruse to help Halperin get into Harvard Medical School. It was an act of chivalry, designed to help a colleague and friend. When Halperin was not accepted, they amicably ended the marriage.

This explanation is curious. Williams asserted that a seven-day marriage in El Paso would have somehow affected a decision being rendered two thousand miles away. Applications to Harvard Medical School at that time had to be postmarked no later than October 17, 1983. There is no mention of his marriage in his application. On February 15, 1984, thirteen days after the marriage was annulled, Lozano was notified he had been accepted. Halperin received her notice of rejection around the same time. Williams maintained that Lozano and Halperin, two microbiology majors, believed that their marriage—that was solemnized long after the application deadline and that the medical school was never notified of—would somehow telepathically influence the decision of the admissions committee.

When I interviewed Williams in early 1993, she repeated the same story. She did admit that the family was shocked by the marriage and that she thought her brother could do much better. She also said, making a face, that Halperin's teeth were severely discolored.

Lozano and Halperin, however, remained on excellent terms. A month before he departed for Boston to attend medical school, she sent him a card for his birthday on August 2 that read:

Dear Paul: Remember there are many people who care deeply about you and desire your happiness . . . and that you feel more fulfilled . . . I think you've come a long way in your first twenty-two years and who knows what wonderful things will come your way in all the years to come . . . You've got some really beautiful qualities . . . It will always be a privilege to call you my friend. But despite all these serious solemn words, get out there and have a good time! Love Diane.

Bean-Bayog said that Halperin would come to visit him regularly in Boston. "He used to call her up when he got lonely and he was embarrassed to do it, because she would fall right back in. He did not really love her; he exploited her; he would reel her in when he needed her. He saw her as somebody who he simply could, you know—. It's one of those things where somebody's in love with you and you don't let them go."

In 1988, Halperin graduated from the University of Texas at Houston Medical School and was accepted at the Boston City Hospital for a four-year residency in obstetrics and gynecology.

"Her coming to Boston was probably no accident," said Bean-Bayog.

Halperin and Lozano continued an intermittent but intimate relationship, according to the Process Notes. In two of the seventeen letters that Bean-Bayog wrote and gave to Lozano in advance of a three-week vacation to the Philippines, which he was to open one day at a time, she referred to the pair's close relationship. At the time he was recovering from knee surgery. "Hi! I hope you're not in pain. I hope Diane is taking good care of you. Tell her hello, (if you do that sort of thing)." In another letter, Bean-Bayog asked, "Is Diane still there?" Eventually, Lozano and Halperin lost touch with one another.

By the time Drew Meyer had filed the Offer of Proof on March 26, 1992, Halperin had remarried but was still living in Boston. While at the hospital, she first learned of Lozano's death from the initial news accounts and she became upset. "I loved him. I loved him," she cried out. Because she had changed her last name, and had not married in Massachusetts, a medical board official said that later, when he sought to interview her, she could not be located.

After completing her residency in July 1992, Dr. Halperin moved to another New England state where she is affiliated with a regional hospital. She and her carpenter husband reside in a house that he built. Halperin declined to be interviewed.

Halperin was not the only woman in Lozano's life whom Williams apparently disapproved of. According to an entry in the Process Notes, dated "summer '89," Lozano dated and became engaged to Melissa King[4], when he was home. King and Williams were colleagues at the Providence Memorial Hospital in El Paso. Apparently, through Williams, Lozano met the woman who introduced him to cocaine, the drug he later used to kill himself with.

In the summer of 1989, Bean-Bayog wrote:

> (His) sister introduces him to (a) new girlfriend in Texas. (She is a) nurse. (He) describes her drinking and drug abuse. She (is) older. (He) starts (a) relationship. (He) won't listen to warning about her alcohol problem. (He) finally gets mad about it after she introduces him to cocaine. (We) discuss (the) self-destructiveness of using drugs but particularly with (someone suffering from a) mood disorder (like Paul). (He) gets engaged to her but (was) able to break (it) off without marrying her, and telling her it's because she has too many problems.

Gault also recalled what Lozano told him about his cocaine use:

---

4. HER NAME HAS BEEN CHANGED TO PROTECT PRIVACY.

> Well, the one thing that I remember, for some
> reason—you know how these strange things
> stick in your mind—I think he told me twice that
> there was a young woman who was a nurse in
> El Paso . . . For some reason, this nurse and co-
> caine were sort of linked up together. It was
> when he would go out with her, when he would
> see her that he would do cocaine. He implied to
> me that this had happened in the past on a
> number of occasions, although it wasn't clear to
> me exactly how often.

Bean-Bayog was opposed to his relationship with King because of her alleged drug use. It may have been the only time that
Williams and Bean-Bayog unwittingly concurred. Bean-Bayog
said she remembered his ending the relationship in the fall of
1989, because Lozano gave Bean-Bayog an undated and unsigned copy of the letter he had just mailed to his fiancee, breaking off their engagement:

> Dear Melissa, This is a difficult letter to write, but
> I feel I need to finalize things so I can go on with
> my life . . . Hence, I am returning the cards,
> pictures, ring, and necklace because they re-
> mind me of you, your kind and gentle em-
> brace, and your soft blue eyes,[5] which are
> painful for me to remember.

Lozano went on to say that he was breaking off the engagement because her drug abuse—which included marijuana, cocaine, and the theft of Halcion and Valium from her patients—
placed him "at great risk" because of his "history of affective
disorder." He then expressed his regrets for any "angry words

---

5. ACCORDING TO HER DRIVER'S LICENSE, KING IS SIX YEARS OLDER THAN LOZANO,
HAS BLUE EYES, BLOND HAIR AND *WEIGHS 190 POUNDS.*

either Pilar or I have directed towards you." It was a strong but loving and tender letter, in which he did his best to soften the blow.

When I interviewed Williams, she said she remembered a Father's Day "celebration" the family held for Marcos. Lozano had gone out with King the night before, returned home around noon with "hickies all over his neck." Williams could not understand why her promising and brilliant brother found so attractive an older woman who was "big, very big."

Williams told the board's special prosecutor, Jack Fabiano, that King and Lozano happened to meet when they came to visit Williams who was at home recovering from surgery. In her July 1992 deposition, she stated that Lozano briefly dated Melissa King, a fellow nurse at the Providence Memorial Hospital, in the summer of 1990. She said that Lozano was home only for "five to ten days" when he met King. Williams denied introducing them. Under oath, Williams stated:

> (Paul) told me that—this was after he returned to Boston—that he had—during his visit to her home, had discovered some prescription medications, which appeared to belong to some patients that had been patients in the unit . . . I had to report her, which I did do, and she's no longer (at the hospital) . . . He told me about it, and he knew I was going to go to the administration about it.

Williams may have been trying to convey the virtuousness of her upbringing. Both Lozano and she met their legal and moral obligations by reporting King for allegedly stealing drugs from patients.

In February 1993, I called the Providence Memorial Hospital. A spokeswoman in the personnel department said that Melissa King had left the hospital's employ "about a year to a year and a half ago." Hence, at the earliest, King departed the hospital in the fall of 1991, a year after Williams claimed she turned King in and two years after—according to the Process Notes—Lozano stopped seeing her.

If Melissa King was fired or resigned from the Providence Memorial Hospital in the fall of 1991, Lozano would have had little to do with it, having killed himself earlier that April.

10

THE APRIL FOOL'S AFFIDAVIT

On March 31, five days after the first news broadcast, Amy Stromsten, a 49-year-old Cambridge-based social worker, read Bean-Bayog's lawyer's response to the medical board's allegations:

"Mr. Lozano also disclosed to Dr. Bean-Bayog his problems with alcohol and drug abuse, his sociopathic symptoms, such as lying, stealing and cheating . . . He harbored homicidal, violent, and delusional thoughts; and he had periods when he was completely out of control."

This statement enraged Stromsten, the mystery witness, who decided to issue a public statement, because she could not tolerate Bean-Bayog's defamation of Lozano. She believed a Harvard psychiatrist had sexually maligned, in effect, murdered, an innocent, gifted minority medical student and was now continuing to malign him after his death.

On April Fool's Day, Stromsten, wrote out a hurried sworn affidavit and filed it at Middlesex Superior Court. (The misspellings and omissions are hers.)

I am a psychotherapist who was involved in the treatment of Paul Lozano in 1987 (actually 1986) until January 1991. I also was involved in conversations with Dr. Bean-Bayog regarding her sexual attraction to Paul Lozano. I am coming forward and making this statement because I am distressed at the mischaracterizations, un-

true statements and attacks on Paul Lozano's
character by Dr. Bean-Bayog.

I first met Paul Lozano when he was hospitalized at McLean Hospital under the care of Francis Franckenburg. Paul Lozano was also seeing
Dr. Margaret Bean-Bayog. Paul was a likeable
young man. He was honest with a great of integrity. Paul was extremely well liked by his
peers. I found him to be easy-going, somewhat
shy and introverted and not at all violent. At first,
Paul was suicidal. I frequently talked to Paul
while he was in the "quiet room." Before seeing
Dr. Bean-Bayog Paul had no history of psychiatric problems . . .

Though I was impressed that she had been one of the mental
health professionals treating Lozano during his first admission to
a mental hospital, I had to wonder how she could say with such
certainty that he had never suffered from any serious emotional
or mental illness.

. . . During our discussions Paul told me that he
felt inadequate at Harvard because he was a
Mexican American. Paul said he felt out of
place like a little fish in a big pond. He was
afraid he was not up to snuff . . . In clinical case
conference with Dr. Pope, Dr. Franckenburg, Dr.
Bean-Bayog and myself we discussed Paul
Lozano. Dr. Pope and Dr. Franckenburg were
concerned why she was doing analysis on an
individual with major depression, which was not
the usual form of treatment . . . We questioned
releasing him into the care of Dr. Bean-
Bayog . . .

To me, this was significant information. If true, I wondered
why Meyer had not mentioned it—that the hospital staff was so

apprehensive about the therapeutic relationship between doctor and patient that they had openly expressed concern about releasing Lozano into Bean-Bayog's care. Certainly he would have underscored it in his introduction to the Offer of Proof and pointed it out to the press.

> . . . In Spring/Summer of 1990 I joined a supervision group headed by Dr. Margaret Bean Bayog. The group of five social workers and one psychologist met at her home in the same room where she saw her patients . . . In this supervisor's group, Dr. Margaret Bean-Bayog talked about her erotic sexual feelings and sexual attraction toward a Mexican American medical student. I told Dr. Bean-Bayog that I knew the student she was referring to and that I treated him at McLean's. Dr. Bean-Bayog brushed this information off and continued on about her erotic countertransference—her sexual feelings toward Paul Lozano. Dr. Bean-Bayog described how powerful and strong her feelings were toward Paul Lozano in great length. This worried me because I knew there was some chance that Paul Lozano was being sexually abused . . .
> In January 1991, Paul called me and said that things were really bad and that he had to see me. I met with him for an hour and half and he poured his story out to me. Paul told me that he had been having a sexual relationship with Dr. Bean-Bayog for a number of years. Paul said he felt "ashamed, embarrassed, dirty." He described their relationship as "kinky." I asked him why he felt he had to have this relationship with her and he said he wasn't paying her very much . . . Paul also told me that Dr. Bean-Bayog shared her erotic fantasies with him and asked him to act them out with her and that they did.

> Paul was in no way delusional . . . Paul felt to-
> tally rejected because Dr. Bean-Bayog sud-
> denly terminated him since she was about to
> adopt a baby . . . I told him that he had been
> sexually abused by Dr. Bean-Bayog and what
> Dr. Bean-Bayog was doing was wrong. I also
> told him I knew what he was saying true be-
> cause Dr. Bean-Bayog had discussed her sex-
> ual attraction to him in the supervision group . . .

That statement troubled me. I felt that Stromsten should not
have told a patient with multiple admissions to mental hospitals
that his psychiatrist was going around confessing her sexual
attraction for him.

> . . . I referred him to Michael Lew of Newton
> Lower Falls who specializes in sexually abused
> men (in childhood). Michael Lew verified that
> Paul Lozano had indeed been sexually abused
> by Dr. Bean-Bayog . . .

I wondered how Lew could have "verified" that Lozano had
been sexually abused. Even if Lozano, who had a history of
serious psychiatric disorders, admitted to Lew that he had been
sexually involved with Bean-Bayog that is hardly verification.

> . . . In May 1991, I contacted Dr. Bernard Levy of
> the impaired physician's committee who I knew
> had a close and confidential relationship with
> Dr. Bean-Bayog. I asked him about Paul Lozano
> and he told me that Paul had committed sui-
> cide. I asked if the investigation was still under
> way and he told me that Dr. Margaret Bean-
> Bayog had masturbated in front of Paul and
> that they had a kinky relationship but that the
> investigation was over and that I should still refer
> patients to Dr. Bean-Bayog. I was outraged that

> Dr. Levy was covering up Dr. Bean-Bayog's serious misconduct.
>
> At no time has any member of the Board of Registration of Medicine contacted me or asked me what happened to Paul Lozano.

The first thing reporters did was to seek comment from Dr. Bernard D. Levy, a noted Newton psychiatrist, who told them that Stromsten's claims were patently false. He denied knowing anything at all about Bean-Bayog's alleged sexual abuse of Paul Lozano until the media broke the story several days before. Levy, who was placed on administrative leave pending the outcome of the investigation, considered launching a lawsuit against Stromsten for libel and slander, and accused her of violating state law because she herself had not reported the allegations to the state medical board in January 1991 when Lozano first reported them to her. Though Stromsten had not mentioned it in her affidavit or to the press, she suddenly claimed that she had, indeed, filed a complaint with the board in "the first two weeks of January 1991." The board, after scouring its files, reported it could not find her letter. The press was skeptical of the board's record keeping, because it had also misplaced both Becker's and Gault's initial letters of complaint sent in December 1990. Stromsten expressed her own skepticism, saying that apparently her letter had been "mysteriously lost." Next, she told the *Herald* that board officials had acknowledged they had received her letter. Attorney Alexander "Sandy" F. Fleming, the board's executive director, responded by denying that his agency ever acknowledged receiving it.

After she filed her affidavit, Stromsten granted interviews to the *Globe, Herald, Harvard Crimson, New York Times,* and *Los Angeles Times.* She was flooded with calls from "Geraldo," "Hard Copy," "Inside Edition" and other TV tabloids, begging her to appear. She told *New York Times* reporter, Fox Butterfield, that:

> (T)o her knowledge, Mr. Lozano's problem was depression that could be treated with drugs.

Therefore, she said, she and some senior colleagues questioned why Dr. Bean-Bayog had used psychoanalysis on him during four years of intensive therapy, in which the psychiatrist posed as his "mom" and encouraged him to think of himself as her infant son.

The *Los Angeles Times* reporter Elizabeth Mehren, who is Butterfield's wife, wrote:

If Lozano was sexually abused as a child, Stromsten says, "then regression therapy would be absolutely counterindicated." In cases of sexual abuse, she and others say, "the last thing in the world you would do is retraumatize someone by regressing them. That would be heinous."

Stromsten also became an investigator. The *Harvard Crimson* reported that "Stromsten said she suspects that several physicians, including Harvard Medical School professors, are involved in covering up Bean-Bayog's alleged sexual relationship with Lozano."

Her appearance on center court, however, was brief. Her problems began because reporters found in the Offer of Proof the entire records of Paul Lozano's two admissions to McLean Hospital. These contain page after page of physiological tests, medications, handwritten notes of doctors, nurses, and social workers, and two discharge summaries written by Frankenburg, the psychiatrist in charge of Lozano's care. Many of the handwritten notes are hard to read, because of the quality of penmanship, photocopying, or both. But in one particular case, the notes of a social-work intern are legible. They are the notes of Amy Stromsten.

For example, in the fall of 1986, Stromsten wrote in Lozano's records:

Paul was scapegoated in the family and appears to have suffered emotional abuse . . .

(Paul) never dated at West Point and when he transferred to U. Texas he met his wife, Diane. His parents said that if he kept seeing her they would tell her medical school that she had once been hospitalized for depression. In anger, Paul retaliated 2 days later by marrying Diane . . . He finally annulled the marriage to please his family.

In Lozano's second McLean admission, Stromsten noted:

When he told his parents (that he had decided to take a leave of absence from medical school), they were very upset, and (Paul said that) his mother said, "I'll probably die in the next year and not see you graduate." Paul said that "She'd probably do that just to spite me. . . ." The pressure from Paul's parents is enormous. Their response to his wish to take a year off was "This will be another West Point."

Also, in his first admission, Stromsten recorded that the "Patient refused [to give McLean Hospital permission to make] contact with his family." In his second, she scribbled, "He refuses to allow family members to know that he is in McLean."

Finally, she wrote:

I met with Victor Gonzalez, a roommate and close friend of the patient, on 9/27/86. He gave extensive information about a car accident in January. (Paul was hit while crossing the street) and family history. There were many incidents of abuse in Paul's childhood. He told Victor that his siblings frequently locked him in a closet and ignored his cries, and he said that this was only the tip of the iceberg.

The *Herald*, which had quoted her earlier without attribution, did not confront Stromsten on the fact that this information contradicted her affidavit, but she did anticipate that a reporter might challenge her. She told the *Herald,* "My impression was that there is some family trouble there. But don't forget that he was in a psychotic depression at that point. It's possible that it's true. It's possible that it's not. There was never any evidence of that."

Stromsten's more experienced superiors, however, found no evidence of Lozano's psychosis. Nowhere, in any of Lozano's McLean hospitalization records is he described as psychotic. Frankenburg stated in Lozano's medical records that he was suffering from "Major affective disorder, depressed, without melancholia, and *without psychotic features* [emphasis added], probably recurrent." Pope, Lozano's psychopharmacologist, also agreed that Lozano was not psychotic.

Stromsten, who was a social-work intern with limited experience and authority, was mistaken about Lozano's being psychotic at that time. Yet the press regurgitated her comments and analysis for digestion by millions of readers.

Over at the *Globe,* Stromsten's contradictions did not go unnoticed. On April 9, reporter Alison Bass ran a tough front-page story:

> A social worker who filed an affidavit in court last week saying that Paul Lozano had no history of psychiatric problems before being treated by Dr. Margaret Bean-Bayog acknowledged yesterday that she had written in his medical records that Lozano had a history of depression and had been abused as a child . . . When confronted with that inconsistency and asked directly if she knew that Lozano had a history of problems prior to his therapy with Bean-Bayog, Stromsten said, "Yeah, but what this really comes down to is what the treatment should have been."

After that, the mystery witness dropped from sight, referring all calls to her lawyer.

11

APRIL 2, 1992

Late in the afternoon of Thursday, April 2, 1992, the same day
that Stromsten's affidavit hit the front page of the *Globe,* the
clerk of the Middlesex Superior Court unexpectedly and incon-
spicuously placed the Plaintiff's Offer of Proof back into the
public record.

Within minutes, this information somehow wended its way to
the *Globe* newsroom.

At the same time, rumors that a motion had been filed by
Bean-Bayog's lawyers to seal all documents in the lawsuit and
that Judge Connolly was mulling it over also reached the newsroom. (Critics of Bean-Bayog's lawyers, including the client herself, would later charge that they should have sealed the
documents before Meyer had a chance to put them into the
public record.)

So when these two bits of information collided in the newsroom late Thursday afternoon, metro editor Bradlee, ordered me
back to photocopy the Process Notes before the rumored gag
order went into effect. He wanted the *Globe* to have a complete
copy of the documents, because this story was like the blob, a
voracious organism that inexplicably kept growing.

At 8:30 A.M. on April 3, one week after the story broke, I was
the first one through the door when the Middlesex County
Courthouse opened. I grabbed the notes and began photocopying the equivalent of two reams of paper. Over the past week, I
had written out checks for $1,500 to the clerk of the Middlesex
Superior Court to cover the costs. A few reporters from *People*
magazine and *Newsweek* meandered in as I was finishing up. By
noon, I was back in the newsroom. I dumped the notes on
Bradlee's desk and turned to go. He gruffly told me to read them

and submit a story in seven hours for tomorrow's paper.

"Impossible," I said, smiling. "How about for Sunday?"

"Fine," he said, as he hurried out to play lunchtime basketball.

I stood there and did some simple arithmetic. I had about twenty-four hours to decipher and absorb 987 pages of scribbled notes, roughly forty-one pages an hour. A few of the pages were blank, some only partially filled.

In the reader's heart of hearts, only one thing really mattered: Did she or didn't she make the beast with two backs with Paul Lozano? Other questions, such as acceptable psychiatric standards or manipulation of the press, were tangential. The common man and woman were salivating over sex and I was determined to try to provide them with an answer. And my father probably could help.

I called him in Washington D.C. and he agreed to cancel his Saturday plans and read a thousand pages of hieroglyphics before his son's deadline. I made another copy and shipped the notes to him overnight.

The deadline for the daily *Globe* is 7:30 P.M. For the Sunday edition, it is 5 P.M. The earlier deadline allows the Sunday paper to reach the news stands by 10:30 P.M. Saturday night.

I rushed home apprehensive. I wasn't sure I could read and digest all of these notes and write a coherent story in eighteen hours. I brewed a pot of strong coffee, shut off the phone, and began to read. The Process Notes were the notes that Bean-Bayog took down during virtually every therapy session and every phone call with her patient, Paul Lozano. Since most psychiatrists hardly take notes at all—my father never took any— this was a relatively unique tome of a kind that virtually never becomes public. Her hard work was impressive. But I had a hunch it wouldn't be hard to listen in on what really transpired between doctor and patient. When she wrote down this material, she never thought it would be someday scrutinized by lawyers and reporters. Additionally, I would benefit from bouncing my callow impressions off my father.

As I began reading, I tried to imagine myself in the room with the two alleged lovers. When two people become romantic, the tone changes. Formality evaporates. Tenderness seeps in. Some sign of vulnerability would show up in the notes. I believed that my antennae would pick up echoes of intimacy, unguarded comments. She couldn't have rapidly scribbled down this much material without inadvertently leaving behind a few damaging, incriminating tidbits.[1]

At first, I had trouble reading Bean-Bayog's script. One word in particular stumped me. It appeared again and again. When I finally deciphered it, I found myself more fluent in her penmanship. The word was "angry." From the first session until the last, Lozano expressed much anger and humiliation. Also, I eventually began to understand her symbols and shorthand notations. For example, "pt" was patient; a triangle, (the scientific symbol for catalyst), stood for change; and the ancient Greek letter "Psi," which looked like Satan's pitchfork, represented "psychiatry."

In the first two years of therapy, Bean-Bayog wrote down much of what Lozano said, occasionally switching between third person and first person as he spoke. In fact, 93 percent or 920 pages cover the first two years of the four years of therapy. The final two years of therapy are covered by a mere sixty-seven pages of notes. Later, Bean-Bayog told me the reason she took fewer notes in the last two years is that his condition greatly improved. Indeed, Lozano managed to stay out of the hospital from July 1987 until March 1990.

---

1. LATER, I EXAMINED THE ORIGINAL PROCESS NOTES. THEY WERE IN TWO GRAY THREE-RING NOTEBOOKS, EACH WITH A FRONT INSIDE POCKET STUFFED WITH MISCELLANEOUS MATERIALS. THESE INCLUDED "OUTSIDE THERAPIST NOTES" THAT BEAN-BAYOG HAD WRITTEN FOR THE FAULKNER HOSPITAL, A FEW LETTERS AND BIRTHDAY CARDS TO BEAN-BAYOG FROM LOZANO, AND A FEW ITEMS, SUCH AS CARTOONS AND ARTICLES, THAT HE HAD GIVEN HER. MOST OF THE PROCESS NOTES WERE WRITTEN ON WHITE-LINED, PREPUNCHED PAPER. A FEW WERE WHITE AND UNLINED; OTHERS WERE YELLOW. SOME OF THE PAGES WERE WRITTEN ON BOTH SIDES. A FEW WERE WRITTEN ON HOTEL MEMO PADS WHEN SHE WAS OUT OF TOWN AND HE TELEPHONED LATE AT NIGHT. THE PAGES WERE UNNUMBERED. IT WAS MEYER WHO HAD PAGINATED THEM. ON A SMALL POST-IT ON EACH INSIDE COVER, SOMEONE HAD WRITTEN, "COPY FRONT TO BACK." THE MATERIALS IN THE FRONT POCKETS, HOWEVER, HAD NOT BEEN COPIED AND WERE NOT INCLUDED IN THE OFFER OF PROOF.

"He became merely neurotic and lost most of his suicidal impulses," Bean-Bayog said, adding that she no longer had to listen carefully—by writing down as much as possible and reviewing it later—for the subtle harbingers of his suicide attempts.

Only when he returned to his medical school clinical rotations in January 1990, did his mental illness rekindle.

Occasionally, when Lozano said something noteworthy, Bean-Bayog would place his words in quotations. Periodically, she made marginal notations, such as "patient standing up," "furious," "frantic," or "giggling." She usually placed her own private thoughts or verbal responses in parentheses.

Later, Bean-Bayog told me she had never taken such extensive notes and had never fought so hard to keep a suicidal patient alive.

12

THE PROCESS NOTES—THE FIRST YEAR

I knew a little about psychotherapy because I'd seen several therapists, all couples counselors, to explore my reluctance to marry my girlfriend, now my wife, of twelve years. I knew that I was about to embark on a remarkable journey—mysterious, suggestive, and occasionally terrifying, but promising.

Critiquing the therapeutic journey is like judging nonrepresentational art. The journey is abstract, subject to widely divergent interpretation, and virtually never chronicled in detail. No one will ever see a photo or painting or read an account of it, because therapists rarely take extensive notes. However, here was a notable exception, a seeming map into a young man's psychopathology, doggedly logged by his female psychotherapist.

In the early days of the news accounts, the press had repeated, almost verbatim, tufts of documentary evidence plucked by Meyer. In reading the full notes for the first time, I began to glean a narrative structure in them. They told a very sad story, to be sure, one that would lend itself to many interpretations. They also provided the best evidence of what may have happened between Paul Lozano and his therapist.

What follows is my own reading of these notes.[1] I have done my best to preserve as much as possible their character and tone.

---

1. FOR CLARIFICATION, I HAVE CLEANED UP THE PUNCTUATION, ELIMINATED THE PARENTHESES, INSERTED WORDS IN BRACKETS, AND SPELLED OUT BEAN-BAYOG'S SYMBOLS, ABBREVIATIONS, AND SHORTHAND NOTATIONS.

In doing so, I have paid special attention to aspects of the notes that relate to the three principal charges levied against Bean-Bayog: wrongful death of her patient, psychiatric sexual misconduct, and medical malpractice.

In late August, 1984, the Lozanos proudly put Paul on a plane to Boston from El Paso. He had achieved one of the highest honors for any family, immigrant or not: admission to Harvard Medical School. Three weeks later, however, he made an appointment to see a psychiatrist, chosen from a list supplied by the school's health services.

His tentative approach in labeling himself a patient in need of psychiatric care is reflected in the very first pages of notes for September 24 and 27, 1984. My immediate sense was that Lozano had psychiatric problems long before he met Bean-Bayog and long before he began intensive therapy with her two years later.

The words are his as recorded by her:

> Didn't want to come. . . . Since school (began, I've done) nothing. Don't go to school. Could grasp (the material, but I) don't care. Don't like being here. Stayed in bed. Embarrassing. People give right leg to get (into this) place. Feels better to come and talk . . . If I leave this place . . . (my) family won't speak to me . . . Have no one to study with . . . (I was in a) pediatric oncologist (ward.) (I told) jokes about (the) sick kids.

> (I was) married and annulled . . . Embarrassed. No one knows. Parents had liked Diane before . . . One of my sisters called her. So upset with family. Didn't want anything to do with them. Said horrible things. I'm going to medical school one way or other. Don't see point of leave of absence. Discouraged about (these) symptoms . . . If (I) go talk to Mommy and Daddy, maybe don't need treatment.

Lozano did not return to Bean-Bayog's care until the start of his third year in school. In the interim, he attended classes, earned average grades, but flunked anatomy.

He saw Bean-Bayog again on July 3, 1986, the first day of what would become four years of intensive therapy. Apparently, Bean-Bayog realized immediately how suicidal Lozano was, because in the upper right hand corner of the page she jotted down the phone number of McLean Hospital.

On that first day, Bean-Bayog wrote:

> (He) saw me two years ago. "(I've been) think-
> ing about treatment since . . ." (He feels) iso-
> lated. Sits alone. Cringes when sees group in
> cafeteria . . . "(Last January,) I was hit by a car.
> (I was) inattentive," Actually suicidal.

A year later, Lozano admitted to her that he had been drinking, worn dark clothing, and that his stepping in front of the car was a "clear suicide attempt," in which his knee was injured. Eventually, he sued the driver and won a $55,000 out-of-court settlement. Later, when his apartment was burglarized, he thought it was retaliation for his filing a false insurance claim.

During the second therapy session on July 11—the one in which Williams claimed that Bean-Bayog masturbated—Lozano talked about his dropping out of West Point Military Academy. He later told Bean-Bayog one of his major failings at West Point was that he was "bad at making beds." He said that he had reached his limit, been drunk a lot, looked out a window and thought about jumping and drank to "get anesthetized."

While attending medical school, Lozano worked as a research assistant at a variety of labs. At the time he began intensive therapy, he told Bean-Bayog that his job was to kill with lethal injection the beagles that had been used in experiments.

In the third session on July 17, 1986, Lozano admitted shamefully, "Another bad habit. Stuffed animals. Very childish. I like them. I have this cute little dog."

In the news accounts, Pilar Williams had asserted that as an adult Lozano did not have stuffed animals, except those given to him by Bean-Bayog, including the infamous Pound Puppy. I had assumed this was a stuffed animal that Lozano had metaphorically named. In fact, it is a brand name.

According to the notes, for nearly a year Lozano could not summon up the courage to show the Pound Puppy to Bean-Bayog, because he was so ashamed of it.

Williams claimed that Bean-Bayog reduced her brother to the "state of a dependent 3-year-old." But on July 31, the fourth therapy session, in which Lozano described Williams as the person who raised him, the patient appeared to be already regressed:

> Shame. Wish to be a puppy. (I want to be) held.
> Strange. As a kid, talk to self, hate schools . . .
> Brothers and sisters teased me. One sister, nurse,
> kinda raised me . . . Got knife and was going to
> hurt them. Worse, was going to kill self, chil-
> dren's aspirin.

I remembered reading in his hospital records that Lozano had told Bean-Bayog and other psychiatrists of two other childhood suicide attempts, one by hanging, the other by gas. Williams denied her brother attempted suicide as a child.

By early August, 1986, Bean-Bayog put Lozano on Imipramine, an antidepressant. On August 8, he told her, "Each time [a suicidal desire] came, I'd panic. 'It's coming again. It's not going away.' "

But Bean-Bayog felt confident enough in his survival to go away on vacation. At first, his reaction to the antidepressant was an "immediate placebo elation, which collapsed while [I] was away on vacation." She didn't see him again until September 4:

> Previous suicide attempts untreated depres-
> sion. 13 tried to hang self in basement.
> "I never told my family. Hard to hide rope
> burns, petechiae eye spots. They brushed it off.
> She probably suspected . . . Again in col-

lege . . . Gas inhalation . . . What if parents walk in. Dad smokes. About to black out. Cramps in hands and arms. Terrible hangover. Really guilty about it . . . Sister would flip out. Bad deportment (in) junior high. Took long way home. Talking to self . . . Never felt (I) belong here. Half the (medical school) class (from) the same ten (prep) schools . . . always think bottom will fall out . . ."

Discussed . . . (he) shouldn't be in medical school now if (he) thought he'd suicide if patient died.

"(I) feel really good about self doing something about this (depression)"

By mid-September, Lozano admitted that he went jogging late at night in a park near the marginal neighborhood he lived in, hoping to get mugged: "If I go running in park, woods, if something happens, that's okay. [I] did. In park yelling OK. Go ahead! That's what I'm here for, aren't I?"

He also told her that he had purchased a container of Morton's Lite Salt (KCL) and was contemplating killing himself by injecting some of it: "It doesn't matter if it's sterile if you're using it to check out . . . I wouldn't want to botch this. It would be all over in about four minutes unless someone had a defibrillator."

He was also reading veterinary journals learning how to painlessly kill large animals. Lozano said:

Don't expect to live to my dad's age . . . There is a defect in the machinery. It's important to be logical about this. Some people just aren't going to make it. When a computer shorts out, no one makes a fuss . . . I've been telling myself I didn't feel this way, but it's a relief to admit I *do* feel it. What has fueled me for years is I was going to show them. Medical school is very important. Without it there would be no reason to go on being.

Lozano's black sense of humor reflected his sense of doom. He again visited a pediatric oncology unit and found the children's shaved heads "like it was all hilarious, horrible things, went to bathroom and roared." Later, he laughingly told Bean-Bayog that, if he shot himself in the head with his father's gun, his landlady would come in and find "half [my] brain splattered all over the wallpaper. She makes such a fuss over everything. She'd have to change it."

His desire to kill himself intensified. He visited the thirteenth floor of the Harvard School of Public Health and thought about jumping. He calculated how long it would take to hit the ground: "Skulls break in very characteristic places. It would be a bad one or two seconds but pain is short."

On September 22, 1986, he told Bean-Bayog that he was,

> Furious. Feel(s) good to say, "Fuck you." Before didn't kill self for parents. Tired of living for them. Finished . . . Suicide makes sense because of suffering and hopeless. I *am* hopeless, really tired . . . Pain's short. Don't wanna botch it. Wish you'd been my mother. Sister would never believe I was seriously suicidal until I was *cold* . . . Only thing kept me alive is you. Not for you I'd be dead. (I'm) gonna be dead, so (let's) take afternoon off . . . Arrogant, but just don't wanna say Paul couldn't take it. That's what kept me from talking to anyone, coming to see anyone. Can't pretend anymore. Out of hand. Suffering could stop. I was gonna do it. I was gonna do it. I was gonna do it . . . At least I can talk now. Frozen. Couldn't talk. Couldn't talk. Couldn't talk. When realize gonna be dead, (I) can do whatever (I) want . . . Lots of good organs. Two corneas, liver, kidneys. Only good as cadaver.

Bean-Bayog had no choice but to act. On September 24, after a mere eight therapy sessions, she had Lozano admitted to McLean Hospital. He was diagnosed with a major recurrent depression. Because of "urinary retention," his psychophar-macologist, Dr. Harrison Pope, changed his medication from Imipramine to Desipramine and increased the dosage. After that, his condition improved.

At this point, I stopped reading for a moment. Why, I wondered, would a psychiatrist who had foolishly and bizarrely masturbated in front of a patient during their second meeting allow him to be examined by other psychiatrists, who might elicit this information? It made no sense. It disturbed me that I, along with other professional news people, had simply accepted the claim. But that didn't mean it wasn't possible, only improbable. Again, I made a mental note to search every word of these records for the slightest false note, the slip that would convey some suggestion of intimacy, anything that would suggest Bean-Bayog had misbehaved toward her patient.

About eight weeks later on November 19, Lozano was discharged from the hospital. His prognosis was only fair and Frankenburg had astutely urged him to put off his psychiatric rotation as long as possible.

He continued therapy with Bean-Bayog; and on the day of his discharge, he signed a fee agreement with her:

> I agree to reimburse Dr. Margaret Bean-Bayog payment in full @ the rate of $80/hr. for services rendered. (signed) Paul. A. Lozano.

Below his signature, Bean-Bayog scribbled in:

> Discussed courtesy reduction for medical students. Patient wants to pay if he can, with deferred payment when out of school if he can't. "Like a taxi meter."

Though the press had reported that Bean-Bayog had not charged Lozano for therapy, that was not quite true. Not only had he promised to pay after graduating from medical school, but a small portion of the bill was picked up by his student health insurance. Additionally, he had written out six checks to her totalling $1,535. And in July 1989, Lozano wrote out a $9,000 check to Bean-Bayog from the $55,000 he received in the settlement of his car "accident." Nonetheless, at the end of therapy in 1990, Lozano's outstanding balance was sizable. He owed Bean-Bayog $25,692.

Soon, his sexual desires toward his therapist and his desires to be a "safe" 3-year-old began to haunt him. In November 1986, she wrote:

> (He) mention(ed) having sexual feelings out-
> side office. Felt very guilty about this. Wouldn't
> talk (about it. "You'd be angry," (I) explained
> he didn't choose his feelings and they might
> bother him less if he talked about them. "(I'm)
> still terribly ashamed of feeling like a three year
> old," We invented a baby version of him who
> might have something on his mind. Maybe he
> could make friends with his three year old self.

At that time, Bean-Bayog began using a cognitive-behavior technique of providing Lozano with a list of instructions, reminding him not to drink, to take his medications, to get plenty of sleep, and to call her at any time if he began feeling suicidal.

In December 1986, he revealed that his childlike behavior may have predated his therapy with Bean-Bayog, something the family may have known about but denied.

> Patient made the blanket in my office into a
> transitional object. I gave it to him. He was
> deeply ashamed and felt I would be angry
> when he was "like this," i.e., three years old,
> because his family couldn't stand it.

In February, Lozano revealed that he felt more comfortable if someone was angry or critical of him. When shown affection or praise, he said it "makes me feel sick to my stomach," because he viewed himself as a fraud.

Another character trait was for Lozano to play one person off against another in order to elicit sympathy and solicitude. For example, Bean-Bayog noted in March 1987:

> Patient may be telling Dr. Pope I told him to discontinue drugs. Patient after talking to sister decided to stop his antidepressants without consulting me or Dr. Pope, (led to) acute withdrawal reaction.

One of the dangers in treating patients with certain kinds of mental disorders is the intense dependence they develop on their therapist. Psychodynamic psychiatrists, including Freud himself, are often criticized for treating only the "worried well;" i.e., mildly neurotic patients. Lozano did not fall into that category. Whatever the cause of his psychopathology, it is evident from the notes that he was extremely angry, easily humiliated, and suicidal. His extreme dependence was also frightening.

Bean-Bayog wrote in several notes of April 1987:

> Patient came in feeling humiliated . . . with a bag of intravenous equipment and drugs. He initially would not part with them. Was a very intense, exhausting session where we discussed how he wanted to shoot himself but had no gun, wanted to overdose with his antidepressants but really didn't think there were enough to really do the job right. He seemed amazed that I wanted him to give me his bag of drugs so badly, that it really mattered to me that he was alive.

> Still (had) substantial suicidal impulses and thoughts. "My father has a gun. I keep thinking about it. I don't want to do a half-assed job. If you put a gun to your temple you may survive. But if you put it in your mouth . . . The only reason I didn't was I don't have a gun."

Describing his reaction to my first weekend away when he shot up trilafon. He felt I was angry with him . . . associated to repeated experiences when his mother was angry.

Lozano's injecting himself with Trilafon, a hazardous drug with myriad side effects, was a dangerous, self-destructive act. His suicidal gesture was a response to the fact that his therapist, his lifeline, was unavailable for a weekend. He found her absence very threatening. Lozano's reaction was the beginning of a pattern that would have profound consequences in the eventual litigation against her. Whenever any of the mental health professionals, including Bean-Bayog, with whom he had forged a therapeutic alliance, went on vacation, Lozano felt abandoned and rejected, increasing his suicidal rage. A year later, in December of 1987, the measures that Bean-Bayog took to keep her patient alive during her three-week vacation to the Philippines and Hong Kong became a focus of the Lozano lawsuit and hence of the press.

By late April 1987, Lozano, manipulative and threatening, had become increasingly suicidal. On May 3, Bean-Bayog wrote:

12:30 A.M. Patient called slightly drunk, having shaken off his roommate, from the 13th floor of Harvard School of Public Health, where he had spent 15 minutes dangling his legs out and thinking of jumping. I arranged to meet with him immediately at my office.
Patient: "We'll just talk?"
Me: "We'll talk."
Mercifully he came, and mercifully did not run out when I told him we had to go to the hospital. I drove him there. He said on the way over if I had called police, ambulance, etc., he would have run. Even so, when we got to the hospital and security got in the car to guide me to the building, he did run. Again, mercifully, he was

caught and put himself through a whole har-
rowing scene of being physically subdued,
held (by two uniformed security guards), and
(put) in 4-point restraints.

Lozano's second admission resulted in several significant events. First, he took a leave of absence from Harvard Medical School lasting for nearly three years. Second, his confinement in four-point restraints, in which his limbs were tied to the side rails of the bed, became one of the central themes of his repeated sadomasochistic sexual fantasies about Bean-Bayog. And finally, Lozano informed his family, who knew nothing of his prior admission, that he was a patient in a mental hospital and allowed them to visit him.

Frankenburg raised with Bean-Bayog the issue of her possible overinvolvement with her patient. In psychotherapy, overinvolvement is somewhat routine, an issue that therapists deal with fairly often. Lozano's response was "What do they know?" Bean-Bayog told him self-critically, "They may have a point."

Overinvolvement, though common, should be monitored. Mechanisms exist, like consultations, for dealing with it. However, there are no clearly defined protocols. Essentially, it's a judgment call. Psychiatrist-patient relationships are complex and volatile. What's more, preventing a patient's suicide may require unique and heroic action by the treating therapist.

Bean-Bayog did, however, obtain consultations from three fellow psychiatrists.[2] Two of them, Drs. Dan H. Buie, Jr. and Gerald Adler, are nationally known analysts, affiliated with the Boston Psychoanalytic Society and Institute, where Bean-Bayog was a candidate. They enthusiastically supported her treatment. The third, Dr. Shervert Frazier, the psychiatrist-in-chief of McLean Hospital, told her in a brief phone call that the patient might need some kind of protection from the intensity and re-

---

2. BEAN-BAYOG SAID SHE ALSO CONSULTED REGULARLY WITH DRS. BETH BROWNLOW AND SUSAN ADELMAN, WHO COVERED FOR BEAN-BAYOG WHEN SHE WAS OUT OF TOWN. SHE ALSO CONSULTED OCCASIONALLY WITH DR. TOM GUTHEIL.

gression in the therapeutic relationship with her. Frazier also believed that Lozano was manipulative and seductive, and was using treatment for gratification. However, Frazier was unable to schedule a conference with Bean-Bayog before the patient was transferred out of McLean when Lozano's insurance ran out.

There is broad disagreement on how to treat disruptive patients like Paul Lozano. Even my father agreed with Drs. Frazier and Frankenburg's position that borderline patients should be treated with harsh doses of reality and limitations, not empathic explorations.

In a word, Frankenburg preferred antidepressant medication, limit setting, and reality testing to deal with Lozano's depression, and what she would later diagnose as his borderline personality disorder. Bean-Bayog preferred antidepressant medication, some limit setting and reality testing too, but also the empathic exploration of his psyche and of his feelings. Frankenburg refused to discuss with Lozano why he wanted to feel like a 3-year old. Bean-Bayog, however, was willing to listen. Both psychiatrists were aiming for a functioning patient and both would have preferred to hospitalize Lozano for a year or two.[3]

On May 6, 1987, Bean-Bayog jotted down her conversation with Frankenburg:

Met with Dr. Frankenburg who was concerned I was overinvolved, inappropriate, and dangerous to the patient who was "torturing you."
How would you feel if he had killed himself?."
"Upset, but I'd get over it."
"Not relieved? Aren't you angry with him?"
"I don't think so."

---

3. THOUGH BEAN-BAYOG TRIED TO ARRANGE FOR PAUL'S LONG-TERM HOSPITALIZATION, INSURANCE COMPANIES AND HEALTH MAINTENANCE ORGANIZATIONS WOULD NOT PAY. PILAR WILLIAMS DID NOT WANT HER BROTHER COMING HOME TO TEXAS'S "SNAKE PIT OF STATE MENTAL HOSPITALS." BECAUSE THEY ARE SO OVERCROWDED AND DISCHARGE PATIENTS LIKE LOZANO AT THE FIRST SIGN OF THERAPEUTIC IMPROVEMENT. ONLY THE VERY WEALTHY CAN AFFORD LONG-TERM ADMISSION TO A PRIVATE HOSPITAL.

"Who pays for his treatment?"

"He is running up a tab. Currently, he isn't paying."

"And didn't it occur to you to blame him for (your) miscarriage?"

"No, it hadn't crossed my mind."

I was a little startled. No, I didn't think I was so angry with him. Tired, yes. He was very hectic, panicky a lot, and with the blackmail of suicide in the background. No, I wanted him alive, and I think if I had been ambivalent he would've picked it up. Told her I had had various discussions about him with consultants and was scheduled to see both Dr. Adler and Dr. Buie. (Dr. Frankenburg) thought I was being conned. I thought she was being unempathic. Then I realized he had replicated his family structure in the split he set up between her and me. She is his mother, physically and sexually abusing him. I am probably Pilar, who dotes on him, and the rest of the staff are the siblings who tortured him and vice versa.

Later, that day, Bean-Bayog met with Lozano:

Clarified reasons I can't touch him. "It's confusing. It needs to stay all talk. Otherwise it's not safe and you need a safe place."

"You're very careful. It really helped the other night when you touched my hand when you left. I was so frightened I couldn't move."

"Even shaking hands is too confusing."

Frankenburg's reference to Bean-Bayog's miscarriage was important. In press interviews, the Lozanos claimed that the intimacy between Bean-Bayog and Paul was implicit because she was sharing personal and intimate details about herself with her patient. They also alleged that Bean-Bayog's desire to have a child of her own was so ardent she temporarily created one in Lozano, later "dumping" him when she thought she was about to adopt a baby in the summer of 1990.

In late April, 1987, there was an important development. Bean-Bayog began to speculate that her patient was a victim of incest, because Lozano told her that he "couldn't tell if his Mom was also his girlfriend."

I wondered why Bean-Bayog so resolutely latched on to the theory of childhood seduction. Couldn't his statement about his mother being his girlfriend have other interpretations, perhaps an early example of psychotic thinking, not echoes of incest? Shortly after his second McLean admission, Bean-Bayog shared with her patient an article on child abuse that had just been published in *Psychiatric Annals*. It was called, "Psychological Damage Associated with Extreme Eroticism in Young Children: Evaluating Suspected Cases of Child Sexual Abuse."

I found the contents of this article astonishing:

> Assessing the emotional damage sustained by children who have been sexually abused is extraordinarily difficult . . . (W)hen a 4-year-old boy (has had) an incestuous involvement with his mother . . . The youngster is (usually) attracted to older females . . . Very few eroticized children are referred for intensive, long-term therapy; the culture views them as behaviorally rather than emotionally disturbed . . . When these children become adults, they often view post-discovery events as more damaging than the molestation itself . . . The children need to develop intense nonsexual relationships that will serve as alternatives to the original, intensely sexual relationship . . . For therapy to be effective, the therapist must form a close relationship with the child. The eroticized child reacts to the therapist as if the therapist were soliciting sexual

favors. When the therapist is consistent and kind, but firm, the child desists—but not until every strategy has been tried . . . (I)t is difficult and dangerous for male therapists to treat these (female) children. Male therapists must contend with intense countertransference reactions and they must be constantly alert and able to handle constructively a child's seduction. When in a state of negative transference, a child may complain to others about the therapist's sexual advances. As child and therapist have been alone together, it is the child's word against the therapist's word in a culture that believes that children never lie about sexual molestation . . . With intensive, long-term therapy, the nonsexual therapeutic relationship can become as intense and invested as was the original, sexualized transference to the parent . . . Male and female therapists become sexually aroused when they treat eroticized youngsters. This is especially disturbing to male therapists. Therapists need to accept this response as a manifestation of the countertransference; they can learn a great deal about themselves through understanding the reaction rather than suppressing or denying it.

The article was written by Dr. Alayne Yates, chief of child and adolescent psychiatry and a professor of psychiatry and pediatrics at the University of Arizona College of Medicine. Her phone numbers were scrawled twice in the margins. Bean-Bayog's notation read: "Article given to patient [in] early May [1987], reviewed repeatedly while hospitalized and after."

Since the article was also about the treatability of such patients, her reason for sharing it with Paul may have been another way of giving him something to hang on to, a comforting object.

An intense relationship between doctor and patient did develop. One result was that Bean-Bayog wrote down the notorious "sexual fantasies." According to Pilar Williams, they were an account of actual sexual activity between doctor and patient. According to Bean-Bayog, they were her own very private way of dealing with a powerful countertransference, and learning from it.

However, I had to wonder how Yates could have known that very few eroticized children are referred for long-term therapy and that the patients view post-discovery memories as more damaging than the molestation itself. I had to also wonder in reading this article whether Lozano would have been better off with a male instead of a female therapist, and hence, did Bean-Bayog err in not referring him to one.

Bean-Bayog's key working hypothesis for Lozano's psychopathology was his mother's sexual abuse. In the notes, she repeatedly advanced this theory upon her patient. I wondered why. Psychotherapists certainly make suggestions and offer observations but should they push their speculations on their patients? The notes of June 3, 1987, reflected this pressure:

> "Just gets bent over all the time. Gets fucked over by everyone. Dr. Frankenburg gets off on it."
>
> "Connection to talking about your family abusing you, lying, covering up sexual abuse?"
>
> "It *hurts*. I don't maybe want it to hurt anymore. It felt awful after. Depression, guilt, shame, awfulest feeling is that it also felt good."

The mention of his family's "lying, covering up sexual abuse" referred to the family meeting at McLean on May 26, attended by Frankenburg, social worker Roberta Goldwyn, Pilar, Paul, and Epifania. Williams emphatically denied that her brother had been abused in any way, rather he had been doted on and pampered.

After the meeting, Lozano was concerned that the McLean staff would view him, rather than his family, as a liar:

Intense reaction to split between hospital staff
buying his family version.

"Dr. Frankenburg flashes her understanding
eyes and says, 'We don't think you're lying' . . .
All a mistake on my part. I made it all up . . .
Sister said, '. . . I don't know where he gets all
these ideas. We've always loved him . . .' I have
all this anger. If my childhood were happy, so
where could it have come from? . . . Made me
feel really crazy. I don't think I was lying. I think
I do remember those things."

"(You're) not sure?"

"I know what I remember and why'd they tell
me things (I) didn't remember and didn't want
to . . . You probably think I'm distorting too."

In mid-June, Lozano told Bean-Bayog: "I am doing better
with my parents. Before I'd call and lie to them. Now [I] just
don't call. I'm past caring."

In reading the notes, I realized that Lozano's ethics were not
exactly exemplary. In September, he noted that the new application for medical licensure requested any information on the ap-
plicant's psychiatric history. "I guess you lie. I do. I've gotten
into the habit of lying."[4]

Also, Lozano had committed insurance fraud on his car accident. He confessed to Bean-Bayog that he had falsified research
data, shoplifted, stolen books from the Countway Medical Library (which has elaborate security), had done "a little breaking
and entering" while on vacation in Texas, drove drunk without
insurance or registration, and thought about running a child
prostitution ring.

The notes imparted the inescapable impression that Bean-
Bayog was an industrious psychiatrist, who was undaunted by
challenges. In fact, she seemed to feed on them. She probably got

---

4. BEAN-BAYOG OMITTED HER 1984 DRUNK DRIVING CONVICTION FROM HER 1986
AND 1987 MEDICAL LICENSE RENEWALS.

writer's cramp scribbling out these 987 pages. She willingly and empathically took Lozano's late-night phone calls when he was feeling troubled; many of the notes are of telephone calls. She wrote out detailed outside therapist notes for each of his first four hospitalizations in order to familiarize the staffs with Lozano's history and condition. Moreover, she penned a detailed ten-page "Note on P.L.'s Suicide Risk" with scholarly references. She shared this monograph with her colleagues, and—most significant—with her patient.

Bean-Bayog simultaneously explored a variety of avenues in her treatment of him: psychodynamic psychotherapy, cognitive-behavioral techniques, drug therapy, and hospitalization. She also appealed directly to his considerable intellect and to his own ample knowledge of medicine. Doctor and patient discussed Yates's article on childhood sexual abuse, an article on borderline personality disorder, Bean-Bayog's extensive treatise on his suicide risk, and an article on transitional objects.

After reading the first year's notes, I took a break and brewed a third pot of coffee. The press had painted her as a sexual deviant who had employed bizarre therapeutic techniques. I realized that whatever else was true, Bean-Bayog had worked very hard to keep her patient alive. Lozano realized this too. On June 6, 1987, he said, taunting her: "Go ahead. Break your ass trying to get me better. I'll watch a while."

13

THE PROCESS NOTES—THE SECOND YEAR

A strange, but not untypical, quirk in Lozano's health insurance was that though his coverage had run out for care in a private psychiatric hospital, it had not run out for care in the psychiatric ward of a general hospital. Consequently, like so many others, Lozano was bounced by the system from the relatively posh surroundings of McLean's 240 acres of tree-lined hills and woodlands to a general hospital in Boston, where even the best professional care could not match the attention he had received during his seven weeks in suburban Belmont. On June 22, 1987, Lozano arrived at Faulkner General Hospital in Boston for the first of four admissions.

When McLean discharged him, Frankenburg had declared his prognosis as "extremely guarded." Lozano was still taking Desipramine, but its therapeutic effect was beginning to wane.

McLean Hospital may have been comfortable, the rooms clean and airy, the staff outnumbering the patients by three to one, but Lozano found its no-nonsense, intentionally unempathic approach to his attempts to gain sympathy harsh and unpleasant, nothing like the support he had been able to elicit from Bean-Bayog. In fact, just before his transfer, he talked his way out of the hospital on a brief pass for ice cream. He went to his favorite haunt, the thirteenth floor of the Harvard School of Public Health and contemplated leaping to his death. The hospital placed him on escape status but he returned on his own. He refused a toxic screen because he was drunk and did not tell the staff that he had considered jumping off the thirteenth floor of a building. Actually, this was the second time in a week that McLean had placed Lozano on escape status. Thus, he was surprised that he had been allowed to leave the hospital at all for "ice cream." He told Bean-Bayog it showed that either the hospital staff did not appreciate the severity of his condition, or didn't care, or both. Oddly, it was the general hospital, where accommodations were not so comfortable and the staff far more thinly stretched, that Lozano found what he considered sympathetic attention. In that environment he became less angry and more cooperative.

It was a few days after his transfer to Faulkner that Bean-Bayog told her patient:

> "(I) can speculate what happened with your mother. Psychotically depressed. Over-stimulated. Pilar taking over."
> "She felt more like my mother. Good thing she was there."
> "(You had a) lot to survive."

Bean-Bayog continued to speculate about the childhood interaction of Lozano and his mother. Following Lozano's plea at the end of June 1987, that Bean-Bayog not "give up on the boy. Please keep hugging him," the notes from July 14 and 15, displayed the intensity of their exchanges.

> "I was really angry with you . . ."
> "Because of restraining you and hospitalizing you?"
> "Yes, (I) guess (it) generated a lot of other feelings too, which even spill over now. (I'm) getting aroused feelings more often. Hope it's OK to talk about these feelings."
>
> (He) described wanting to put me in restraints.
> (I) explained how what is going on between us is information.

"Maybe what's happening now is what happened to you when (you were) little. Very scary, intense experience like small child . . . How (do) you feel about talking about it?"

" . . . I'd been carrying them around so long, feeling they were terrible. I guess they seem lot less horrible when they're discussed openly . . . I guess I never thought you'd understand that I had those two different sets of feelings—being degraded and aroused. I never expected it to be discussed. Seems we've gone quite a way in one year. Guess (it's) not just my private badness. Not so private, not so bad."

"I'm glad I talked to you about this. I think it's a good idea . . ."
"I think that's wonderful."
"I think you're wonderful."
"I think you're better."
"I'm afraid to get started because . . . then I'd have a lot of other things to say."
"Like?"
"You're just (my) type of person, very understanding, constant force in my life. Besides, your work precedes you according to Dr. Gregory. Said you were really well known and respected in this city."
"Would not've known it from McLean."
"He's a second-year resident and he's heard of you. I'm pretty lucky anyway."
"So am I."

Lozano also said, "When you were talking about how the boy wasn't real, just a fantasy, my heart started pounding," because Bean-Bayog repeatedly reminded Lozano, the adult, that the "boy" was just a therapeutic tool.

A week later, the relationship had evolved to a point where the patient needed from his psychiatrist objects that kept him in touch with her.

Transitional objects are articles or symbols that provide comfort and reassurance. A child may have a toy or stuffed animal for comfort. As adults, certain objects and experiences may also provide comfort and solace, such as a wedding ring, a cross, a Star of David. According to Bean-Bayog's curriculum vitae, she had done a residency in child psychiatry and therefore had many children's books in her office library. Because Lozano asked for them, Bean-Bayog gave several to him as transitional objects.

The note of July 22, 1987, on transitional objects read in part:

> (We) review use of transitional objects to comfort him. Won't always need them. Will outgrow. But as (he is) leaving hospital, Baby can have blanket and *Goodnight Moon*. Toddler can have *Owl at Home*. Boy can have *Alexander and the Terrible Day* (and) *Where the Wild Things Are*. Medical student can have N(ew) E(ngland) J(ournal of) M(edicine) articles (and) Dr. Yates's article about sexually abused children being treatable.

Patients in psychotherapy often have fantasies about their therapists. I know. I've had them myself. (My first therapist was a dazzling beauty to whom I would have been attracted in or out of therapy.) Paul Lozano repeatedly voiced his sexual desires for Bean-Bayog, which she permitted with limitations. On July 25, 1987, she wrote:

> Reviewed safety, that he can feel anything and talk about the feelings but (we must) keep boy safe.
> "If we slept together, all the work we've done together would go all to smash."
> "I guess it would."
> "You can want to, you can make me want to, but we can stay in our chairs, keep boy safe."

In the meantime, Bean-Bayog continued to speculate on his mother's incest. On July 31, 1987, three days after his discharge from the Faulkner Hospital and shortly before he began working as a research assistant, she wrote:

> He brought Pound Puppy to show me. Sequence of getting aroused, describing (a sexual fantasy), then using Pound Puppy to comfort, calm self down.
> "Must have done that when (you were) sexually abused as (a) baby. Few ways to protect self: Go to sleep, blanket, Pound Puppy."
> (He then) describes wanting to be three years old and *"That's all.* You wouldn't do anything else. You might read to me but I'd just be three years old and *that's all."*

Apparently, Bean-Bayog theorized that, since a patient usually transfers his feelings for a parent onto his therapist, if Lozano had been sexually violated by his mother, it might explain why he had such intense and violent sexual fantasies about his therapist. To me, that sounded like a big leap in logic; there could have been many other plausible explanations for his fantasies.

However, one of the pivotal issues in this case was Bean-Bayog's countertransferences, that is, her private and complex feelings for her patient, most conspicuously manifested in her sexual fantasies. Evidence of her countertransferences do appear in the Process Notes, almost invisibly. In fact, tired and reading too quickly, I almost missed them in the early hours of the morning.

For example, on August 14, 1987, she noted that she had a:

> strange countertransference reaction to his improvement. Sad at losing the tight sense of where he is, not wanting to let go. In fact, just like his mother's and sister's reaction to him and his brothers leaving home.

Her admittedly "strange countertransference" of "not wanting to let go" because his condition appeared to be improving
and hence might soon lead to the end of his therapy, is an honest
admission. Psychiatrists are human. They sit, often for years,
listening to a patient's suffering. They can't help but feel some
human attachment and hence some sense of loss when all contact
is about to end.

Indeed, the key question was whether Bean-Bayog managed to
control and not act upon her countertransferences, not whether
she had them. Essentially, most psychiatrists involved in talk
therapy have them. Also, the passage raised the question of
whether she discussed her countertransferences with Lozano. If
so, that would have been inappropriate. Though reading very
quickly and unable to decipher some of her handwriting, I did
notice a few ambiguous passages that needed clarification, passages that I would ask her to explain if I ever got the chance to.

On August 21, 1987, she wrote:

> Only three year olds get to play like this with
> their moms."
> "Sexual games?"
> —(He began) hyperventilating.
> Gave (him) bag to rebreathe. Explained what
> was going on. Made sense out of my experi-
> ence. He and I were in the middle of a perver-
> sion, like how the love between him or a baby
> and his mother got distorted, destroyed, twisted,
> poisoned by her molesting and abusing him.
> That was what he felt was happening and I had
> parallel experience, raw, overwhelming, him
> molesting me, me molesting him.

At the time I did not realize the potential gravity of that last
clause. If I ever interviewed her, I would ask what she meant by
"parallel experience?" Was the "parallel experience" her own
sexual fantasies? And what exactly did "me molesting him"
mean? Is it her countertransference or is the "molestation" the
dilemma of the therapeutic bond? If she brought him in too close

(as his mother may have), Lozano would start to panic; if Bean-Bayog coldly kept him at a distance (as Frankenburg did), he would also panic and become infuriated.

More notes from the same therapy session may provide some clues:

> (I) shared mother-child incest fantasy (with him). Pretty raw, but that's what (I) think she did. Patient agitated, aroused, furious, regressed . . .
> "I don't remember. I don't want to remember."
> (He) fell asleep. (I) woke him.
> "(You have) Too much to deal with at once, but this is the stuff that's making you suicidal, that got you into McLean, that repeated the abuse by (your) mother. As much as (you) can stand (it), we have to understand it."
> Hypervent(ilating): "I don't remember. I don't remember what you said."
> "Maybe just as well."
> Panicking: "Don't leave me."
> Was hard to end (the) session. (He) took several transitional objects.

The following day, they spoke by phone:

> "Don't wanna talk to you."
> "(I) don't blame you after what I talked to you about (yesterday). (I just wanted to) check to see if (the) boy is safe."

During this period Lozano seemed particularly confused, which is reflected in the notes of early September:

> Acting aroused . . .
> "Dilemma is to keep (the) boy safe without making him feel rejected."
> "You mean I don't have to stop having these feelings?"

"No, you can't choose what you feel. Just keep (the) boy safe."

Described detailed fantasy of touching, exploring, undressing, stimulating (me), ignoring (me), trying to stop me, finally both (of us) making love. (He became) calmer.

"(The boy) seems to be OK as long as he's sure I'm not making love to him no matter how he feels or how seductive he gets."

"(But he) wants you to though."

"Yeah, but if there was any of that, (it) would destroy him and all the work we've been doing in here."

"(I) spent (the Labor Day) weekend with Diane (his ex-wife). Nice to see her. Strange feelings comparing her to you. Not fair. She didn't measure up. Maybe (I'm) idealizing you. We slept together and I felt sleazy . . . (I) told Pilar (that) she was graduating next year . . . This is odd. You'll think it's strange, silly. Well, there has been something sexual in here and it's like it would hurt your feelings. Or this is pretentious. Make you jealous."

"That you'd have a real relationship and not just this talk which frustrates you endlessly? Why wouldn't I be pleased something good happened in your real life?"

After reading the entry of September 9, 1987, in which Lozano voiced a typical sadomasochistic fantasy about his female psychotherapist, I was beginning to have misgivings about the growing number of improbabilities and discrepancies of the Lozano case—including Pilar William's claim that Bean-Bayog had masturbated in the second session, that she had given Lozano the Pound Puppy, and that his family had been unaware of his childlike behavior before entering psychotherapy.

Bean-Bayog continues describing Paul's fantasies:

"I had a specific fantasy about you. You were lying on the bed, had just had a shower, taken together, unbeknownst to you. I started kissing, caressing you, touching thighs, breasts, vaginal area, very lightly, not to hurt you . . . then you go on top of me and were making love up and down and then got off and you were kissing my penis, I was wild, asking you to get back on and you did, you had your reasons. Guess some people think of movie stars. Me, it's my psychiatrist. Do other patients do this?"

"Sexual feelings on both sides are very common. But we're also understanding that something may have happened to you that this is a memory. It doesn't only happen with me. Not everyone would describe being tackled by two policemen and locked in restraints as a deflowering, or having their way with you, or rolling over and having a cigarette afterward. You experience lots of situations as assaults, sexual, degrading, humiliating, when maybe they aren't. We need to find out where the feelings come from."

I remembered that in the introduction to the Plaintiff's Offer of Proof, Meyer had quoted Bean-Bayog saying that "sexual feelings on both sides are *much*." What she actually wrote was "sexual feelings on both sides are *common*." There is a significant distinction between "much" and "common." I wondered whether Meyer had misquoted or mischaracterized anything else.

Also, I noticed that Bean-Bayog never addressed him as "Paul" and he never called her "Margaret." When she spoke to him in person, she called him "Mr. Lozano." In her notes, she almost invariably referred to him as "patient." Orally or verbally, Lozano always called her "Dr. Bean." Furthermore, I remembered reading the seventeen letters she had written in advance of her 1987 Christmas three-week vacation. Bean-Bayog wrote these letters as the "nonabusive mom" to the 3-year-old "boy," and some of the letters began with "Hi!" Others begin with no salutation at all. It seemed clear that doctor and patient were not on a first-name basis.

On September 13, she wrote out a typical reminder for her patient to take home with him. It was not addressed "Dear Paul" and was not signed "Margaret."

> P(aul) L(ozano), Keep yourself safe, Do not drive home, Take (the) subway, Come back for (your) car when you clear up, Go home to sleep, Call me when you wake up, Come see me tomorrow, Do not drink, Do not hurt yourself, Call me for God's sake if you want to hurt yourself. (signed) MBB MD.

Such messages were used to mitigate Lozano's suffering and his belief that suicide would provide relief, which were reflected in his statements of mid-September:

> "I'm just *worthless.* (I) should just *realize* it. (I) want to end it. Should just finish it off."
> "What (do you) want to do?"
> "Nothing specific. Actually, I am follow(ing) the directions on the yellow sheet (that you gave me). That's why I called."

> "I get so angry at self. I hate it. That's when I start wishing I was *dead* . . . What am I waiting for? I'll never be happy . . . Today, rain. Feel like getting in a car accident or coming home and taking all those pills I have on the counter."
> "Feel like that now?"
> "That's what I was feeling. Changed out of my wet dirty clothes, curled up with (my) blanket, read your note, pictured all the 3-year-olds lying down to take a nap."

> "Thank goodness."
> "And I woke up to talk to you . . . You must get
> tired of hearing me. I get tired of hearing me.
> You do a lot. I wouldn't be in medical school
> without you.[1] I might not even be alive. I
> wouldn't *be* without you. Such a spool of nega-
> tive thoughts. They won't go away . . . Dr. Bean
> I really love you. Please don't get tired of me."

I was beginning to wonder whether Lozano had been sexually
molested by his mother. However, I found intriguing his overreaction to, of all things, a bronze statue of a nude mother
holding a nude child.

The brown statue, titled *Mother and Child,* stands on the lawn
just outside a cafeteria of the Massachusetts General Hospital.
One of the mother's nipples is close to the baby's mouth and the
thumb of her left hand is almost touching his penis. For Lozano,
this was apparently a very erotic work of art.

On September 24, 1987, Lozano told Bean-Bayog:

> "(Some)thing I didn't want to talk to you about.
> Weird. This statue at Mass. General: mother and
> baby. Well, she was naked. Strange . . ."
> "(You've) just been talking about (your)
> mother's sexual abuse . . . What might hap-
> pen?"
> Hesitantly: "She might touch me . . . rub me
> when I was little . . . I remember seeing her do
> it to my nephews, changing them, or bathing
> them. She would kind of kiss and fondle
> (them)."
> "The little boy's penis?"
> "Yes."
> "How did you feel?"
> "(A) little mad. Maybe not just a little."
> "Furious?"

---

1. ACTUALLY, HE WAS ON A LEAVE OF ABSENCE.

"Yes. I could remember her doing it to me if I
tried really hard, but I think I don't want to."
"Because."
"(I) might get angry . . . Didn't think I was going
to tell you this today . . . (I've been thinking
about it) for a few weeks. (It) would start to
come up and the boy would get scared and
you would sense it and cools things off. Now (I)
feel sad."
"So do I."
"(Does the boy) have to give up the feelings?"
"Why would he have to give up the feelings?"
"Because you said (he'd have) to."
"I said (we could) protect the child but not give
up all sexual feeling. You can't do that."
"I can still have fantasy of making love?"
"Yes, just keep (the) boy safe. He mustn't be
raped anymore."
"Where there's a will, there's a way," (said
Lozano referring either to resisting the tempta-
tion to have sex with her or continuing to pres-
sure her to.)

About a month after mentioning the statue, Lozano's therapy
reached a crisis when he confessed that he had broken into her
office and stolen materials from his file.

"I did something else. I took the folder with the
McLean summary out. None of my business.
Saw things about (your) miscarriage. I'm sad for
you."
"Stole it out of (my) file?"
"Not hard."

I was surprised that she did not record more of her own
reaction to the fact that her office had been burglarized by her
patient! The following day, November 3, Lozano exploded with
homicidal rage over his treatment at McLean Hospital:

"(I'm) angry at Dr. Frankenburg. (I have) lots of feelings."

"Yes, but just feelings. (You're) not talking about pushing (her) off (a) cliff or raping her or suing her."

"(I'm feeling) so confused, painful . . . There's another fantasy that bothers me. It's me wanting them to put me in restraints. It (is) arousing me, wanting her to do that to me, then (I feel) ashamed. They turned me on (my) back; (they) could all see my erection. She did it on purpose. She ate it up. (I'm) wanting you to do that; too humiliating to admit."

"Better to admit than act out, because if you think that's what's happened, like the fantasies, the boy freaks out," (said Bean-Bayog).

"Yeah, he hates it."

"That's what he wanted to rape her for."

"I'd never do that. They wouldn't let me back in school. I'd find subtler means. Get a lawyer to rape her for me(!)"

"Except now you see this abuse experience didn't start with her, or me, but repeats what your mother did."

"And like me screaming obscenities when they had company."

"Or when you'd massage her when she was washing dishes."

Screaming: "*I don't want to talk about it. I don't!* My father used to say, 'You really like your mother's bread basket' . . . *I don't want to remember.*"

"(How are you) feeling?"

"So humiliated, I think I'll leave."[2]

---

2. ACCORDING TO MY FATHER, THIS EXCHANGE IS A GOOD EXAMPLE OF WHAT GOES ON IN PSYCHOTHERAPY.

Bean-Bayog did not report the burglary of her Cambridge office to the local police. She should have. It would have strengthened her defense in the civil and administrative complaints that eventually followed.

Perhaps, Bean-Bayog did not think of filing a police report, because she was too busy trying to prevent Lozano, who had stopped taking his antidepressants and whose rage continued unabated for many days, from murdering Frankenburg, or killing himself, or both.

This possibility seemed to be supported by her notes of November 18, 1987:

> (Lozano was) threatening to shoot McLean staff. Had gun permit application in and (was) absolutely furious . . .
>
> "I have to get away from you, you bitch. You gave me to them. You let them do that . . . I'm giving my Pound Puppy to Children's Hospital . . . I don't make a practice of rifling through someone's things and taking things out."
>
> "But you just did," (said Bean-Bayog, referring to his burglary of her office.)
>
> "I know you must be mad."
>
> "Yes. Look what it did to you. There were reasons those things were confidential. You should not read that stuff without discussing it."
>
> ". . . Well, they'll be lucky if I don't shoot them all, Frankenburg, Frazier, Pope, fucking shrinks. I'll show them. They'll get theirs . . . I wish I never mentioned the word lawyer. I got you thinking this is a lawsuit."
>
> "Sure made it sound like it."
>
> "Crazy people don't sue anyone. They don't sue McLean. It's a joke. They have an army of lawyers . . . It's like suing my mother, a little perverse."
>
> "If that abuse experience comes from child-

hood, she might be who you need to be angry at."

"I guess I thought I could get back at them, get a lawyer. I don't know. It's all me. It's all coming from me."

"I think (it's coming) from your childhood abuse and stopping (your antidepressant) pills . . ."

"I talked to those gun (club) people today . . . They were really enthusiastic. 'C'mon over. We have training sessions. *We'll provide you with a gun*, training, if you don't have (any)' (I) wanna call you Mommy now. Not supposed to but I'm going to."

Legally, Lozano could demand that McLean Hospital provide him with a copy of his own medical records. Instead, in a 1987 written request, he instructed McLean to forward them to Bean-Bayog. When he broke into her office, Lozano stole those records and read her Process Notes, a claim that Pilar Williams did not dispute. What they did dispute was Bean-Bayog's assertion that, unknown to her, he had also purloined her sexual fantasies. The Lozanos contended that she shared them with Paul, which he secretly photocopied, and that they had acted them out. Bean-Bayog, through her lawyer, had already stated that she kept them in a locked drawer. The only fantasy she thought Lozano had stolen was the mother-child fantasy.

Two days later, there was a key and controversial passage:

More storm about reading the discharge summary . . . Have identified the issue of why Dr. Frances Frankenburg's opinion is so devastating as a major focus. Revives experience of (his) mother's abuse. Patient makes connection of disappointment in his family to these feel ings . . . Spent last part of session reviewing the fantasy which he also reread when he got the discharge summary—with *the alternation be-*

tween torturing and turning me on. (Emphasis added.) (He) spent time reading the discharge summary, working me over and over in his mind. (He was) furious. Proceeded as in (the) fantasy. Also: would have me in a device like stirrups. Could get at my inner thighs and vagina better. He reveled on control. (He felt) cold sadistic pleasure in turning me on and then hurting me. Sometimes (he had me) in restraints on the floor as in the fantasy. Sometimes would turn me over. Sometimes he would have me clamped against the wall, so I couldn't move and had (to) do whatever he wanted . . .

"I can't call it making love. It would be being done to you. You would never know what I was going to do. I would leave and say I was coming back. You thought I was going to keep you there forever. I would begin to touch your breasts, running my finger around your nipple, and then touching your inner thighs and labia, you would get moist. I would keep doing it, and rubbing your clitoris. I would feel it get erect. You would be moaning and pressing me, begging me to fuck you. I would keep doing it until you were absolutely wild with need. Then I would just walk out and leave you. You would be shouting names at me, 'bastard,' 'mother-fucker.' I would have a light trained on you, so I would look at you from outside the room. I would stay outside for a long time. When I came back I would make you apologize and of course you would. I might slap you a few times. Then I'd put you up against the wall. You'd be standing but you couldn't move your hands or feet. I'd touch you everywhere, running my hands all over, turning you on again and then I'd just enter you thrusting you against the wall, and explosively come."

". . . Bring back the stuff (you stole) from the chart."

Sheepishly: "It would be a relief,"

Later, turned out my asking him to bring (the) fantasy back made him *Furious.*

"You're just covering your own ass. If I kill myself and my family finds it and sues, all you care about is what happens to you. Had fantasy of bringing it back and then killing self. Then you'd be happy. You'd have what you wanted."[3]

Lozano had a gift for prophecy—at least in this instance. He warned her that he had a vindictive personality, who might do harm to the "messenger," i.e., his therapist, even though he admitted she had done nothing to deserve it. For example, in early October as he was expressing his ubiquitous anger, he told her:

I guess I'm not a very nice person. I haven't been since I was a child. (I have a) tendency to be vindictive. I'm not gonna let you fuck me twice again (regarding her hospitalizing him again). That's vindictive, as a matter of fact, I'm gonna make you pay for it. I'm going to make you pay.

At that time, Lozano gave two cartoons to Bean-Bayog. The first portrays a duck kicking a woman down a flight of stairs with a portrait of Sigmund Freud on the wall. At the bottom of the stairs, another duck is distracting her. The caption read: "As the first duck kept Margaret's attention, the second one made its move." In the second cartoon, two bears are standing in a trophy room. One of the trophies is an amputated hand. The caption reads: "And that's the hand that fed me."

---

3. LOZANO DID NOT RETURN THE MATERIAL FOR A YEAR. ON DECEMBER 4, 1988, BEAN-BAYOG WROTE: "RELIEVED. GAVE BACK FANTASY. WANTING TO GET RID OF THAT STUFF. 'WE'VE BEEN WORKING ON GETTING YOU RID OF IT.' "

As November wore on, Lozano's sadomasochistic sexual fantasies intensified. Bean-Bayog continued logging their graphic details.

Here are some of the Process Notes for November 27, 1987:

> "Seeing you wakes up these internal longings I didn't know I had. I'm at the same time angry and love you. The 3-year-old is around all the time. Helps to talk."
> "Any of this have to do with you taking the fantasy about the mother/woman seducing the baby out of the chart?"
> "I better go."
> "Hard to talk about it?"
> "It's just the same over and over. I get aroused, I think you're gonna take those feelings away, be critiical, think I'm degenerate."
> "You don't choose the feelings. Kids who get overstimulated have tons of them."
> "I do all the time. I see your stockings, skirt, how it fits, well, looking at your stockings, thinking of . . . having my head right between your legs. Sometimes I want to rape you, stroking between your legs, labia, your clitoris now and my fingers in your vagina. You'd be asking me to fuck you, but I wouldn't,"
> "What happens to the boy?"
> "He's OK as long as I'm sure you're not touching him. This relieves some kinda tension to talk about it . . ."
> "You still haven't said anything about taking the fantasy about the mother seducing the little boy out of the chart."

Bean-Bayog then noted that Lozano grabbed his "blanket" and became more "regressed," adding "I think some of this is too hot for him to handle."

However, I noticed that in her responses to his sexual fantasies, she either deflected or responded to Lozano's graphic sexual talk with a therapeutic question. This forced him to focus on his place at that moment, a kind of reality check, but also to check his pleasurable emoting. Like the rest of her language, it is quite devoid of intimate or carelessly seductive phrases or insinuation. Also, she reminded him over and over that they could not touch and, despite his earnest requests, could not have sex because of the damage it would do to "all the work."

Three days later, the focus shifts from sexual fantasies to the reality of her imminent three-week vacation.

> "Notice I get really angry about you leaving?"
> "Think any of this is a reaction to my saying we could electively hospitalize you at Faulkner while I'm away?"
> "Maybe."
> "Hospital's a fighting word."[4]
> "Can be. Good thing you didn't mention that other place . . . Well, if I had to stay anywhere it would be Faulkner. Guess that settles it."

Lozano's anger and apprehension about her absence began to grow as the day of her departure approached. He had decided to reject the prophylaxis of hospitalization. In mid-December, to keep him alive for such an extended period of time, she had to ply him with transitional objects:

> *Very* suicidal . . . finally cajoled, coerced into sitting down.
> Sarcastic: "Oh, I got you this last night for Christmas (*Inquisition, a Bilingual Guide to the Exhibition of Torture Instruments from the Middle Ages*

---

4. LOZANO NOW APPEARED TO BE IN A PARANOID STATE ABOUT PSYCHIATRIC HOSPITALS. HAD BEAN-BAYOG COMMITTED HIM INVOLUNTARILY, IT PROBABLY WOULD HAVE SPELLED THE END OF THE ALLIANCE OF THE THERAPEUTIC RELATIONSHIP.

to the Industrial Era.) Some of them made me think of you —breast ripper, vaginal pear, couple others." (He inscribed the book: "To my favorite inquisitor.")
(Then Bean-Bayog told him a comforting story.)
"How can you tell me a story full of hope when I give you a book like that?"
"He was only three. His mother abused him. Can he keep safe? Shall we put him in the hospital?"
"No."

"(I feel) guilty about hurting you. You have the patience of a saint . . . It hurts too much and I need you and I don't want you to go away and I want you to be my Mommy. I want it to be true. I need you so much."
(We) review how he can have parts of me: books, tapes, notes. Gave Winnicott article on transitional objects.
"You can use them to stop being suicidal."
"That would help. I feel so *lost* out there . . ."

(We) read flashcard set. (We) read 'Morning' set. (We) read 'Cookies.
"We've done a lot of preparation. I think (my being away for three weeks) will go well."

(We) made more flashcards about distortions . . .
Reviewed preparations. Read 'Shots' and 'Restless' for the tape recorder. (We're in) good shape.

" . . . What about the boy? . . ."
Sharply: "The boy isn't here. He's going with you. He'll stay in your back pack the whole time."

All of the material she had prepared before her Christmas departure seemed to be an extension of the many cognitive reminder notes that she had prepared for him to take home and read whenever he felt suicidal. With the exception of her three-week vacation in August 1986,[5] over the past seventeen months of therapy, Bean-Bayog had not been absent for more than a few days. Even those absences caused him intense anxiety. Now she would be vanishing for three weeks.

Lozano survived her long vacation apparently by using her audio cassette recordings of children's stories, and flash cards, including:

> "I think you're my mom."
> "Right, you are. I'm your mom and I love you and you love me very, very much. Say that ten times: You're my mom and I love you very very much."

Another one read:

> "Do I love you? Yes, absolutely. Lots. I'm keeping you in my heart all the time I'm away and afterwards."

From Pilar William's initial statements, as well as Meyer's introduction to the Plaintiff's Offer of Proof, I and my colleagues got the impression that these devices had been employed throughout the four years of therapy. In fact, they appear to have been employed, because of the particular circumstance of her three-week absence, only during the late fall of 1987. Again, I felt somewhat misled.

Bean-Bayog made back-up arrangements at the Faulkner Hospital should Lozano need to be hospitalized. Doctor and

---

5. DURING HER THREE-WEEK VACATION IN 1986, LOZANO DID NOT FEEL REJECTED AND ABANDONED BECAUSE HE HAD ONLY JUST BEGUN THERAPY AND AN ALLIANCE BETWEEN DOCTOR AND PATIENT HAD NOT YET BEEN ESTABLISHED.

patient also scheduled two phone conversations in advance, one from Manila and Hong Kong. On December 31, Bean-Bayog returned home and they spoke again by phone.

When they met for the first time after her vacation, she gave him a high five for staying alive during her long absence.

In the first half of 1988, his need for the transitional objects began to diminish and he began to lay them aside, suggesting that they indeed had had their usefulness. In February and March, he said, "I haven't [read my children's books] for a while . . ." and "Don't need to be three years old so much."

Though many of the same issues persisted—his anger, suicidal impulses, his resistance to taking his medication, his sexual fantasies about Bean-Bayog, and his hinting at his mother's alleged sexual abuse—Lozano's condition began to stabilize and improve.

For example, on January 29, he asked:

> "Can I suck my thumb? I get too excited. I hate this. There was a game we played. I'd crawl around and around, but I can't tell you. You might do it too."
> "The boy is only three. I don't touch him."
> "I know you don't but she would. I'd crawl around and end up under her skirt, hot and moist . . . I was her favorite. She loved me the most."

In mid-April, Lozano admitted—as Dr. Yates had predicted in her article—how difficult it was for him to consciously face his mother's possible molestation.

> "(I) want to really *have* sex with you. I'm *tired* of talking about it."
> Discuss(ed) why (we) can't. (It would be an) act just like his Mom('s). Exploitive.
> "You *did* write those things about what happened with my mother. I thought you were

doing it to me. It was harmless. Those experiences happened *inside* of me. (In) some way you understood I couldn't talk about them. I couldn't, so you described them for me. I can't believe the things I say. It helps to say them. I used to feel those feelings would just blow me up sooner or later."

"They very nearly did. You were gonna shoot yourself or all of us. (It) drove you bananas."

"I felt hopeless. I never thought I could talk about them. Every relationship, if I started to get close, just blew up, sooner or later. Always had (been) better to avoid having relationships,"

"See why all we do is talk?"

"Yeah. Safer."

Also, with the new year, some of the cast of characters changed. He redirected his anger from Frankenburg to a Dr. John Collins,[6] who was working with Lozano on an experiment at the Department of Muscle Biochemistry of the Boston Biomedical Research Institute. He told Bean-Bayog he wanted to kill Collins. In fact, Lozano wrote a long letter to Dr. McPeek, one of their superiors, accusing Collins of plagiarism.

> . . . I feel compelled to inform you about some unfortunate incidents involving an individual on the anesthesiology staff, Dr. John Collins . . . I would not trouble you with these quarrels except that recently John and another scientist who is collaborating with our lab . . . attempted to plagiarize ideas which I had shared with them. I realize that this accusation is a serious one and should not be made lightly, but I feel that I can substantiate my claim . . .

6. HIS NAME WAS CHANGED TO PROTECT PRIVACY.

Bean-Bayog persuaded her patient not to mail the letter.

Later, Lozano wrote and submitted a paper to the journal *Anesthesiology,* on which the other scientists who collaborated did not wish to be listed as co-authors. The paper was rejected as too amateurish.

Lozano also became excited about and then furious with Dr. Harrison Pope, who apparently continued to be Lozano's psychopharmacologist, over a brief business collaboration.[7]

On April 21, Bean-Bayog recorded what her patient told her in a long phone conversation:

> "(I) saw Pope. The other guy knew I'd been there. Told him my ideas. My name. Divulged nothing. . . . Injecting pigs with Haldol, combination with Lithium, (I recalled that in Paul's autopsy Haldol and Lithium were the two prescribed drugs that Paul was taking when he killed himself with cocaine) . . . Dr. Pope takes what I say down —I don't know, I told them what any reviewer would say . . . Problem. I was patient . . . I told them I'm broke —they'd pay for reagents . . . what (this test) could really be used for is it could screen every patient against NMS (Neuroleptic Malignant Syndrome)—(it would be) malpractice not to. About 50 cents a test — we'd split that, half a million to 1,000,000/yr . . . I won't get that excited—strange—royalties, haven't even done experiments and they're splitting royalties . . . He's my doctor . . . You always told me I had knack of exciting people. He said—let's just not let things (go) beyond 3 of us right now. Spooky . . . I started feeling like he

---

7. POPE AND LOZANO BELIEVED THEY MIGHT HAVE STUMBLED ACROSS A LUCRATIVE TEST, WHICH WOULD IDENTIFY THOSE PATIENTS WHO WOULD HAVE AN ADVERSE, AND OFTEN FATAL, REACTION TO ANTIPSYCHOTIC DRUGS. THE CONDITION IS CALLED NEUROLEPTIC MALIGNANT SYNDROME.

was like my parents and I wanted to make 'em happy. They'd get real excited . . . Pope's my Dr., then two minutes later switched. Weird . . . With you I just think you're my mom, safe. I have (it) cemented into place. He's not my Dad but he's my doctor. Nothing changes that fact. Feel kinda indebted to him. Another thing too. Wanted to show him I was something besides a flake in quiet room. Show you too . . . Pope said, "Call me Skip.". . . I should be happy . . . (I'm on a) first name basis with world renowned psycho-pharmacologist. (He) said if I dropped by (his) house he'd let me use his daughter's pony. People from Southwest like horses . . . He's probably trying to be nice . . ."

After reading that entry, I thought the medical board should not limit its probe to Bean-Bayog. On the other hand, Lozano, an admitted liar, could have made the whole thing up.

In mid-May, his collaboration with Pope ended because the experiments failed to produce the desired results. When Lozano told him the bad news, he claimed that Pope "left [him] in parking lot at McLean." Lozano quickly left the grounds and took a bus home.

Meanwhile, typical exchanges between Bean-Bayog and her patient continued, though less frequently. In May 1988, she wrote:

(He had) angry, rape fantasy, locking (me) up (in)restraints, whispering, arousing, leaving me, making me hold still while he kissed my clitoris. "Like (your) mother?"

Lozano changed the subject.

As it began to get light outside my kitchen window, I came to an entry for June 17, 1988. I had less than seventy pages to go.

More elaboration of (his) confusion, fear.

"Think this has to do with your mother?"

Shouting, clutching his blanket: *"I can't tell you, I can't tell you, I can't tell you."*

"What (are you) afraid of?"

"You'd do what happened *then*. You'd pick me up, all cozy, but I'd know you wouldn't stop. You'd caress my head and then down my body and between my legs, repeatedly. If I pushed your hand, you'd slap me hard and tell me to hold perfectly still. You could do what ever you liked and keep doing it. She would. She would even if I tried to stop her, she'd hold me down and keep doing it, even be glad I was angry. She'd stroke me and spread my legs and kiss me and kiss and lick me till finally I wanted her to continue. I can't go on. I'd do anything to get her to do that. I'd get into her lap and push her legs apart, get under her skirt and do just what she did to me, caress and kiss her or her nipples, I could get her to stop doing anything else. And then she'd make me stay still and do whatever she wanted, as long as she wanted over and over and over, all those things Mom's just do."

"And you want me to be your *Mom*?"

Frantically: "Not like that, not like that. I want to be 3 years old and have you be just my mom who'd never touch me. You'd just read to me or give me soup, and you'd never, never touch me."

I'm not sure why, but I began to cry.

14

APRIL 5, 1992: ON THE SUNDAY COVER

About fifteen minutes later when my wife shuffled downstairs to brew her morning coffee, I was still crying. In part, I was exhausted and my blood was saturated with caffeine, so I was more vulnerable than usual. The conclusions I held when I had begun reading the notes were foreign to those I had just come to. To me, there now seemed to be considerable doubt about Bean-Bayog's guilt. In my view, the allegations, once litigated at the hearing or in court, probably could not be proven.

Later that afternoon, however, I spoke to my father. He had received the notes at 9:30 A.M. and had spent five hours reading them. His reaction stunned me. He said he was neither persuaded nor moved by what he had read. My father did agree that the consistently professional tone throughout the notes strongly suggested that no sex had occurred between doctor and patient, though she may have been tempted—temptation is hardly malpractice or negligence. But my father was not at all swayed by Lozano's descriptions of incest with his mother. Borderline patients can be extremely perceptive and creative, sensing the vulnerabilities of people they wish to manipulate and exploit, he said. He also told me that between 1895 and 1897, Freud had been similarly duped. He read me the following from *An Autobiographical Study,* published by Freud in 1925:

> Before going further into the question of infantile sexuality I must mention an error into which I fell for a while and which might have had fatal

consequences for the whole of my work . . . (T)he majority of my patients reproduced from their childhood scenes in which they were sexually seduced by some grownup person. With female patients the part of seducer was almost always assigned to their father. I believed these stories and consequently supposed that I had discovered the roots of the subsequent neurosis in these experiences of sexual seduction in childhood . . . When, however, I was at last obliged to recognize that these scenes of seduction had never taken place, and that they were only fantasies which my patients had made up or which I myself had perhaps forced on them. I was for some time completely at a loss . . . When I had pulled myself together, I was able to draw the right conclusions from my discovery: namely, that the neurotic symptoms were not related directly to actual events but to wishful fantasies, and that as far as the neurosis was concerned psychic reality was of more importance than material reality. I do not believe even now that I forced the seduction fantasies on my patients, that I 'suggested' them. I had in fact stumbled for the first time upon the Oedipus complex, which was later to assume such an overwhelming importance, but which I did not recognize as yet in its disguise as fantasy."

Freud's controversial rejection of these stories of childhood seduction is a precursor of today's debate on childhood sexual abuse and "recovered memories." Stories of childhood sexual abuse by parents or priests have become a regular part of the news, not to mention a part of psychotherapy.

My father agreed that there was no question Lozano was pathologically enraged over something. Since seductions, rapes, and the pummeling of small children by parents, relatives, and priests actually do occur and are repressed, Lozano may have indeed been sexually molested by his mother. But it is also possible, if one accepts any part of Freud's theories, that he mistook his Oedipal fantasies for reality, seizing them as a convenient rationale for his unremitting anger. At the same time, by "confirming" her hypothesis, Lozano pleased his doctor and secured her continued and dedicated attention.

On the other hand, Bean-Bayog worked intensely with this patient for four years and drew on her perceptions of his symptoms, her experience in treating difficult patients, and her own expert knowledge and judgment. As intense as my own reaction to the Process Notes was and as helpful as my father's observations were, neither my father nor I, nor any of the many psychiatrists and other experts quoted by the press had more than a superficial acquaintance with Paul Lozano or his psychological troubles. The press's knowledge in particular came predominantly from information supplied and characterized by Drew Meyer, Pilar Williams, and Amy Stromsten.

Researchers have pointed out that severe childhood traumas, including incest, do not necessarily poison the psyche. Some victims adapt. Some are strengthened by the abuse. Even creative talents can arise from these violations. Psychological reactions to human experience are as varied as human experience itself.

"We'll never know if Paul was molested by his mother," my father said, "and if he was, whether that was the thing that did him in."

Bean-Bayog, however, was convinced that Lozano was raped by his mother. "He then got others to do to me what others had done to him as a child," she later told me.

During his March 1990 psychiatric rotation at the Massachusetts General Hospital, Lozano suffered a breakdown after listening to a patient describe how she was a victim of incest. He was immediately readmitted to the Faulkner Hospital on March 15.

On that day, Bean-Bayog wrote an outside therapist note for the staff, summarizing the patient's life over the previous year.

Since his discharge from his first admission here, Mr. Lozano has done well in three-times-a-week outpatient treatment, and despite a variety of symptoms, he did not need to be rehospitalized ... He was gradually able to rebuild his life, get a grant, do research, get a nice apartment, get himself into Harvard graduate school in biology. His self-esteem and ego strength improved. Work with him was often stormy and demanding, but the alliance was solid and for the past year he functioned basically at a neurotic level and with excursions into more serious symptoms. He was not psychotic and, though he repeatedly tested and attempted to discontinue his antidepressants, resulting in withdrawal symptoms and collapse in mood, he generally took increasingly good care of himself. His present decompensation probably began at Christmas time, when he broke up with a girlfriend (who was probably alcoholic). In January he continued his PhD research and excelled in his parasitology course, but he dreaded beginning medical school again, predicting that he would not be able to continue psychotherapy and that I would be glad to get rid of him. He performed well on his February gynecological elective, but was escalating with me, unable to see me but once a week because of his schedule, and disorganized in those contacts. He began retrieving vivid memories of his early childhood physical and sexual abuse by his mother. He became convinced that I was intruding on him and arousing him, and at the same time intensely clingy and dependent. It was terrifying for him. He was also panicked about his psychiatry elective, unsure if he could be a doctor and finding that he was overwhelmed and overstimulated by watching interviews with paranoid suicidal sexually abused borderline patients. He was seeing me four times a week but his alliance with me deteriorated; he became paranoid. Just before his psychiatric rotation, three weeks ago, without calling me, (he had) paranoid delusions and accusatory and command hallucinations, which he obeyed. My voice was telling him he was bad, I wanted to get rid of him, and he should inject himself with toxic substances. Because he was sure I had been present at the suicide attempt (when he intravenously injected fentanyl, a synthetic morphine, and then nalozone, a reversal agent, and later, a mix of lidocaine and ketamine, which produces psychosis), he did not tell me any of this till 10 days later. "Why should I tell you when you were there and already knew." . . . (W)hen he failed to show at his 7 A.M. appointment this morning and was groggy and disoriented on the phone, I sent the police to bring him here. He is pretty angry and humiliated about needing admission.

It was now noon, five hours to deadline, and I had not written a single word. I called a friend and *Globe* colleague, Peter Canellos, and explained that I was exhausted and emotionally drained. We met in the newsroom a few minutes later and pounded out a story. Moments before the deadline, the story was filed. That evening, I picked up a copy of the *Sunday Globe* at 10:30. The story ran in the upper right hand corner of the front page. The headline read: BEAN-BAYOG'S NOTES CONVEY DETAILS OF FANTASIES, NOT OF SEX:

The 987 pages of handwritten notes of Dr. Margaret Bean-Bayog describing hundreds of psychiatric sessions with Paul Lozano reveal in graphic detail Lozano's sadomasochistic fantasies about his psychiatrist, but provide no references to an actual sexual relationship between the doctor and patient. The notes, which Bean-Bayog would have known could be subject to independent scrutiny, amount to a sometimes daily diary of Lozano's four years of treatment, in which she transcribes in his approximate words Lozano's sexual, and sometimes violent, free associations toward her . . . the notes clearly label as fantasy the many violent and sadomasochistic desires that Lozano expresses to his psychiatrist . . . References to the notes are featured prominently in the Lozano family's lawsuit against Bean-Bayog, as supporting the family's contention that the Harvard psychiatrist had a sexual relationship with her patient, which later drove him to suicide.

Later, that morning, my tennis match was interrupted by a call from Meyer. The Process Notes meant very little, he told me. "You're only looking at a slice of the pie . . . It would be improper at this point to draw any conclusions when there is much evidence to be forthcoming."

"Sure sounds like you haven't been shy about drawing conclusions yourself, Mr. Meyer," I replied.

He told me he was just doing his job. I replied I was just doing mine. Meyer then threatened to write a letter to the editor-in-chief protesting my involvement in the story, for a variety of vague reasons, among them that my father was a psychiatrist. People threaten reporters all the time. We get inured. I cordially proffered the editor's name and hung up.

Between sets I called my editors and informed them of Meyer's threats. Their reaction was to suggest I immediately write another story. In fact, I wrote two.

The first ran the next day on the front page. The family

claimed that the etiology of Lozano's psychopathology was Bean-Bayog's gross negligence and bizarre behavior. Until he fell into her wicked clutches, Lozano had been fine, just a little lonely. I wrote:

> **Detailed notes taken by Dr. Margaret Bean-Bayog during the 3½ years she treated Paul Lozano indicate she believed that he was suicidal from the first day of his treatment with her. This would appear to contradict the contention by Lozano's family that Lozano had no suicidal tendencies before he began seeing Dr. Bean-Bayog.**

Later, I got another call from Meyer. He apologized for his threats the day before but criticized the story I'd just written. He insisted that the family had never claimed that Lozano did not have serious psychological problems prior to meeting Bean-Bayog, merely that her unconventional therapy had exacerbated them and caused his death.

I contradicted him by reminding him of a statement Williams made to the *Herald* in an April 1 story: "There was absolutely no history of psychiatric problems with my brother prior to the time he walked into her office," which is also precisely what Stromsten had written in her affidavit of the same day. Indeed, Williams knew that something was profoundly wrong with her brother long before he ever met Bean-Bayog, because ten days before Lozano was transferred to Faulkner from McLean, social worker Roberta Goldwyn wrote in his medical records, "[I] talked with patient's sister by telephone . . . At that time, she said she had talked with him [two days earlier] and that he sounded the best he had sounded since the start of medical school."

Also in that *Herald* article, Williams said, "Another thing we take great exception to is she called him a liar, a cheat, a thief. What is she basing that on? Another sexual fantasy?"

This too appears to be another serious discrepancy, because in the Process Notes, Frankenburg told Bean-Bayog that Williams said her brother had "distorted things." And nearly a year later, when I interviewed her in El Paso, she repeatedly called him "a liar" and "a fibber." And in the Process Notes, I remembered reading that even Lozano considered himself a habitual liar.

In the second story, I looked at yet another discrepancy. The family claimed that Bean-Bayog had callously and abruptly ended her mother-child relationship with Lozano because she was about to adopt a child of her own. This was the theory championed by Stromsten. The notes indicated, however, that Bean-Bayog had insisted that Lozano join the impaired physicians committee,[1] a group that monitors physicians impaired by mental illness or substance abuse, to ensure that they remain drug-free and competent to treat patients. Lozano's refusal to accept this condition was, according to her notes, the crucial factor in her decision to end his therapy. According to Blau, there were other reasons. Lozano had come to her home in March 1990 when she was not there and pounded on her doors and windows, frightening her two stepchildren, Franz and Ruby. Lozano's bill had grown to more than $25,000, larger than she ever expected. She wanted him to pay her at least enough to cover her expenses. Finally, she and her husband expected to adopt a baby that summer and she wanted to take a four-month maternity leave from all of her patients, not just Lozano.

I went back to my beat in Cambridge but the Bean-Bayog coverage continued unabated. In March and April, the *Globe* and *Herald* ran at least seventy stories. The *New York Times, Los Angeles Times, Washington Post, USA Today, Time, Newsweek,* and *People,* ran prominent articles. Local TV news coverage

---

1. IT'S OFFICIAL NAME IS COMMITTEE ON PHYSICIAN HEALTH OF THE MASSACHU-SETTS MEDICAL SOCIETY. IT WAS HEADED BY DR. BERNARD LEVY, THE PHYSICIAN ACCUSED BY STROMSTEN OF COMPLICITY IN THE CASE. BEAN-BAYOG IS A FORMER COMMITTEE MEMBER.

continued. "Hard Copy," "Inside Edition," "Geraldo," and "Nightline" weighed in. Also, two Hollywood production companies began preparing TV movies.[2]

Meyer, however, did not appreciate the shift in coverage at the *Globe*. "What you're getting now in the press is an analysis by newspaper reporters, by most media or at least the *Globe*," he told *Globe* columnist Tom Palmer. "What we're seeing is, to a great extent, news reporters reading the records and commenting on those records and attempting to analyze them."

On April 10, Bean-Bayog secretly flew to a western state to meet the family of a teenager, specifically to show them the *Globe* newsclips about the scandal that had broken around her. The next day, Bean-Bayog returned to Boston.

"We had been chosen by this 17-year-old girl in January. And so after the news broke I let them know that they didn't have to go through with this if they didn't want to, that this is who I was, and the stuff that I was being accused of was very bad. And then I had to meet with the social worker who is a Baptist missionary. I had to meet with the family . . . It was horrendous. I was more scared of [the father of the pregnant girl] than I was the [medical] board . . . because the stakes were higher. Losing my license was one thing, but losing the adoption was another . . . We were going to back out of it, but they wouldn't let us . . . What happened was that we had to have a second home study and this social worker said, 'How will you feel if this family and this pregnant girl are attacked in the tabloids the way you have been?' And [my husband] Roger said that, 'We can't do that. We can't do that to someone else.' But the girl's mother said, 'I trust my judgment.' She said, 'I just have got a feeling. I don't think you'd be out here talking to us, showing us all the news clippings.'

---

2. I WAS HIRED AS TECHNICAL CONSULTANT FOR A VERSION THAT WAS TO STAR JAMIE LEE CURTIS ON NBC. A COMPETING VERSION, TO WHICH THE LOZANOS HAD SOLD THEIR RIGHTS, WAS TO BE AIRED ON ABC. BOTH VERSIONS WERE EVENTUALLY CANCELED, BECAUSE OF UNACCEPTABLE SCREENPLAYS.

On April 25, Bean-Bayog secretly flew back and adopted a two-day-old Hispanic child,[3] a volatile piece of news that the press never discovered. She and the baby remained on the West Coast for six weeks before boarding a plane and landing in Boston on June 3.

Sixteen days later, I met with Bean-Bayog for the first time.

---

3. TECHNICALLY, BEAN-BAYOG AND HER HUSBAND REMAINED FOSTER PARENTS UNTIL THE ADOPTION PROCESS WAS COMPLETED. "WE WERE SCARED THE WHOLE TIME THAT THE ADOPTION WAS GOING TO COLLAPSE," SHE SAID. EVER FEARFUL OF THE PRESS, THE ADOPTION WAS FINALIZED IN MIDDLESEX PROBATE COURT ON MARCH 17, 1993, AT 7 A.M. WHEN THE COURTHOUSE WAS DESERTED.

15

FACE-TO-FACE WITH BEAN-BAYOG

Though I was no longer covering the story for the *Globe,* my father and I were thinking of writing a book about the case. I continued calling Blau, pleading for an interview with Bean-Bayog. Finally, he agreed. He said we could meet with her for a one-hour, off-the-record interview. No notes, no tape recorders, no substantive questions, and not a whisper to anyone. This would merely be a "get-acquainted" meeting.

On June 19 my 68-year-old, white-haired father flew into Boston and took a cab to my home in Harvard Square. I was grateful not to have to face Bean-Bayog alone. He would be an invaluable asset. I knew she would be drawn to him, feel at ease, and reveal herself.

At 11:30, I hung my laptop computer bag over my shoulder and we took the subway downtown for the rendezvous at Blau's office with his mysterious client.

At this embryonic point in our investigation, my father had already leapt confidently to a conclusion. Bean-Bayog and her seriously disturbed patient, Paul Lozano, had fallen into a *folie à deux,* the psychiatric term for the condition in which two closely associated people develop similar delusions, transmitted like a contagious disease from one to the other.

Sounded pretty good to me.

We arrived at the offices of Blau's downtown law firm, McDermott, Will & Emery, told the receptionist that we had an appointment with Blau, and sat down in the lounge and waited nervously. I made a few phone calls. Then suddenly, I saw her.

She was sitting in a lit, glass-enclosed conference room forty feet away, talking to Blau. Moments later, she stood up, left the conference room, and walked right by us, no more than six feet away. She looked directly at me, not my father, and nodded. I smiled weakly—my throat suddenly dry—and nodded back.

My father leaned over and whispered, "Obviously, she prefers younger men."

Moments later, she returned, presumably from the rest room, and walked by again, this time without making eye contact. She reentered the conference room and continued talking to Blau.

Bean-Bayog appeared to be five-and-a-half-feet tall, her weight average for her size. She had straight blond hair with bangs. Except for a solitaire diamond engagement ring and wedding ring, she wore no jewelry. She was wearing a light blue suit. It looked like the same one she had worn when she trooped through the early morning gauntlet of cameras and reporters on March 31. Her hemline was at mid-calf and her slip was showing.

To my father, who squeezed my hand when he saw it, it was a Freudian slip. He leaned over again and whispered, "I'll bet she wore that long skirt to counteract the reports of her wearing miniskirts without panties during therapy. And as far as the slip is concerned, it's the mark of a sloppy woman." He then deduced that because she was sloppy, her office was probably disheveled, with papers and books piled helter-skelter. That might explain why she hadn't noticed her sexual fantasies missing for three years after Lozano broke into her office and stole them. I knew that my father is prone to fits of psychoanalytic exegeses, based on great leaps of faith, and that I would have to rein him in. This investigation would have to be solidly grounded in concrete fact.

"Dad, to quote Sigmund Freud," I said deferentially, " 'Sometimes a cigar is just a cigar.' "[1]

Suddenly, Michael Blau was standing before us. Surprised, we got awkwardly to our feet. I introduced him to my father.

---

1. LATER, I TOLD BEAN-BAYOG WHAT MY FATHER HAD SAID ABOUT HER SLIP. "I'D LOST TEN TO FIFTEEN POUNDS BECAUSE OF ALL OF THIS AND THAT'S WHY MY SLIP MAY HAVE BEEN SLIPPING; IT HAD NOTHING TO DO WITH FREUD," SHE SAID.

Blau, also the son of a psychiatrist, was a little taller than Bean-Bayog, had a slight frame, a thin moustache, and short light brown hair with a bald spot. His face was pleasantly, but delicately, featured. I don't know why I remember this, but his eyelashes were perfectly formed and beautifully curved. However, in at least one forum, Blau, a graduate of Harvard College and Georgetown Law School, is a force to be reckoned with. If you are a physician facing disciplinary action before the state medical board, you go see him.

Blau invited us to the conference room to meet his client, who stood as we entered.

Though her Nordic skin looked washed out on camera, she was much more attractive in person. In fact, Meyer, who had deposed her in his office seven days earlier, had told me that he too was surprised by how attractive she was. He even called her "cute."

Her composure impressed me. She looked me in the eye, thanked us for meeting with her, and told me how grateful she was for the balanced stories I had written. I wondered whether, if I had been in her shoes, I could muster such forbearance.

Blau introduced her to my father, who pursed his lips, bowed slightly, and shook her hand.

"Nice to meet you again," she said.

My father was too nervous to grasp the implications. When had they met before? Why didn't he ask her to refresh his memory? Why didn't I think of asking? He assumed she had heard him give a speech or lecture at Harvard Medical School since she was a student when he was a professor there. Still, it was a lost opportunity to dissolve the awkwardness everybody was feeling.[2]

The two psychiatrists and the two sons of psychiatrists finally

---

2. ACTUALLY, MY FATHER HAD MET BEAN-BAYOG ONCE IN 1970. LATER, WHEN I SHOWED HIM HER BROWN-HAIRED MEDICAL SCHOOL YEARBOOK PHOTO, HE REMEMBERED HER IMMEDIATELY. SHE TOLD ME THAT WHEN HER HAIR STARTED TURNING GRAY, SHE BEGAN BLEACHING IT AND THAT THE REASON SHE HAD MET WITH MY FATHER OVER TWENTY YEARS AGO WAS TO DISCUSS THE PSYCHODYNAMICS OF ALCOHOLISM FOR AN EXTENSIVE ARTICLE SHE WAS WRITING, "ALCOHOLICS ANONYMOUS," THAT APPEARED IN *PSYCHIATRIC ANNALS* IN 1975. SHE CITED ONE OF HIS BOOKS IN HER REFERENCES.

sat down. Blau reviewed the conditions of the interview: We could not talk about the specifics of the case and could not take notes. Then my father spoke. He wanted to show off to his eldest son.

"Dr. Bean-Bayog," he began pedantically, "from what I have seen and read, if you are guilty of anything, you are guilty of trying too hard."

Bean-Bayog stared back and said nothing.

Clearly, his start was a faux pas. Trying to reassure her that we believed in her innocence made it sound like he was reinforcing the charge of her overinvolvement.

Sensing a blunder, he quickly blundered again. He moved to their shared area of expertise by asking about her personal history of alcoholism.

"I don't want to talk about that," Bean-Bayog replied, nodding to Blau. "I'd rather talk about who I am."

Chastened, my father folded his hands and hardly spoke again.

It quickly became apparent how eager she was to pour out her bottled up feelings and thoughts. When she began to uncork, the gush of words was like a rain-swollen river bursting its levees. She talked essentially uninterrupted for a solid hour and would have continued if Blau hadn't cut her off. She never fumbled for words or paused between thoughts. Her thinking was clear, well organized. She saw and thought in patterns, shapes, and relationships. At times, her imagery approached the poetic. Since she was annoyed with my father, she looked mostly at me. I stared back, never taking my eyes from hers. If she digressed momentarily, she always resumed her theme or point. She never once lost her train of thought. If her confidence had been unhinged by the onslaught of this calamity, she was a master of concealment. She seemed undaunted by the catastrophe. At times, she seemed amused by it. But she regularly eye-checked with Blau to make sure she had not transgressed. As spontaneous as her speech seemed to be, she nevertheless took her cues from her lawyer.

Bean-Bayog began recounting her childhood. She spoke of her father, a nationally influential family doctor, his 200 books and

800 articles, and how he had influenced her philosophy as a physician: "You give to your patients without thinking of yourself." Her grandfather had been a productive and well-known physician and anthropologist. She hinted at the travails she had endured with her perfectionistic mother, an artist, who was jealous of her. At age 13 when Bean-Bayog was sent off to St. Katharine's boarding school in Davenport, Iowa, she was freed from "the enormous pressure to perform and produce." When she attended Radcliffe College, she never told her parents of her long-cosseted dream to become a physician. They learned only after she had been accepted at Harvard Medical School. Her parents, particularly her mother, "were shocked" by the news. During her psychiatric rotation, Bean-Bayog had "an epiphany." She realized that psychiatry would allow her to explore herself and to make good use of her verbal skills, raw enthusiasm, and irrepressible optimism. Relating to people had always been one of her "strong suits," she said, adding that she loved taking on the most challenging patients, the ones her colleagues tended to refuse or had given up on. She was also past president of the American Society of Addiction Medicine and was proud of how much the organization had grown. She described marrying her husband and "taming" her newfound family. Clearly, challenges energized her.

I interrupted and asked if she took copious notes with all patients. Before Blau could stop her, she said, "I usually don't take many notes at all." Blau then reminded us we could not pose questions relating to the Lozano lawsuit.

After graduation, Bean-Bayog continued, she got a "mountain" of training in psychotherapy and "is still in training" at the Boston Psychoanalytic Society and Institute.

Blau did allow her to vaguely venture into the Lozano realm. She said she expected to be fully exonerated, that the charges against her were "absurd," and that she anticipated that she would take something "disastrous and turn it into something positive." I wondered to myself how she ever expected to do that.

I asked her how she was holding up emotionally. (My father had privately told me that he thought she might commit suicide.)

Bean-Bayog replied that she did not feel "devastated" by the media hurricane, "because I have a strong sense of self" and that the experience seemed surreal. It was as if she were a character in a "fiction." It was like "attending my own funeral service." But at the same time, her life had, indeed, been devastated. Her family was suffering deeply. She was "champing at the bit" to let the world know her side of the story, but viewed herself a hapless "lightning rod" for the many conflicts in the psychiatric world, and that the vitriolic attack against her was in large measure because of her gender. No man had ever been treated like this.

Apparently on a prearranged signal, the telephone rang exactly one hour after the interview began. Blau picked up the phone, listened for a few moments, and hung up. He announced that our meeting had to end.

We quickly went through the rituals of thanking her, offering our sympathies, wishing her luck, hoping to meet with her again.

My father and I hurried down the street to Boston City Hall and commandeered the office of one of the mayor's top lieutenants, one of my best sources. We scribbled down everything we could remember while it was still fresh. However, we agreed that the meeting had not gone well. We had not "hit it off" with Bean-Bayog. She would probably never meet with us again.

Yet less than a month later, ten days before the much-anticipated public hearing on July 20 that would decide her fate, Bean-Bayog did agree to see me again.

I had been explaining to Blau how important it was for Janie James[3], a screenwriter hired by NBC, to get a sense of Bean-Bayog. It was in his client's best interest to have her portrayed accurately, sensitively, and, of course, sympathetically. The two women had to meet—completely off-the-record, of course; I could arrange it. Blau inquired if the producers might consider contributing to a legal defense fund that Bean-Bayog was about to set up to help offset her mounting legal bills. I said I'd pass along the request, which I did half-heartedly. In fact, I advised them against it. Any financial link between the movie and Bean-

---

3. HER NAME WAS CHANGED TO PROTECT HER PRIVACY.

Bayog would taint its integrity. I said nothing of that to Blau. I did tell him that I appreciated the access he was providing but wanted him to understand that if I stumbled across any evidence that implicated his client, I would not hesitate to include it. Understood, he said.

The second meeting went much better than the first, because of a strategy Janie James devised that I would have never countenanced. Just before we walked into our meeting, James announced that she was going to tell the doctor that she too was a recovering alcoholic. I had no idea whether it was true and never asked.

The four of us sat down in a smaller conference room on the seventeenth floor with no window view. Same conditions: no taping, no notetaking, no substantive questions. It was late in the afternoon. Bean-Bayog seemed more relaxed than before. Almost cavalier. This time she did not sit stiffly but lounged back in the chair as if she were about to put her feet up on the table.

I gratefully faded into the background, allowing James to run the interview. As before, my job was committing to memory all topics covered.

James was a brilliant interviewer, intuitively anticipating positions Bean-Bayog espoused. Though James had strong opinions and didn't hesitate to express them, nothing she said seemed to vex Bean-Bayog. James confessed her own recovery from alcoholism. Bean-Bayog beamed at her and gave her the thumbs up. James returned it. An affinity was instantly established, the shibboleth correctly enunciated. Speaking in lingo common to support groups, they discussed their likes and dislikes of Alcoholics Anonymous. James asked if she was still going to meetings. Bean-Bayog said she'd like to but her lawyers wouldn't allow it. I glanced over at Blau sitting at the far end of the table and caught his eye. We silently concurred that we were both third wheels.

For James's benefit, Bean-Bayog recited her family's belief in overachievement. James had read my notes of the first meeting but listened without interruption. This time, willing to talk about her alcoholism, Bean-Bayog pointed out how she was the typical "enabling caretaker" of her current family, "which is exactly what alcoholic children do. They try to make everything okay, which is what I tried to do with Lozano."

James wondered aloud if she should return from Los Angeles in ten days for the hearing. It should be included in the screenplay, shouldn't it? Both Blau and Bean-Bayog said nothing. Blau then confided that their defense would be that Lozano was a brilliant liar, who, by design, had kept his illness from his family and had "designed the whole thing so his parents would be financially secure." Both Blau and Bean-Bayog speculated that Lozano had left behind a suicide note, suppressed by the family, which exonerated her.

At one point, Bean-Bayog said, she was "actually having fun with all of this." She looked over to Blau and asked, "Aren't you having fun too?" He nodded, half heartedly. Was she serious? Sarcastic? We didn't dare ask.

Though it was clear that Bean-Bayog was confident of imminent vindication, she was bitter about the sexist subtext of the attacks against her and the damage done to psychotherapy. Still, she did not hint at countersuits.

I asked how Lozano could have known about her miscarriage. I already knew the answer from having read the Process Notes but wanted to hear her response. She confirmed that when he broke into her office, Lozano read in the notes about her miscarriage during her meeting with Frankenburg. She added that she and her husband had been trying very hard to have a child. Between 1984 and 1989, she had had nine miscarriages. "Five big ones and four little ones," she said.

In fact, Meyer had told me earlier in the week he was trying to subpoena Bean-Bayog's gynecological records to establish the paternity of the miscarried child that Frankenburg had questioned her about. Obviously, if Bean-Bayog had confided in her doctor that Paul Lozano was the father, Meyer wouldn't have to spend another cent on the case.

I asked her why she had written down her fantasies. Catharsis and self-control, she explained. "The challenge is to have all those feelings but not act on them."

Bean-Bayog then explained what she meant by seeing herself as "a lightning rod." To oversimplify, the civil war in psychiatry is being fought by the biologically oriented psychiatrists, who believe that mental illness can be managed with medication, against the psychodynamically oriented ones, who believe it can be managed with medication and talk therapy.[4] Most psychiatrists, including Bean-Bayog, do not neatly fall into either category. They employ a combination of techniques, hoping that one or all will do some good. She said that she was "furious that her case had put psychotherapy in jeopardy, because the seriously ill, like the sexually abused, will no longer have a place to go because therapists will be afraid of treating them, fearing this will happen to them."

If she were not cleared, she said, "They are going to be surprised in what a good Joan of Arc they have in me." She called herself a Joan of Arc three times. James and I understood that she was envisioning her own martyrdom, but, we both admitted later, were afraid to ask her to elaborate. We didn't want to queer the rapport.

I asked her how the case had affected her private life. Life was hell, she said. One of her best friends, a fellow psychiatrist, had suddenly stopped talking to her. She received hate mail, obscene phone calls. Teenagers drove by her house almost on a daily basis, shouting her name, spitting out profanities, calling her murderer. People stopped her in the supermarket. Some told her they thought she was disgusting. Some expressed sympathy or support. Some said she was being attacked because she is a woman. A 40-year-old inmate at Walpole prison wrote to her and asked "Will you be my mommy?" Someone broke into her garage and spray painted MURDERER and obscenities on the passenger door of her late-model Toyota Land Cruiser.[5] *Hard Copy*

---

4. THIS IS AN EXTENSION OF THE AGE-OLD AND HOTLY CONTESTED DEBATE IN PHILOSOPHY AND PSYCHOLOGY OVER WHETHER "NATURE OR NURTURE" EXERTS MORE INFLUENCE IN SHAPING THE MIND. FOR EXAMPLE, DESCARTES AND KANT BELIEVED THAT THE MIND WAS IMBUED WITH INNATE IDEAS. LOCKE AND OTHERS BELIEVED THE MIND WAS LIKE A TABULA RASA OR UNEXPOSED FILM, WAITING TO BE FILLED WITH IMPRESSIONS.
5. LATER, THAT HALLOWEEN, THE BAYOGS HIRED A PINKERTON GUARD, BECAUSE THEY FEARED THEIR HOME WOULD BE VANDALIZED.

had trespassed onto her property as she was gardening in the backyard. She and her husband were weighing whether to sell their home, and start afresh somewhere else. Even though her number was now unlisted, she feared answering the phone, opening the mail, opening the front door. Nearly everyday she suffered a "body blow" of some kind, a reminder that she had suddenly become an international pariah. She had nightmares. She couldn't sleep.

Blau ended the interview seventy-five minutes after it began. We asked if we could meet with her again. She said that was up to her lawyer. Blau said, "I don't know. Maybe."

16

THE HEARING IS DELAYED TWICE

To my surprise, the day after my second and probably final meeting with Bean-Bayog, a brief news story appeared in the *Herald:* MEDICAL BOARD NAMES PROSECUTOR IN PSYCH-DOC CASE. Apparently, the board, prompted by the gravity of the case, had chosen an outside attorney, John G. Fabiano, to serve as its special prosecutor. Fabiano was the head of the litigation department of Hale and Dorr, a law firm redolent of Old Boston and New Money.[1] In June, the board had discreetly approached several Boston law firms seeking the pro bono services of a top litigator to prosecute Bean-Bayog. If a special prosecutor failed to win the case, the board couldn't be blamed. Also, the case was beginning to overload the board's meager resources.

There was a lively response to the board's inquiries. The board considered several interested candidates and made its final selection on July 10. Many of his peers consider Fabiano the city's top and toughest litigator.

Fabiano's arrival meant that the hearing had to be delayed so he could prepare for the case. On July 10, he and Blau appeared before Judge Tierney, who granted Fabiano's request for a continuance. The new hearing date was set for September 1. Hence, both Blau and Bean-Bayog were aware, when James and I interviewed them later that day, that the hearing had been postponed.

---

1. GOVERNOR WILLIAM WELD WAS A PARTNER IN HALE AND DORR BEFORE HIS ELECTION IN 1990 AND IS ACQUAINTED WITH FABIANO. WELD APPOINTED CONSUMER AFFAIRS SECRETARY GLORIA LARSON, WHOSE AGENCY OVERSEES THE MEDICAL BOARD, WHICH IN TURN SELECTED FABIANO.

Fabiano's arrival changed far more than the timing of the hearing. It entirely altered the legal topography of the case. Instead of an overworked, underpaid medical board attorney as prosecutor, Blau and Bean-Bayog would now face a private attorney whose resources were commensurate with those of McDermott, Will & Emery.

From early April, Blau and his team of eight attorneys had been working steadily, without regard to cost. For example, the Process Notes had been painstakingly transcribed at a cost of $35,000; a virtual concordance of the notes had been prepared, including every instance in which Paul Lozano mentioned suicide, drug or alcohol abuse, or childhood sexual abuse. Every deposition was dissected; private investigators scoured Ohio and Texas; videotapes of every news broadcast had been transcribed; and copies of every newspaper story had been collected so that all public statements of Pilar Williams and Amy Stromsten could be scrutinized and compared to their statements in depositions, to Lozano's medical records, and to private interviews with the medical board. In addition, Blau and his colleagues had delivered a blizzard of legal requests and motions that threatened to overwhelm the board's legal staff.

Already wincing from protracted criticism, the board suddenly found itself under a blitzkrieg of denunciation, incited by Meyer, for failing to act more quickly on the Bean-Bayog complaint, filed more than a year earlier. Executive director Alexander Fleming would later admit that the Bean-Bayog complaint had indeed been considered: "not a very high-priority case . . . When we received the allegations . . . we looked into the case somewhat, soon thereafter the patient died. What we were left with basically were some unsubstantiated allegations of a nebulous sexual nature. What we had left was essentially a psychiatric malpractice case, a psychiatric malpractice case with one-and-a-half investigators and six prosecutors, compared with some of the other actual sexual misconduct cases, cases where there was really patient risk involved. This case did in fact take a back seat . . . The standard that [the board] applied as to whether to kick this case up to be a priority case or an emergency case is whether, based on the facts, we had a doctor that presented an immediate and serious threat to the public health, safety and welfare . . . The answer to that was no, that this doctor did not present an immediate and serious threat to the public health, safety, and welfare."

Fleming added that he knew of no other complaint against Bean-Bayog prior to or as a result of these allegations, except for a few crank calls.

Even Meyer later admitted to me in a taped interview that Bean-Bayog was not a repeat offender: "Let me put it in a different way. Do I think this is a repetitive practice with her? I don't think so." If her alleged substandard care of Lozano was unique and not part of a pattern of patient abuse, she was not a threat to society. Therefore, expeditious action by the overextended board was hardly imperative. Meyer's critics charged that the only purpose served by the voluminous Offer of Proof was to cow the defendant into settling the civil suit. For Meyer, a contingency-fee lawyer, settling the suit was cheaper and less risky than going to trial.

So what changed on March 26? Certainly not the facts in the case. The medical board already had the voluminous documents. The difference was that Meyer had supplied to the media sensational documents with, what Blau called, an imaginative analysis, which made it seem that Bean-Bayog was a serious and immediate threat to the public welfare and that the board had been remiss in its duties. Fleming, who had been the agency's director only since September 1990, knew that if the board failed to successfully prosecute the case, the public outcry would cost him his $52,000-a-year job. So he decided to hire a prominent outside prosecutor.[2] Fleming knew that if

2. IN JANUARY 1992, A BLUE RIBBON TASK FORCE, APPOINTED BY SECRETARY OF CONSUMER AFFAIRS GLORIA LARSON TO ANALYZE THE MEDICAL BOARD'S PROBLEMS, ISSUED A NUMBER OF RECOMMENDATIONS. FOR EXAMPLE, IT CALLED FOR THE BOARD TO "DEVOTE A SIGNIFICANT PORTION OF ITS INVESTIGATORY AND PROSECUTORIAL RESOURCES TO DISCIPLINING DOCTORS EXHIBITING AN ESTABLISHED PATTERN OF SUBSTANDARD CARE." BEAN-BAYOG, HOWEVER, DID NOT FALL

someone of Fabiano's stature could not win this case, no one could. Blau theorized that the board was trying "to cover its ass." When asked to respond, Fleming coyly replied, "That's an interesting theory."

Blau was furious over the hearing's delay. "We were put on an expedited schedule at the request of the board and we've been going around the clock to be ready by July 20," he told the *Globe*. "And now they have asked for an extension. All of this has incurred extraordinary cost to the doctor and this extension will seriously disrupt her practice."

The hiring of a special prosecutor was almost unprecedented. The only other instance happened more than a decade earlier. A prominent private attorney was hired to prosecute a group of surgeons at a nearby hospital suspected of responsibility for an unusually high death rate from open-heart surgery. The board's extraordinary step in hiring Fabiano fueled speculation that a woman was being singled out for attack. Bean-Bayog's detractors, of course, were delighted by his selection. I didn't necessarily believe my father's prediction that Bean-Bayog was actually contemplating suicide, but her bizarre cheerfulness in the face of the impending hearing, especially since she had known of Fabiano's intrusion, made me wonder why she had referred to herself as Joan of Arc. If not suicide, perhaps martyrdom was her temptation.

One thing was certain. With Fabiano aboard, there was now parity on both sides.

I continued trying to arrange another interview with Bean-Bayog but to no avail. I sent her several letters. In one of them I included a copy of the August edition of *Boston* magazine's "Best and Worst," which had named me "Best print investigative reporter, 1992." But that produced no response from her. Blau

INTO THAT CATEGORY. ANOTHER TASK-FORCE RECOMMENDATION WAS TO "EX-PLORE WHETHER EXPERTISE AND TIME MIGHT BE DONATED BY CAREFULLY SELECTED PRIVATE LAW FIRMS TO ASSIST THE BOARD IN HANDLING THE MORE COMPLEX SUB-STANDARD CARE CASES." ON THAT SUGGESTION, FLEMING DECIDED TO ACT. HIS ONLY REGRET, HE LATER TOLD ME, WAS NOT HIRING FABIANO SOONER.

said I couldn't meet with her again at least until the hearing was concluded, and most likely not until after the pending civil suit went to trial, which was scheduled for the summer of 1994.

In the heat of August, things slowed down, at least on the surface. On August 10, the *Globe* reported that the hearing had been postponed a second time to September 21, allowing attorney Michael E. Mone, recently hired by Bean-Bayog as her co-counsel, time to prepare. The real reason for the delay, however, was that Bean-Bayog's lawyers and the special prosecutor had begun negotiating a settlement. These negotiations were never leaked to the press.

Medical board hearings are usually held in a small room that seats about forty people, including judge, attorneys, and support staff. However, Larson's agency had received requests for credentials from scores of journalists, some as far away as Japan and Europe. "48 Hours," CNN, Canadian TV, *Vanity Fair,* the wire services, as well as all local media, wanted to send reporters. "Court TV" had made arrangements to put a satellite dish on the roof of the state office building, in which the hearing was to be held, to provide live nationwide gavel-to-gavel coverage of the hearing, expected to run for several weeks.

"It's going to be a circus," attorney Lee Dunn, who had defended doctors at medical board hearings, told the *Herald.* He said that the hot glare of media coverage would pervert the process. "[It's] one of the things that has gone wrong here."

Stephen Wallace, assistant secretary of consumer affairs, told the *Herald* that one of the reasons for relocating the hearing to the 600-seat Gardner Auditorium was to accommodate the press: "It's a case that has a lot of sex appeal and it's gotten an enormous amount of attention both from local and the national media."

Lozano's mother, who would speak through an interpreter, would probably be Fabiano's first witness. Next, Pilar Williams. There were also rumors that Fabiano was planning to call Bean-

Bayog to the witness stand and have her read aloud her sexual fantasies. All fifty-five pages of them.

On the morning of September 17, four days before the hearing, Michael Blau called. He asked me to drop by his office at five that afternoon. There was going to be an important announcement. He wouldn't tell me what it was over the phone.

17

JOAN OF ARC AND THE SECOND SUICIDE

It was about 5:15 P.M. when I got off the elevator on the seventeenth floor of McDermott, Will & Emery. I was surprised and disappointed by what I saw. Several camera crews from local TV stations were milling in the lobby. I thought Blau was going to give me an exclusive.

I asked the receptionist to tell Blau that I had arrived. He appeared moments later, looking harried but excited, and invited me to his office.

"She's going to resign," Blau told me. "At least it looks that way. I have some stuff I want you to read. As soon as we finish making some copies, I'll give you one."

I took a deep breath, wondering what on earth influenced her decision.

"So, no hearing," I said.

"Doesn't look that way." Blau handed me a four-page letter from a pile of papers, files, and documents.

The letter was addressed to Dr. Dinesh Patel, chairman of the medical board. I read the first clause: "As of today I am resigning . . ."

I stopped.

"Can I call the *Globe* and get one of my colleagues over here to get a copy of this stuff?"

"Sure."

"How did all the TV people hear about this?"

"Not from me. Maybe they were tipped by the board. They arrived only moments before you."

"Would you mind giving this stuff to the *Herald* much later, like a few minutes *after* deadline?"

He avoided a direct answer. I called Bradlee and alerted him. I then went back to her letter.

As of today I am resigning my license to practice medicine in the Commonwealth of Massachusetts. I understand that this resignation is irrevocable, permanent, and nationwide—that is, by resigning I can henceforth never again practice medicine. This is an unspeakable loss for me and, I believe, a loss for my patients and the community at large.

I have been driven to this extreme because it is far more important that my family and patients be spared the trauma of another public assault on me than it is that I receive justice and pursue my career. To avoid this assault, I realize that I am electing an outcome that is far more severe than would ever have been imposed on me through a hearing process.

The damage inflicted by the media repetition of the false allegations against me . . . was mammoth. I refuse to now subject myself to a legal but destructive hearing organized with a degree of media intrusiveness and exploitation which no other physician in the Commonwealth of Massachusetts has ever had to endure. This process is entirely out of proportion to the legitimate issues in this case.

My family, my patients and I have already suffered through an undeserved and unimaginable ordeal, and I will endure no more. I refuse to endure any further false allegations from Paul Lozano or his family; I refuse to endure any further denial of the severity of Paul Lozano's mental illness and suicidality, or the effectiveness of my treatment in keeping him alive; I refuse to endure any further gross distortions purveyed by the Lozano family's unscrupulous malpractice attorney; I refuse to endure any further the segment of the news media that reports before it investigates; I refused to endure, at my expense, any further pandering to the public appetite for preposterous, salacious scandal; I refuse to endure any further the Secretary of Consumer Affairs' immense overreaction to the groundswell of misinformed opinion in this case; I refuse to endure any further the unprecedented procedures, employed in this case for purely political purposes (e.g., summary suspension hearings conducted without prior notice, unrealistically expedited proceedings, appointment of a Special Prosecutor, and trial in a six hundred seat auditorium to accommodate the press and gavel-to-gavel national television coverage); I refuse to endure any further the prejudice against "Harvard-educated", "women", "psychiatrists"; I refuse to endure any further the burden of overcoming common fears and misconceptions about the practice of psychiatry; I refuse to endure any further being condemned by certain "experts" who pursue doctrinaire goals by criticizing competing but respected schools of thought; I refuse to endure any further standards and approaches in my profession; and I respectfully decline to serve any further as a lightning rod for all of these converging forces.

I am not resigning because I fear the potential outcome of this hearing process. It is the process itself, which has already taken a heavy toll on me and my family, and not any potential verdict, that I find daunting.

In July, I was prepared to appear at the hearing with a clear conscience and considerable serenity of spirit. And, I remain confident that if this case went to hearing I would be largely if not wholly vindicated. Top psychiatric experts have thoroughly reviewed this case and are prepared to testify that my treatment of Paul Lozano was, in all respects, within applicable standards of care. My attorneys, who have strenuously advised me not to resign, are prepared to expose the mistaken assumptions on which the prosecution's case is based, as well as the lies about my conduct which thrust this case into the public spotlight.

I emphatically deny that I engaged in any form of sexual misconduct with Paul Lozano.

What has changed since July is not my innocence, which remains, but the way this particular case is being conducted by the state. It has changed from having some semblance of fairness into a media circus.

After it was announced that the hearings would receive national television coverage, I attempted to avoid this horrible hearing process by exploring the possibility of a settlement. I was offered a suspension that could be stayed after one year. But the settlement included a statement of facts and conclusions that were so outrageously false that I could not agree with them without perjuring myself. It required me to confess to conduct I did not commit and profess beliefs which neither I nor a respected segment of the psychiatric community hold to be true.

The Special Prosecutor refused to provide any reasonable alternative to an appalling hearing process. He made my integrity the price of avoiding it. I cannot relinquish that. With that settlement option foreclosed, I am forced to take the drastic step of resigning.

I am saddened to be left with no other choice. I have been able to channel all of my own life experiences into an identity as a healer. I can't imagine life without my career as a physician. It is in my bone marrow, my ancestry, and all my dreams. I loved it so . . .

But no matter how much I love the privilege and commitment to practice medicine, it is not worth the excessive price I am being asked to pay. I choose to relinquish my license before I permit any further threat and damage to my family and patients, and my personal welfare. The price is higher than the awful price of giving up my profession.

I have a story to tell, a powerful story. I believe what I did was a good faith effort to do what was right and was life saving not only for the patient who has falsely accused me, but also for the other physicians this patient intended to harm. But this story cannot receive a fair hearing in this venue. And no one should be subjected to the assault which has been prepared for me.

I know that the Board did not intend this runaway process and will be appalled at this outcome. I believe that we have all been entrapped by the same political forces.

The only wonderful thing in this whole debacle is that I have found out how many people love me without having to wait for my own funeral, although this feels like one. I want to thank all the people who have loved and supported and written and prayed for me: my husband and children, friends and colleagues, patients and strangers. I ask you to continue to keep me in your prayers.

I looked up at Blau who was just putting down the phone. He asked me what I thought.

"Very moving. Very powerful. Did she write this herself?"

"Yes. I made a few minor changes."

"So, she's resigned. Stabbed herself in the heart. Michael, just between you and me, is she guilty? Is that why she's resigning?"

"No, she's not guilty. She just isn't willing to endure this anymore."

"So, is that it? It's over?"

"Not quite. We have a one-percent chance that she won't be allowed to resign. I've given the board a way out, a chance to do justice."

"How so? Sounds like she's resigned to me."

"Read this."

Blau handed me a letter he had composed, which had been delivered to the board about half an hour earlier.

> **This is to respectfully request that the Board of Registration in Medicine either (1) accept Dr. Bean-Bayog's resignation tendered today, or (2) do justice in this case by ordering an appropriate disposition that serves the public interest, without resort to an exploitive hearing process. If the Board wishes to be fair and fashion a just result, rather than force Dr. Bean-Bayog to the draconian step of resigning, we request that the Board defer the hearings presently scheduled in this case while it reviews the enclosed materials.**

I looked up. "What materials?"

He smiled and handed me an eighty-five-page bound volume, called the Respondent's Evidentiary Submission, which he said he had written over the weekend. An associate Professor of Psychiatry at Harvard Medical School, Dr. Thomas Gutheil, one of Bean-Bayog's expert witnesses who had met with Lozano twice, supplied the scholarly basis of the treatise. Blau then handed me an appendix, nearly 400 pages long, which was a collection of thirty-two exhibits attached to the submission.

"What's all this," I asked.

"It's a well-documented defense of her treatment of Paul Lozano, showing that everything she did had numerous precedents in psychiatry and that she was always operating within accepted standards of practice, which is what this case is all about."

I went back to Blau's letter.

> As you are aware, resignation is a far more severe sanction than could ever have been imposed on Dr. Bean-Bayog after a hearing process. She has decided to tender her resignation and present this case to the Board for final disposition at this juncture because she is otherwise faced with two alternatives, both of which are intolerable. On the one hand, she can submit to a hearing process, with a level of intrusiveness and media exploitation that no physician in the Commonwealth has ever had to endure. Or, on the other hand, she can perjure herself by accepting settlement terms offered by the Special Prosecutor which include false statements of fact, and conclusions diametrically opposed to the expert opinions we submit today.

"I had no idea that there'd been an attempt to settle," I said. "Was anything put in writing? Can I get a copy of the terms?"

He lifted from the floor another 300-page volume, called the Agreed Statement of Facts, Conclusions of Law and Jointly Recommended Sanction. I groaned. I would have to review this, too. I went back to Blau's letter.

> Dr. Bean-Bayog will not submit to the appalling hearing process that the state has designed

for her. No psychiatrist should be hauled into the
state's largest auditorium, under the glare of national television cameras, to be interrogated
about intimate disclosures made by a severely
mentally ill patient in a confidential therapeutic
context. The hearing arrangements are clearly
designed to make a public spectacle out of
these proceedings.

Blau went on to write that the board should accept the en-
closed documents as well as any materials Fabiano chose to
submit, make a summary decision without a public hearing, and
that Bean-Bayog would accept whatever sanction the board applied without appealing its decision. In other words, the board
should make its decision based on a submission of written documentation and she would abide by the punishment, if any, the
board decided to mete out.

"Does this maneuver have any chance of succeeding?"

"I doubt it."

"What happens if it doesn't."

"We have one other trick up our sleeve."

"What is it?"

"I can't tell you. You'll find out tomorrow. You ought to get
over to the board. They'll probably be issuing a statement, hold
a news conference. Maybe Fabiano will be there."

"How do you feel about her resigning?"

"It is absolutely her decision. I'm strenuously opposed to it. I
don't take a case of someone's who's going to resign. Why
bother?"

My feelings were mixed. Bean-Bayog's sudden decision had
angered and puzzled her lawyer. It had also inflicted a little
narcissistic injury on me. Just when I thought I had a handle on
this story, it turned out that I didn't understand it at all.

Preoccupied and feeling pretty stupid, I hurried from Blau's
office. Before I had gone more than a few steps, I saw what in my
muddled state seemed like an apparition. Bean-Bayog, not more
than twenty feet away, was fast approaching. I halted, non-

plused. She smiled and said buoyantly, "Hi, nice to see you again." She seemed relaxed or relieved, not saddened. Her Dutch-boy haircut covered much of her face including her eyebrows. She looked younger than her age, because the furrows in her forehead and crows feet around her eyes were hidden by her hair. For the first time, I noticed a discoloration, perhaps a birth mark, on her right cheek, made almost invisible with makeup. I opened my mouth again to speak but nothing came out. I kept staring at her and she at me. I wanted to tell her how sorry I was, to wish her good luck, to say something comforting. Then, I recalled what she said at our last interview in July. "They are going to be surprised in what a good Joan of Arc they have in me." A Joan of Arc, indeed, confident and serene in her decision.

When I got to the medical board several blocks away, the hearing room was crowded. Six videocams were already set up. On the dais were several pink armless chairs behind a long, V-shaped purple formica table on which was a jumble of black-and-white nameplates.

Suddenly, attorney Paul Gitlin, the board's vice-chairman and spokesman, walked out on the dais and made an announcement.

"We are in the process of considering the filing from one of the parties . . . We will have a decision within an hour . . . Thank you."

Many of us retired to a bar/restaurant across the street to eat and wait. Finally, at around 7:30 P.M., we learned the board was convening and would make an announcement.

Back in the hearing room, the seven board members and several board staff filed in, seated themselves, and arranged the nameplates. One stocky man, without a nameplate, in a dark blue suit and silk tie with short black hair and black glasses, was seated among them. I guessed correctly that he was Jack Fabiano. On the table was a cardboard box filled with the materials that Blau had given me two hours earlier.

After some preliminary statements, Gitlin said, "At 4:45 P.M. today, the board received a voluminous filing from the defendant in the matter of Dr. Margaret Bean-Bayog . . . The filing included a resignation but stated that the resignation should be accepted if the board, after review of these materials, concluded that resignation was appropriate. Under these circumstances, the board does not believe that a valid resignation has been filed with it . . . [T]he board is not accepting this filing and will refer the matter to the hearing officer [Judge Tierney] assigned to this case at DALA [Division of Administrative Appeals] . . .

"The Board of Registration of Medicine throughout this case," Gitlin continued, "has tried to do what we believe is appropriate, in such a way that the public interests are protected and a person's, who has not been adjudged guilty of anything yet, rights are protected. I don't think there has been any attempt on the part of the Board of Registration to avoid its responsibilities. It's a very difficult responsibility that we have. It's a hot potato . . ."

In other words, the board did not believe that it was in its jurisdiction to make a decision on Bean-Bayog's request for an immediate decision, based on written evidence submitted, which would nullify the hearing. That decision would have to be made by Tierney, who would meet with Blau and Fabiano at 9 A.M. the following morning.

Then Fabiano spoke, clearly agitated, yet carefully, precisely, and cogently.

"I view this as a highly improper attempt to circumvent normal trial procedures. She is attempting to carve out some exception, to get around the trial process. I'm ready to try my case."

He then took questions. I asked him about the attempt to negotiate a settlement. He said, "Her attorneys approached us a month ago for a resolution but we couldn't come to an agreement." I asked if he would be disappointed if there were no hearing. He said it made no difference to him. I told him that it appeared to me from reading her resignation letter and the one written by Blau that Bean-Bayog had clearly resigned but had hoped that the board would consider another option. Fabiano fired back, "My opinion is her resignation is invalid. If she is still a physician on Monday morning, I will appear at the hearing."

I then asked rather impertinently why he seemed so upset over this development.

"[Because] she is trying to try this case before you gentlemen with these filings," he said, pointing to the box of documents on the table.

Another reporter asked Gitlin if the board had rejected her resignation. He replied, "We have neither accepted nor rejected it," adding that the doctor's move was very unusual and that he was "somewhat perplexed why her attorneys hadn't asked for a closed hearing."

A few moments later, I telephoned Blau at his office. He was anxious to know what had happened at the news conference, so I summarized it. I asked why he hadn't requested a closed hearing. "Why should we ask for a closed hearing? We have nothing to hide. And there could never be any such thing as a closed hearing. Everything would be selectively leaked to the press and appear on the front page the next day." I asked if he had had any contact with Fabiano. Blau said he called him just before the news conference and that Fabiano had said, "You little sneak," and slammed down the phone. Blau, sounding amused, said, "He's a little angry because the rug has been pulled out from under him." I asked how Bean-Bayog was holding up. He said, "She's sitting right here. I'll ask her. Gary wants to know how you're holding up." I could hear her respond with flat affect, "Fine."

Later the next morning, Blau and Fabiano sat down at a table directly across from Judge Tierney to address Bean-Bayog's "special request." Blau called the nature of the hearing "unconscionable" and equated his client's predicament to that of Anita Hill's. In requesting the waiver of a hearing, he said, "What [Bean-Bayog] asked for and what she wants by way of those documents is justice. She wants justice without an exploitive hearing process." Tierney then told Blau that "The board has a right to submit their case to prove their allegations . . . You can proceed as you wish," implying that Bean-Bayog was free to boycott the hearing, which would commence as scheduled on Monday morning. Blau threatened to seek a preliminary injunction to stay the hearing, but admitted to me later that he knew it was futile.

In mid-afternoon, Bean-Bayog submitted a one-page "official" resignation,[1] requesting that it go into effect on November 10 "to provide for an orderly transition of my patients to other physicians."[2]

A few hours later, the board voted unanimously to accept Bean-Bayog's resignation. Because the board no longer had jurisdiction over her, Tierney had no choice but to cancel the hearing.

Fabiano called it "the second suicide."

Blau told the *Globe* that "What drove her to this was not the merits or facts of this case, but simply this horrendous, appalling, horrible process which she had already been traumatized by once but would not be traumatized by again."

Meyer, who told me that this was "the worst possible outcome" for Bean-Bayog, knew that her resignation would probably persuade her malpractice insurer to settle the civil suit out of court for a sizable sum. But he didn't seem overjoyed with his victory. Meyer did say the Lozanos felt vindicated. "When someone turns in their license in the face of a hearing, it speaks for itself," he said quietly.

And on the eleven o'clock news, WCVB-TV 5's Chet Curtis said that "For the family of Paul Lozano, her action amounts to an admission of guilt."

Contacted in El Paso for her reaction, Pilar Williams was feisty with victory. She was asked if she actually believed that Bean-Bayog's therapy had been tantamount to voodoo, because it allegedly reduced her brother from a "strong, independent young man" into a toddler.

---

1. ACTUALLY, BLAU HAD SUBMITTED AN EXACT COPY OF THIS "OFFICIAL" RESIGNATION THE DAY BEFORE WITH THE RESPONDENTS EVIDENTIARY SUBMISSION, WHICH UNDERCUT FABIANO'S CLAIM THAT BEAN-BAYOG'S RESIGNATION WAS "INVALID."

2. SEVERAL DAYS LATER, BEAN-BAYOG RECEIVED A LETTER FROM HER INSURER TERMINATING HER COVERAGE EFFECTIVE ON THE DAY SHE ANNOUNCED HER RESIGNATION, NOT ON THE DAY IT WENT INTO EFFECT.

"It appears that Margaret Bean-Bayog has made history, then, because that is in fact what happened. I still stand behind what I said. If she felt so strongly, she should have gone to trial on Monday. I was willing to go in and say the very same thing on Monday. I'm not the one who backed out of this; she did," Williams told the *Globe*.

18

MCHUGH'S MANIFESTO

I was intrigued that there had been an attempt to settle the case with the medical board and chastened that I hadn't known about it. I wondered why Bean-Bayog, who had so staunchly declared her innocence, had been willing to settle. Was it a tacit confession of guilt or an admission of weariness? I was curious to know whether she had been offered the chance to plead to a lesser charge or accept sanctions without conceding wrongdoing, so common in civil and criminal cases. Over the weekend, however, I carefully read through the proposed settlement agreement and discovered that Bean-Bayog had been offered an agreement that seemed harsh and absurd. She would have been required to admit to violations that seemed unprovable. What I read did not smack of compromise at all.

So I was anxious to interview Fabiano right away. How had he arrived at his conclusions and why had the deal fallen through?

I met with Fabiano in his law office on September 25, four days after the canceled hearing. Frankly, I didn't expect the interview to last long or go well. Though he had attended Andover Academy, Harvard College, and Harvard Law School, he had also grown up on the tough streets of Somerville, a blue-collar suburb. I was sure he wouldn't hesitate to kick me out the minute he saw my face, because I had asked him an impertinent question at the news conference.

We shook hands and sat down across from one another. I placed the tape recorder on the table and nervously turned it on.

So far so good. He asked me if I wanted a cup of coffee or glass of water. I declined. Was he being cordial or forgetful? One of the first things he asked me, to my relief, was whether I had attended the news conference. I nodded without making eye contact and began the interview. I had come with a long list of carefully prepared questions.

As we have seen, in the year before the news blitz, Margaret Holland, the medical board's chief investigative attorney had sought unsuccessfully a local expert witness for the Bean-Bayog complaint.

After the board issued its allegations in late March 1992, the matter was handed over to Richard Waring, one of the board's staff prosecutors. He suddenly found himself without an expert witness and hard pressed to locate and prepare one for the July 20 hearing. He decided to consider major medical centers on the East Coast other than the Boston area. Because he had graduated college from Johns Hopkins, Waring decided to call his alma mater's medical school and talk to the director of the department of psychiatry. He reached the department's chairman, Dr. Paul R. McHugh, and asked him to suggest a prominent psychiatrist who might serve as a paid expert witness for the government. McHugh, who knew of the Bean-Bayog brouhaha, suggested himself.

When Fabiano was hired on July 10 and the hearing delayed, he was free to hire his own expert witness but choose to retain McHugh.

I asked Fabiano to provide a brief chronology on the attempt to settle the case with the medical board.

"July 28, McHugh was here working on his case preparation with me," said Fabiano, "and I got a phone call from Mike Mone and the phone message said that he wanted to talk to me about Bean-Bayog . . . [Mone] told me the next day that he was brought in [as co-counsel] because some people that knew her— and he was not any more specific than that—had decided that he should get involved to see if the case couldn't be settled. And he was going to attempt to settle both the civil case and the discipline case . . .

"I told him truthfully that I had never discussed settlement with anybody, either at the board or anywhere else, that the first day I was in the case I went up and filed a motion for continuance because the case was supposed to start in ten days. And I walked back down the hill with Blau afterwards and with Richard Waring from the board, and Blau said, 'You know, I don't think this case could ever settle. You know, I don't see any way that it could.' I said, 'Well, okay' . . . and we walked down the hill and I never thought about settlement again until Mone called me.

"And then at that point I talked to the board staff about what their interest and goals were. And one of the things they wanted, was they wanted a clear public resolution of the case.[1] They wanted some principles or some facts on which they could develop guidelines or principles for other doctors to follow. And they felt that some severe punishment was indicated. But they sort of left the details to me . . . [O]ne thing the board staff had indicated was that the board would probably be more comfortable with doctor's words than lawyer's words. So the notion that I had was that I would . . . append McHugh's expert opinion, so they would have a medical summary." he said.

Mone and Fabiano continued meeting and speaking on the phone over the next two weeks trying to hammer out a deal.

Fabiano said to Mone, " 'I'm going to append a psychiatric report [from McHugh] explaining it all' . . . [Mone] said, 'Well, do I get to append a psychiatric report too?' I said, 'Well, as long as it doesn't undercut the agreed statement of facts, you know, yeah. If you want to say, "Yes, she did all of that but, you know, she did good too and this is why she was good," yeah, what do I care. We'll have to work out how we do it.' So he said, 'Okay,' and [Mone] thought it was worth me trying a draft," he said.

By now, Fabiano said he had "some knowledge of the facts" because he had read the Process Notes, the depositions, and the witness interviews.

---

1. A MEMO SENT BY FABIANO'S ASSOCIATE, STEPHEN A. JONAS, TO THE BOARD'S EXECUTIVE DIRECTOR ON AUGUST 18, SUGGESTED INFLEXIBILITY: "IF DISCUSSIONS WITH BLAU AND MONE LEAD TO A SETTLEMENT *ON OUR TERMS* (EMPHASIS ADDED), FINE, BUT WE WILL BE PREPARED TO BEGIN THE TRIAL ON SEPTEMBER 21."

"So I spent a night in a conference room here with everything spread out on a table, and I did an outline of what I thought would go into [it]. It was a pretty extensive outline. It went on for pages. I think like eight pages. I sent it to McHugh. I sent it over to the board. McHugh gave me some input. I don't think the board people gave me that much input, although maybe they did. But McHugh was the guy I was trying to please."

Fabiano then gave the draft to Mone and Blau for their review.

A few days later, Blau, who, according to Fabiano, had indicated a willingness to settle, sent the special prosecutor his own draft.

"And his draft blamed everyone in the world except her," said Fabiano, "and suggested that she should get a so-called 'stayed suspension,' which means we suspend you but we immediately stay its effects so you can continue to practice medicine. It's kind of, talk about your oxymoron[2], but it strikes me as one, but I read it and I said, 'This is not acceptable. You know, we don't have a deal. We'll continue to prepare for trial . . .' I thought that I could prove every fact that I had put in the initial draft."

Then summer vacations began to intrude. Since Fabiano was scheduled to depart on an eight-day vacation to Wyoming on August 14, and two days later, Mone was set to fly to the Baltics for two weeks and would be completely unreachable: "[Mone] said, 'Let's go talk to Tierney about getting the case continued.' I said, 'What will we tell him?' He said, 'Well, we'll tell him that we're working on, you know, reaching an agreement and we both request additional time . . .' "

"I was in the airport in Jackson . . . and I called [my associate], Steve [Jonas], and he said, 'We got two things yesterday. One, we got a letter from Mone who is now in the Baltics, saying "I believe the case is going to settle. Essentially, we're in agreement with your draft. Blau will work out the details with you." And then we got a letter from Blau which says, "Your draft is unac-

---

2. IN CRIMINAL PROCEEDINGS, THE OXYMORON IS KNOWN AS A SUSPENDED SENTENCE, A NOT UNCOMMON SANCTION.

ceptable. Here's a new draft . . .' " So I said to Steve, 'Gear up for trial.' "

However, when Fabiano returned from vacation, settlement negotiations with Blau and Mone continued.

Fabiano said, "And they said, 'How about a comma here, how about an adjective there. Can we delete this sentence? Can we move that sentence? . . . I won't take out that adjective. I will move this comma.' I mean we were at that level of discussion. And then I said, 'About this psychiatric report that we had talked about back in the beginning. Where is your report? I want to look at it.' And Blau said, 'I'm not going to show it to you.' I said, 'Well, if you don't show it to me, we can't have a deal . . .' So Blau said, 'You're not going to censor my expert.' I said, 'Well, I don't intend to censor him but I've gotta see what it is or else we can't do a deal.' He said, 'Well, my expert doesn't agree that there are boundary violations.' I said, 'Well, then we've been wasting a lot of each other's time because that's the entire premise of this . . . Everyone has to buy into that . . . If she is going to say that she agrees to all those things in the agreed statement and then have [Dr. Tom] Gutheil come along . . . and say, 'Oh, but she didn't really do anything wrong,' then we don't have any agreed statement at all. At that point they left. Mone called me the next day and said that he was sort of bowing out."

But Mone did not bow out. A few days later in the first week of September, Mone and Blau told Fabiano that Bean-Bayog was seriously contemplating resignation.

"I said to both of them, 'Do you understand a resignation under the rules, if there is discipline pending against you and you resign, it's forever . . . I remember saying to Mone, 'It would be a lot smarter for her to do the agreed statement than to do this. This is crazy.' You would have to ask Mone but he certainly indicated his agreement with me. That it would be a lot smarter to do the agreed statement . . . I again said, 'If she does that she's killing herself. It's a death sentence to avoid a trial . . . At one point Mone said to me, 'I told her that if she did this she would be the second suicide in the case.' "

On Monday September 14, Blau called Fleming, the board's

executive director, and tried to negotiate a voluntary resignation for a limited period of time. Fleming, who told Blau that he should be negotiating only with the special prosecutor, immediately called Fabiano.

"I called Michael and said, '[Fleming's] right. You should be talking to me, not with him. The answer is 'No.' If she wants to resign, I can't do anything about that. If she doesn't want to resign, we either go to trial or you sign the agreed statement you now have a written copy of.' "

At that point, I decided to ask Fabiano about the guts of the settlement agreement, the so-called conclusions of law—eleven of them—that he was convinced he could have proven and that he had insisted Bean-Bayog admit to. Namely, that she had

(a) failed to perform a proper initial evaluation of Lozano's psychiatric illness or to perform a comprehensive mental status examination;

(b) failed to prepare a formal treatment plan;

(c) failed to delineate carefully for Lozano the respective roles of therapist and patient;

(d) failed to indicate any consideration or analysis of alternative methods of treatment;

(e) failed to obtain consultations from professional colleagues in determining the appropriate treatment for a patient whose illness was more severe than any she had previously treated;

(f) failed to obtain meaningful consultations for professional colleagues when criticized for being "overinvolved;"

(g) responded inappropriately when criticized for being "overinvolved;"

(h) failed to monitor the progress of the therapy and compare that progress to goals set forth for the therapy;

(i) permitted repeated and serious violations of

the proper boundary between patient and psychiatrist and failed to take appropriate corrective action;

(j) continued the therapy after termination became necessary and appropriate;

(k) failed to provide subsequent treating therapists with information necessary for an appropriate transition; and

(consequently) Lozano was harmed by Bean-Bayog's failure to conform to standards of accepted medical practice prevailing at the time.

To me, the above claims were at best unprovable and at worst absurd. How had Fabiano so adamantly come to what I thought were untenable conclusions? As far as I could see none of the above transgressions could be matched against any written standards, and congeries of expert witnesses would sharply disagree on what the standards, if any, were.

When my father, who did not agree with Bean-Bayog's theory of treatment for Paul Lozano, read the settlement agreement, he snorted, "Every psychiatrist in private practice in the state would have to be disciplined. This is the most ridiculous thing I've ever read."

I myself had seen three psychotherapists. None took any notes during or after the session. None had written up an initial evaluation, a comprehensive mental status examination, or a formal treatment plan. My father told me that in his many years of private practice with hundreds of patients in his office at the Massachusetts General Hospital, he had never taken a single note. Many other psychiatrists told me essentially the same thing. Fabiano was implicitly claiming that an overwhelming majority of psychiatrists in private practice in Massachusetts had failed to conform to accepted medical standards. I had assumed that accepted standards were determined by what most local psychiatrists were doing. Since there were no written standards on what is acceptable "consideration or analysis of alternative methods of treatment," or "meaningful consultations for professional colleagues when criticized for being 'overinvolved,' " or "information necessary for an appropriate transition," how had Fabiano so confidently drawn these conclusions?

If many psychiatrists in private practice did not take notes and Bean-Bayog had conscientiously taken so many, why should she lose her license for failing to draw up a "proper initial evaluation or formal treatment plan." What's more, the many psychiatrists who treated Lozano did not exactly agree on what mental illness he was suffering from and did not agree on what the best treatment was. Hence, since there are numerous recognized methods of treatment of depression and/or borderline personality disorder, it seemed impossible that Fabiano could prove that Bean-Bayog's treatment was inappropriate. Indeed, she herself had used various types of treatment, including medication and cognitive behavior. Indeed, she had pleaded with him to take his antidepressants. She had obtained consultations from two of the most prominent psychiatrists in the Boston area, who enthusiastically applauded what she was doing. And in the third consultation, Dr. Frazier did not appear particularly dismayed by her therapy. He probably knew her form of therapy was a product of a respected and powerful minority in psychiatry; namely, the Boston Psychoanalytic Society and Institute, an organization with which Bean-Bayog was affiliated.[3] There is nearly unanimous agreement that there are few explicit guidelines, written or not, in psychiatry, and much disagreement on what those guidelines ought to be. And if there are not clear guidelines, Fabiano would have been hard put to prove in a court of law that accepted standards of care had been violated, especially the eleven "violations" he had cited.

I asked Fabiano, "Do private psychotherapists perform full medical, neurological, and psychiatric evaluations? Do they per-

---

3. THE INSTITUTE EXPRESSED ITS CONTINUED SUPPORT OF BEAN-BAYOG BY SCHEDULING HER AS A SPEAKER IN AN OCTOBER 17 SYMPOSIUM IT SPONSORED ON "ADDICTIVE BEHAVIOR: PSYCHODYNAMICS AND TREATMENT." AFTER HER RESIGNATION, HOWEVER, BEAN-BAYOG WITHDREW FROM THE SYMPOSIUM.

form a comprehensive mental status exam? Do they perform
treatment plans? If so, what are the bases of this conclusion."

Fabiano's answer startled me.

He said, "Dr. McHugh would have said so in his testimony."

I asked, "Did any other private psychiatrists in Massachusetts
review this question?"

"Not with me. He was my only witness . . . I mean, I have no
background in psychiatry. I have to rely mainly on the chairman
of the department at Johns Hopkins."

I wondered aloud if McHugh had ever practiced outside of a
hospital setting, because procedures may differ radically between
a hospital and private practice.

"I don't know the answer to that . . . I think he has been in
private practice, but you'd have to ask him. I don't know," said
Fabiano.

I almost blurted out, "But perhaps there are enormous differences. You may be applying the standards for one, unheard of in
the other. Why didn't you ask McHugh?" But I held my tongue.

Instead I asked, "What is your basis for concluding that Bean-
Bayog didn't live up to quote "standards of acceptable medical
practice," when those standards have not been defined in the
psychiatric profession itself?"

"The law has always said that there are standards to which
doctors are held and those standards are standards that are
generally known throughout the community and acted upon by
most physicians. Most physicians hold them in common. My
basis for saying it is that I had one of the most distinguished
psychiatrists in America who was prepared to testify that she
departed from good care," he said.

I wanted to tell Fabiano that there are literally hundreds, if not
thousands, of the "most distinguished psychiatrists in America"
and many—in some cases, rather fiercely—disagree about the
standards and directions of psychiatry, as well as how they feel
about one another.

My father, who knows McHugh, told me that he is a warm
and charismatic man but a staunchly biologically oriented psychiatrist.

Later, I asked McHugh, who had been paid about $11,000 in

public funds, for an interview. Though he had granted interviews to others working on the Bean-Bayog case, he told my father that he did not wish to be interviewed because he was thinking of writing his own book on the subject. I immediately wrote to him urging him to reconsider, because his selection as expert witness had been widely criticized and I wanted to afford him the courtesy of responding. He wrote back saying that since I had my father, a psychiatrist, to rely on, no interview was necessary.

The reason so many of his colleagues had criticized his selection was that McHugh hardly represents the mainstream in psychiatry.[4] Even a biologically oriented psychiatrist[5], who agrees with much of what McHugh says and knows him well, called him "somewhat of an extremist."

Gutheil, one of Bean-Bayog's expert witnesses, added, "For [McHugh] to discuss psychotherapy is tantamount to having a Christian Scientist discuss the indications for surgery."

I became better acquainted with McHugh's reputation and positions by speaking with a number of psychiatrists who knew him personally, obtaining his curriculum vitae, reading several papers he had published, and reviewing articles in the *Baltimore Sun* in which he was interviewed.

McHugh, a graduate of Harvard College and Harvard Medical School, is a psychiatrist with a background and concentration in neurology and brain research, but essentially none in psychotherapy. Indeed, he never even did a clinical residency, or any residency, in psychiatry. From 1957 to 1960, he was a neurology resident at the Massachusetts General Hospital. For two of those years, he also served as a neuropathology fellow. After

---

4. HOWEVER, THAT MAY BE CHANGING. IN 1991, DR. JOSEPH T. COYLE, A BRAIN RESEARCHER AND CLOSE COLLEAGUE OF MCHUGH'S AT JOHNS HOPKINS, WAS NAMED AS CHAIR OF THE NEWLY CONSOLIDATED DEPARTMENT OF PSYCHIATRY AT HARVARD MEDICAL SCHOOL, WHICH INCLUDES EIGHT AFFILIATED HOSPITALS. ON HIS APPOINTMENT, COYLE REPORTEDLY SAID, "UNDERSTANDING THE BRAIN—THAT IS THE BASIC UNDERSTANDING OF PSYCHIATRY."

5. SOMEONE I HAVE PERSONALLY KNOWN FOR MANY YEARS BUT WHO ASKED NOT TO BE IDENTIFIED BECAUSE HE DID NOT WANT TO BE OPENLY CRITICAL OF A COLLEAGUE.

that, he had a one-year appointment as a research fellow in psychiatry, under Sir Aubrey Lewis, at a hospital in England. For four years, he was a member of the neuropsychiatry division of the Walter Reed Army Institute of Research. For the next four years he was a professor in psychiatry and neurology at Cornell University Medical School. At the same time, McHugh, who had become board certified in psychiatry and neurology, was the director of electroencephalography, (study of brainwaves), at New York Hospital. He later became its divisional clinical director and supervisor of psychiatric education. After a two-year stint as chair of the psychiatric department at the University of Oregon Health Sciences, he was named head of the department of psychiatry and behavioral studies at Johns Hopkins Hospital in 1975. McHugh is also the director of the Blades Center in Baltimore for clinical practice and research in alcoholism. As he clearly has an interest in alcoholism, I wondered if he had ever stumbled across the reputation or publications of Dr. Margaret Bean-Bayog before he got the phone call from Richard Waring.

In a brief biographical sketch that McHugh forwarded to the medical board, he characterized his career as an effort "to create a model department of academic psychiatry producing leaders in research, education, and patient care by emphasizing concepts of contemporary biopsychology . . . and how the brain-mind problem is embedded in these concepts and affects the thought and action of psychiatrists."

His biological orientation is reflected in his research and voluminous publications, and like many earnest men, he wants to promulgate truths he believes he has discovered. For example, in a lecture delivered in 1991 to the Royal Society of Medicine, McHugh said, "My overall purpose is to show that concepts made explicit at Johns Hopkins are actually embedded in psychiatric endeavor everywhere and can be encouraged to emerge and shape the future of the discipline." He expressed concern over how psychiatry persists "in a 'house divided' [between the biologic and psychodynamic] but we cannot escape its debilitating ambiguity and equivocations."

Apparently, however, McHugh feels that to mend the division

in psychiatry, one camp must surrender to the other. In an article that appeared shortly after Bean-Bayog resigned, he wrote:

> Such sciences as epidemiology, genetics and neuropharmacology, which support and surround psychiatry today, are bringing new power to our practice just as science did for internal medicine and surgery earlier in this century. Only those physicians with critical capacities—who see the conceptual structure of this discipline and can distinguish valid from invalid opinions—will be competent to make use of these new scientific concepts and technologies in productive ways.

I wondered how anyone is able to "distinguish valid from invalid opinions." McHugh went on to express his opposition to sex-change surgery and to declare that the "fads" of multiple personality disorder and recovered memories of childhood sexual abuse "will eventually be discredited and this epidemic will end in the same way that the witch trials ended in Salem." In fact, McHugh wrote that "severe traumas are not blocked out by children but remembered all too well." In other words, he apparently does not believe that traumatic events in childhood may be psychologically repressed![6]

He repeated these views in an interview with the *Baltimore Sun*

---

6. IN APRIL 1993, MCHUGH OFFERED A SURPRISING ADDITION TO HIS DEFINITION OF MALPRACTICE. SPEAKING AT A WEEKEND SEMINAR OF THE FALSE MEMORY SYNDROME FOUNDATION, WHICH CLAIMS A MEMBERSHIP OF NEARLY 4,000 FAMILIES, MCHUGH SAID, "TO TREAT FOR REPRESSED MEMORIES WITHOUT ANY EFFORT AT EXTERNAL VALIDATION IS MALPRACTICE, PURE AND SIMPLE . . . BECAUSE THE MISDIRECTION OF THERAPY INJURES THE PATIENT AND HIS OR HER SIGNIFICANT OTHERS."

SINCE PSYCHOTHERAPY OFTEN INVOLVES UNVALIDATED REPRESSED MEMORIES, MOST PSYCHOTHERAPISTS, ACCORDING TO MCHUGH, ARE COMMITTING MALPRACTICE. MY FATHER AND OTHER PSYCHIATRISTS TOLD ME THAT REPRESSED MEMORIES ARE IMPORTANT IN PSYCHOTHERAPY, WHETHER TRUE OR NOT. VALIDATION IS AN UNREALISTIC, EVEN IMPOSSIBLE, IMPOSITION ON ANY PSYCHOTHERAPIST.

appearing on November 24, 1992, which prompted two letters to the editor.

The first writer, a social worker, wrote:

> After reading of Dr. Paul McHugh's "distaste for three fashions" in the Nov. 24 *Sun,* it is evident why the antipsychiatric movement has existed for 30 years. Dr. McHugh's callous remarks regarding "hidden child abuse," 'victimhood" and memories of sexual abuse indicate how the public needs to be continually educated about incest and sexual abuse, the types of treatment for survivors and exploration of the recovery process.

The second writer was equally vexed by McHugh's views:

> Sigmund Freud, appalled at the number of his patients who had been sexually abused, concluded (under pressure from his colleagues) that they must have been "making it up." And the abuse continued. Dr. Paul R. McHugh claims essentially the same thing. It is difficult enough for patients to accept the fact that those they trusted abused them, or that those with multiple personality disorder developed "alters" to help them survive. But while this esteemed psychiatrist glibly denies the possibly of forgotten trauma, professionals with much less lofty credentials are helping survivors to heal. If you cannot help, Dr. McHugh, do no harm.[7]

The *Sun,* which may have received letters in support of McHugh's views, did not publish them.

The debate over childhood sexual abuse is hardly a "fad" as

---

7. "DO NO HARM" REFERS TO THE HIPPOCRATIC OATH.

McHugh contends; it is more like a hundred years' war. McHugh did not appear to present any scientific evidence to support his dogmatic views, only personal anecdotes and puzzling analogies. He dismisses the notion of midlife crisis as "pure fiction." He refers to some of his colleagues as a "circus of psychotherapists," and apparently he is unfamiliar with adult human development. Despite the fact that many of his recommendations, such as standardizing the practice of clinical psychiatry, seem reasonable, McHugh does not appear to have had much long-term clinical experience with human patients. In fact, in reviewing his numerous scientific publications, I found that a number of them dealt with studies of the digestive systems of monkeys and rats. Indeed, a majority involved the digestive systems of animals and/or humans concerning experiments on eating disorders.

Even if McHugh were correct that psychiatry should be, for the most part, medicalized and that the key to the study of mental illness and behavior is through the brain and its management through medication, that was not the task for which he was hired in the matter of Bean-Bayog. McHugh was not hired to expound his views on what the standards of accepted practice ought to be. He was hired to advise the special prosecutor on what the accepted standards of practice were "prevailing at the time" that Bean-Bayog was treating Paul Lozano.

I now understood why the selection of McHugh, who has apparently little experience in and sympathy for psychodynamic psychotherapy and whose views appear extreme and controversial, was widely criticized. However, in the context of the adversarial process, he was the perfect choice. McHugh would provide expert testimony that would greatly assist Fabiano in winning the case.

Blau said to me that Fabiano should have concentrated on establishing sound public policy rather than a "big win." I wondered if the Canon of Ethics had anything to say on the subject. As a matter of fact, it did:

The responsibility of a public prosecutor differs from that of the usual advocate; his duty is to

> seek justice, not merely to convict. This special
> duty exists because the prosecutor . . . should
> use restraint in the discretionary use of govern-
> ment powers . . . and he should not use his posi-
> tion . . . to bring about unjust settlements or
> results.

Finally, I asked Fabiano, who had been an undergraduate at Harvard at the same time as Bean-Bayog, if he knew her. He was two years behind her.

"Not that I'm aware of. I probably knew five Radcliffe women and I don't think she was one of them. Yeah, I wouldn't have known anyone that was older. I can say it was entirely possible that we were in the same Natural Science II class . . . You know, it's funny because I don't know why her [college] records were even there, but they were in all of the documents that the board sent over here . . . and her premed adviser wrote a letter saying that she was a wonderful student and that she'd taken biology, chemistry, and physics. So I'm pretty sure Natural Science II must have been the physics course that we both took. But I can't truly remember. There are other things. I mean in one of the [sexual] fantasies she has an Ian and Sylvia song called "Someday Soon." I remember that year I had college roommates who played the guitar. She had the words wrong, but other than that. I saw that scene in *Bull Durham* where he says, 'I hate it when people don't get the words right.' But no, I don't think I ever knew her, and I certainly haven't had any contact with her since. And none in this case, too."

I turned off the tape recorder, shook Fabiano's hand, rode the elevator down. I now had a fairly good understanding of what had occurred.

The medical board had, perhaps unwittingly, hired an expert witness whose beliefs and professional orientation placed him in a poor position to judge whether Bean-Bayog had violated accepted standards of therapeutic practice for a very simple reason. McHugh's expertise lay outside hers, just as her own training did not qualify her to judge his work. In fact, the field that McHugh represented was a rival to Bean-Bayog's—a rival for money, academic positions, research funds, and prestige. His published writings show a strong disbelief in recovered memories of childhood sexual abuse, the basis of much current psychotherapeutic work, including Bean-Bayog's treatment of Paul Lozano. McHugh was so much a leading and intransigent opponent of what he often referred to as "fads" in psychiatry that he rejected much of what other psychiatrists practiced every day. He was a zealous reformer, not a judicious assessor, of psychiatric standards. At taxpayer expense, he worked up a set of accusations that focused largely on standards he wished to see imposed on psychiatrists, not on those already in place.

Since McHugh had expressed a particular animus against the doctrine of repressed childhood memories of trauma, he no doubt saw Paul Lozano's "suicide" as an obvious example of psychiatry gone awry, or, as he often wrote, psychiatry responding to cultural fads rather than to the dictates of stern laboratory science. It is no wonder that Fabiano refused to include in the settlement any expert testimony that disagreed with McHugh's. By all accounts, McHugh can be very charming and persuasive. Apparently, Fabiano was persuaded that his expert witness was no less than the pope of psychiatry and recognized as such by most of the flock. But if the case had gone to trial, it would have resulted in sharp "expert" disagreements about acceptable practices and would have become embroiled in a battle of ideologies, just as the case had been drowned in wave after wave of publicity seven months earlier.

The hearing would have made visible the deep rifts in the psychiatric profession. After all, this was not a case of mighty Harvard against a poor student, as the bathetic press stories had suggested and as some chroniclers will, I'm sure, contend. This was an intramural battle among the Harvards, who dislike each other far more than they dislike anyone else. Presented with such a golden opportunity, McHugh struck a blow against an enemy within, a Harvard psychiatrist of considerable reputation. He probably would not have achieved a technical knockout without the assistance of other forces pressing down on Bean-Bayog. The woman who had been portrayed as the protected daughter of rich Harvard was facing the possibility of ruin of a different sort, because the publicity brought to bear on her case had also brought sharply escalating legal costs, something I was unaware of at the time.

I now realized that psychiatric politics had greatly contributed to the sudden end of this case, not a clear resolution of the issues it seemed to crystallize.

19

THE COLOR OF EVIDENCE

At the end of September, 1992, I left the *Globe* to write this book. At about the same time, the medical board placed into the public record three large boxes of Bean-Bayog material. These included twenty-two depositions, internal memos, interviews, letters, and other documents.

I submitted a Freedom-of-Information-Act request for access to the materials. The board promptly misplaced my letter and had to ask me for another.

In the meantime, I now had the time to reexamine Meyer's thirty-page preface to the Plaintiff's Offer of Proof, something I had intended to do since April.

I opened it at random, to see if I could verify the very first citation I happened to come across. Meyer had written:

> (This) clearly indicates that the patient-physician boundaries had been crossed. As early as June 15, 1987, the defendant noted that Mr. Lozano felt that he was "being pulled apart by her (Dr. Bean-Bayog) slowly—*that the* boy *was* clinging to *her and she had* no use for him . . . *that she* should *have* left *him* alone." (Emphasis added.)

I looked up the entry in the Process Notes for June 15, 1987. Lozano is speaking to Bean-Bayog. This is what's recorded:

> Being pulled apart, by *me,* slowly. Vented some spite and rage. Boy *is* clinging to *you. I have* no

use for him. *You* should've left *me* alone. (Emphasis added.)

Something was wrong. I read Meyer's version again. Then the original. Meyer had completely omitted "Vented some spite and rage," and when Lozano said, *"I have* no use for *him,"* he was referring to the "boy." Meyer had quoted it as *"She had* no use for him."

I turned to another page and chose another citation to authenticate. Here is what Meyer quoted from the Process Notes:

Patient (Paul) made the blanket in my office into a transitional object. I gave it to him. He was deeply ashamed and felt I would be angry when he was "like this," i.e. 3 years old.

Meyer ended the above citation with a period after the word "old." However, the actual citation, reads differently.

Patient made the blanket in my office into a transitional object. I gave it to him. He was deeply ashamed and felt I would be angry when he was "like this" i.e. 3-years-old *because his family couldn't stand it.*

A few months later in an April 27, 1987, therapy session, which Meyer did not include in his treatise, Bean-Bayog wrote: "[He was] calmed, much comforted by the blanket. '[It's] different from the other one, you know.' "

So, Lozano did have another security blanket, the one "his family couldn't stand." Rather than Bean-Bayog's regressing him as Meyer contended, the evidence suggested that Lozano had been acting regressed long before he ever met her, and that his family was well aware of it, which they denied.

Indeed, I had just reread Lozano's hospital records and stumbled across a very telling handwritten entry. Despite denials under oath and to the press in 1992, members of Lozano's family privately admitted in July 1987 that Paul had had life-long psychological problems. They made this admission when they visited him again during his first admission to Faulkner Hospital. Psychiatric resident Dr. Robert J. Gregory wrote:

> **Had family meeting today including Paul's 2 sisters (Pilar Williams and Martha Tidball). Parents did not come because of previous bad experience they had at McLean with family therapy . . . Some character disorder is apparently present that Paul has always had. By family account, compulsive vs. borderline vs. schizoid.**[1]

Bean-Bayog later told me that she remembered vividly how regressed Lozano became during his first McLean admission:

"When he got into the hospital, he went into a severely regressed state where he had what is called psychomotor retardation . . . in which you are so paralyzed that your thoughts can't go forward and your body can't move and he would lie in the fetal position in the corner of the quiet room where they would put him and those were the periods in which he was talking to staff about wanting to be a puppy, wanting to be held, wanting to be a baby. And that's where I first heard that he had a desire to be a baby. I remember him standing in the middle of his room wrapped in a blanket, which he had gotten from his bed, not wearing a shirt, wearing a pair of pants and wrapped around the top of his body with a blanket, saying, 'There's something I need to tell you but I'm afraid. I'm afraid that you won't approve of it. I'm afraid you will think it's terrible, but I'd like to be 3-years-old.' "

---

1. AFTER LISTENING TO THE FAMILY DESCRIBE LOZANO'S CHILDHOOD SYMPTOMS, GREGORY INFERRED A POSSIBLE RANGE OF DIAGNOSES: (1) COMPULSIVE—OBSESSIVELY RITUALISTIC IN THOUGHT AND BEHAVIOR, (2) BORDERLINE—VOLATILE PERSONALITY THAT OFTEN FLUCTUATES BETWEEN REALITY AND PSYCHOTIC IDEATIONS, AND (3) SCHIZOID—REASONABLE FUNCTIONING BUT TENDING TO BE WITHDRAWN AND UNREACHABLE.

I went back to Meyer's treatise, flipped a few pages, and selected another passage. Meyer wrote that Lozano became suicidal after Bean-Bayog terminated therapy, severing a "morbid emotional dependent bond":

> In the Malden Hospital admission . . . the discharge summary recorded that in the therapeutic relationship with Dr. Bean-Bayog "there were a number of important and perhaps even somewhat eroticized dependent transferences activated with these leading to a real attachment to this therapist . . . a rather damaging and unfortunate note on which to end."

Meyer's citation, which again misleadingly ends without an ellipsis, came from a psychological evaluation conducted by psychologist Douglas F. Watt. Here is the full context from which Meyer's extractions, highlighted in italics, came:

> In this relationship *there were a number of important dependent and perhaps even somewhat eroticized dependent transferences activated with these leading to a real attachment to this therapist,* an attachment that probably stands in significant contrast to his rather isolative and counter-dependent stance in most of his relationships. He ended up feeling like (a) sizable burden in this relationship and even felt that the therapy had ended because he had become too much of a burden, *a rather damaging and very unfortunate note on which to end* what was from the patient's point of view a promising and important therapy relationship. It is clear that these themes of anxiety about his own dependent needs, particularly fears about becoming a burden and ultimately being abandoned are rooted in many early

experiences. There are signs on his projectives
that he was a rather lonely and awkward young
kid who felt like something of an outsider. There
are also indications that he felt humiliated and
shamed in relationship to his brothers and sisters
and felt that he was somehow different and in-
ferior to them . . .

The most effective illustration of Meyer's creativity was the
following. At the time, none of us covering the story had any
reason to doubt or challenge what Meyer had written:

It was apparent to Dr. Frances Frankenburg,
M.D., the psychiatrist in charge of Mr. Lozano's
care and treatment during this (second) admission, that there was overinvolvement, at the very
least, between the defendant Dr. Bean-Bayog
and Mr. Lozano. It was Dr. Frankenburg's opinion that this "overinvolvement" was undoubtedly contributing to Mr. Lozano's current
problems. Dr. Frankenburg writes in her discharge summary:
"During the hospital (sic) there was some question from the Bowditch treatment (team) as to
the usefulness of his ongoing psychotherapy.
Questions were raised of the possibility of an
overinvolvement on the part of the therapist and
of the intensity of the therapy and the *complete
dependence Mr. Lozano felt on the therapy* . . .
there is also an ongoing question about how
much his present therapy is supporting him *or
rather stirring up almost inconsolable yearnings
and conflictual feelings.*" (Emphasis added by
Meyer.)

I looked up Lozano's hospital records and read his entire
seven-page discharge summary. I discovered that Meyer had

used an ellipsis to join two sentences separated by four pages of single-spaced text! Although this is a common practice in legal textbooks, it seemed to me inherently inappropriate when a person's professional reputation is at stake. Nonetheless, immediately following Meyer's ellipsis, Frankenburg wrote: "This was discussed at length with the therapist, herself, and she obtained consultations with Dr. Gerry Adler, and with Dr. Dan Buie."

Meyer had left out that crucial sentence. He also omitted that Frankenburg then proceeded to cite for nearly an entire single-spaced typewritten page a glowing letter from Buie's consultation, which supported and praised Bean-Bayog's work with Paul Lozano:

> The patient shouldn't lose you, for goodness sake. You have a flexibility in treating him which includes the frequent visits, seeing him for deferred payment, and bringing him to the hospital yourself which is capable of being seen as overinvolved by other people, but which I think is working. What you did is what a lot of us would do. This kind of patient cannot be seen infrequently . . . If he doesn't have a chance to see you, he would lose the possibility of real growth and final resolution of all this. *It would be a question of definitive developmental work versus supportive, and he doesn't seem to be able to make use of the lower level of work.* (Emphasis added.) I think the work sounds very good. Not the kind of work everyone would agree on, including some people at McLean. That is hard because it makes mutuality and team work with the hospital difficult.

In Frankenburg's essay, immediately following the end of Meyer's excerpt, Frankenburg wrote:

However, he and Dr. Bean-Bayog are absolutely committed to continuing this relationship
and she has received support for this from Drs.
Gerry Adler and Dan Buie. Dr. Bean-Bayog will
be meeting with Dr. Shervert Frazier on June 29
for a further discussion of Mr. Lozano's ongoing
therapy.

More and more, I was persuaded of Meyer's untrustworthi-
ness. More and more, even before my one-on-one interviews with
Bean-Bayog, I was becoming convinced of her innocence.

So, I read Frankenburg's deposition, which had just been
released by the medical board to try to determine the basis of her
claim of Bean-Bayog's overinvolvement.

Frankenburg stated under oath that during Lozano's hospitalization her own relationship with him was "a very administrative one," and that his psychotherapy was being handled by
Bean-Bayog. Frankenburg stated that her duties and Bean-
Bayog's therapy did not overlap but "were quite complemen-
tary."

First, Frankenburg had pointed to Bean-Bayog's free treatment of her patient as an indication of overinvolvement, but, as
we have seen, this was not strictly true. Lozano's health insurance picked up some of the tab and he had written out checks to
her for over $10,000. Also, several psychiatrists I interviewed
said they set aside about 20 percent of their practice for pro bono
patients, the category Lozano would have fallen into if he remained unable to pay, which Bean-Bayog told me was her standard too. Some might consider laudable and compassionate the
willingness to provide free therapy to a promising but troubled
minority Harvard medical student on full scholarship.

Second, Frankenburg stated that Bean-Bayog drove to the
Harvard School of Public Health, talked Lozano down from the
thirteenth floor, and then drove him to the hospital. Frankenburg believed that Bean-Bayog should have called the local police. However, in the Process Notes, Bean-Bayog reported that
she talked Lozano down by phone, told him to come to her office

in Cambridge, and then drove him to McLean Hospital. Lozano told Bean-Bayog that if she had called the police, he would have run, as we've seen.

When I later interviewed Pilar Williams, she told me that her brother told her he had never called Bean-Bayog from the thirteenth floor of that building. He was actually calling from a pay phone on the street, threatening suicide.[2]

Finally, Frankenburg claimed that Bean-Bayog conducted a therapy session with Lozano that lasted several hours, which was inappropriately long. Frankenburg may have forgotten that this lengthy session was precipitated by the fact that her staff allowed Lozano to leave the grounds for ice cream. Lozano claimed he actually went to the thirteenth floor of the Harvard School of Public Health and contemplated suicide for several hours. The staff had allowed Lozano to leave the grounds even though Bean-Bayog had warned them that he was feeling suicidal.

Meyer twisted the claim of overinvolvement even further. He wrote:

> This "overinvolvement" was noted by other physicians as well during this admission. Dr. Joan Wheel(is) notes on p. I-13 of the McLean admission, "Evaluate current psychotherapy — ? psychotherapy consult regarding utility of current therapy."

---

2. A FEW DAYS BEFORE THE HEARING, THE MEDICAL BOARD'S STAFF PROSECUTOR, RICHARD WARING, VISITED THE THIRTEENTH FLOOR OF THE HARVARD SCHOOL OF PUBLIC HEALTH TO INVESTIGATE THE PLAUSIBILITY OF LOZANO'S CLAIM. WARING REPORTED THAT:

> In the 13th floor rooms, there are radiators right in front of some of the windows. The radiators are covered with metal caps extending right to the window sill. Lozano could have opened a window and sat on the ledge exactly as he told Bean-Bayog . . . At the time of these events, the 13th floor housed the departments of environmental science and physiology. Lozano was doing research in physiology. He may have had reason to be on the 13th floor and a key to one of the offices or labs.

Again, when the citation is placed in context, Meyer's claim proves misleading. Wheelis, the admitting physician, was simply calling for a standard evaluation of Lozano's psychotherapy and psychopharmacology during the period between his first and second admission to McLean. Meyer conveniently left out the sentence immediately preceding the above citation: "Psychopharmacological evaluation." If we follow Meyer's logic, Wheelis was calling Meyer's good friend, Lozano's psychopharmacologist Dr. Harrison Pope, overinvolved too.

In reviewing Meyer's preface to the Plaintiff's Offer of Proof, I did not find a single instance in which Meyer had employed citations that accurately reflected the context from which they had been extracted. Back in March, I remembered being very impressed with Meyer's exhaustive scholarship. What particularly stood out was one instance in which Meyer made a generalization supported by sixty-three page-citations in Bean-Bayog's Process Notes:

> Dr. Bean-Bayog employed an inappropriate course of treatment with Paul Lozano that focused on regressing this young man to a little boy, three years of age, all the while provoking him with intense sexual stimulation and imagery.

With little relish, I decided to look up every one of the sixty-three citations, which allegedly supported the above statement. It took me two days. I found not a single instance of Bean-Bayog's "provoking" Paul Lozano with intense sexual stimulation and imagery. In most of the citations Lozano or Bean-Bayog mention the "boy" or "the 3-year-old," but that's all.[3]

---

3. THIS IS NOT THE ONLY CASE IN WHICH MEYER'S ETHICS HAVE BEEN QUESTIONED. IN A LAWSUIT HE FILED AGAINST OBSTETRICIAN DR. ILONA LASZLO HIGGINS, MEYER'S OWN EXPERT WITNESS TESTIFIED AT THE TRIAL THAT THE DEFENDANT, HIGGINS, WAS NOT AT FAULT! AS A RESULT, SHE WAS SUCCESSFUL IN RECOVERING $10,000 IN LEGAL COSTS AND EXPENSES, AS WELL AS THE $2,000 TRIBUNAL BOND AGAINST MEYER'S FIRM. EARLIER, ON JULY 1, 1988, MEYER HAD WRITTEN A LETTER TO HIGGINS'S CURRENT

EMPLOYER CLAIMING THAT SHE WAS INCOMPETENT, A LETTER THAT HE AT FIRST ADMITTED WRITING. AS A RESULT, SHE SUED HIM FOR LIBEL AND SLANDER. SUDDENLY, MEYER SWITCHED HIS STORY, CLAIMING THAT HE DID NOT KNOW THE CONTENTS OF THE LETTER. THE FEDERAL JUDGE PRESIDING OVER THE CASE WROTE, ''(T)HE MEYER DEFENDANTS ARE NOW TAKING A POSITION INCONSISTENT WITH THEIR FORMER POSITION THAT MEYER SENT THE LETTER . . . (MEYER) FURTHER ASSERTS THAT HE NEVER REVIEWED THE LETTER THAT WENT OUT UNDER HIS NAME *AND THAT IT WAS HIS COMMON PRACTICE TO AUTHORIZE NONLAWYER SUPPORT STAFF TO SIGN HIS NAME TO DOCUMENTS LEAVING THE FIRM WITHOUT HIS PERUSAL.*[5]'' THE FOOTNOTE READ: ''THIS COURT CANNOT EVEN BEGIN TO ADDRESS THE OBVIOUS VIOLATIONS OF MEYER'S PROFESSIONAL RESPONSIBILITY IF THESE ASSERTIONS ARE TRUE.'' MEYER IMMEDIATELY REQUESTED THAT THE JUDGE ''DELETE THE UNDERLINED PHRASE ABOVE AND FOOTNOTE 5.'' THE JUDGE REFUSED, WRITING, ''THE FACT THAT THIS MAY HAVE BEEN A VIOLATION OF MEYER'S ETHICAL OBLIGATIONS CASTS DOUBT ON THE CREDIBILITY OF THE ASSERTION THAT MEYER NEVER SAW THE JULY 1 LETTER UNTIL AFTER IT WAS SENT.'' HIGGINS'S LIBEL LAWSUIT AGAINST MEYER IS SCHEDULED FOR TRIAL IN THE SPRING OF 1994.

MEANWHILE, MEYER IS FACING ANOTHER LAWSUIT CLOSER TO HOME. HIS FOUNDING PARTNER, DONALD LUBIN, DIED OF A HEART ATTACK IN 1990 AT AGE FORTY-FOUR. HIS WIDOW IS SUING LUBIN & MEYER OVER HOW MUCH IT OWES LUBIN'S ESTATE. UNLIKE THE BEAN-BAYOG CASE, THE COURT RECORDS IN THIS SUIT HAVE BEEN SEALED AT THE REQUEST OF MEYER'S FIRM.

20

STROMSTEN AND POPE

Immediately after the hearing was canceled, I began slipping letters under Bean-Bayog's front door, urging her to meet with me. I did not have her unpublished phone number. Finally, in early October, Bean-Bayog left a message on my answering machine, saying she didn't know what to do, but was giving serious thought to meeting with me. If so, she would call back.

In the meantime, as I anxiously awaited another call from her, I pored over the documents that had just been released by the medical board. I specifically wanted to better understand the crucial involvement of Amy Stromsten and Dr. Harrison Pope in this story.

For example, why had Stromsten, a social worker, stepped forward, exposing herself to the risk of public scrutiny?

One of the issues raised in Stromsten's "April Fool's" affidavit was Dr. Bernard Levy's alleged collusion in suppressing the board's investigation of Bean-Bayog. For example, the *Harvard Crimson* reported in early April that:

> Stromsten said she had called Levy in May 1991 to inquire about the Lozano case. At that time, Levy told her that Lozano had committed suicide, Stromsten said . . . "I was horrified that Levy knew that she had masturbated in front of Lozano and dismissed it," she said in the interview. "He said it was no big deal. He thought the kid was crazy so it didn't matter."

When interviewed by reporters, Levy denied her charges, said he knew nothing about the case until the recent media stories, and questioned the legality of Stromsten's conduct. He told the *Crimson:* "If she knew about sexual misconduct, she should have reported it to the Board of Medicine . . . but she didn't," [Levy] said. "She's in violation of state law for not making that report."

Stromsten immediately claimed that she had indeed filed a complaint in "the first two weeks of January 1991," about three months before Lozano's death. In a confidential interview seven days after she filed her April 1992 affidavit, Stromsten told the medical board's Richard Waring that:

> (In January 1991,) I called the National Association of Social Workers . . . and said, "I have a suspected case of a doctor sleeping with a patient. What do I do, because I know I have a duty to report it", and she said, "You can't report it to us you have to report it to the medical board." So I called the medical board and I got the address and I wrote them a letter.

As noted, the board scoured its files but could not locate her letter. However, Dr. Pope, Lozano's psychopharmacologist at McLean Hospital, contradicted her claim. Under oath, Pope stated he had several conversations with Stromsten in October or November of 1991, nine months after she claimed to have written the letter to the medical board.

> (Stromsten) said that the people at Newton-Wellesley Hospital had apparently reported this alleged abuse to the Massachusetts Board of Registration in Medicine, but that the issue had been dropped or ignored or something to that effect. Finally, she told me that she had further evidence of her own, from her own contact with Paul Lozano, beyond that which was known to the doctors and she was uncomfortable be-

cause *she did not know what her legal obliga-*
tions were. She did not know whether she was
obligated to report her information to the Board
or to come forward in some way. (Emphasis
added.)

If Pope is right, Stromsten had already decided what her legal
obligations were by mailing the letter of complaint but presented
herself to him as undecided.

Waring asked Stromsten to produce a copy of the alleged letter
she claimed the board had misplaced. She said she could not,
because at the time she was living on "the far tip of Gloucester,
like ten miles from a Xerox machine."

In her public affidavit, Stromsten also claimed to have attended a meeting at McLean Hospital with Pope, Frankenburg,
and Bean-Bayog, in which Pope and Frankenburg expressed
their concerns about Bean-Bayog's course of therapy with
Lozano. However, Pope stated under oath "not to my knowledge" had he ever met Bean-Bayog. Bean-Bayog later told me
that no such meeting ever occurred. There was no mention of this
meeting in any of Lozano's voluminous McLean Hospital records. What's more, in an informal interview with the medical
board's Barbara Cullen on June 18, Pope said that he "had no
evidence of [Bean-Bayog's] overinvolvement" and no knowledge
regarding her therapy.

When I interviewed Stromsten by phone, she told me that
Lozano used to drop by to see her for a chat about once every
twelve months. She took no notes of these subsequent meetings
and did not charge him.

In her affidavit, she stated that after meeting Lozano in January 1991, she referred him "to Michael Lew . . . who specializes
in sexually abused men. Michael Lew *verified* [emphasis added]
that Paul Lozano had indeed been sexually abused by Dr. Bean-
Bayog."

On April 8, Stromsten told Waring, "I called Michael Lew
afterwards and I said what do you think and he said he was
clearly sexually abused by his therapist."

But among the records released by the board was Lew's deposition. In it, he contradicted Stromsten's claims. Under oath, Lew stated that Stromsten called him on September 25, 1991, and "told me that Paul had committed suicide and that she and Skip Pope—she called him Harrison Pope—at McLean were pursuing a malpractice suit against—concerning Margaret Bean-Bayog."

Lew said that Stromsten was calling for any information he had about Lozano's relationship with Bean-Bayog. "I told her at the time that, basically, I didn't know too much about this case . . . I didn't think I had anything that would be helpful because I only saw [Lozano] once."

Nowhere in his twenty-eight-page deposition does Lew even remotely "verify" that Lozano "was clearly sexually abused by his therapist."

Stromsten's intervention, while Lozano was still alive, may have had other, far more serious consequences, according to Dr. Gerald Adler, another psychiatrist deposed by Meyer.

Adler, an associate clinical professor in psychiatry at Harvard Medical School, is a noted psychoanalyst in Boston with a national reputation and was Bean-Bayog's personal analyst. When Frankenburg suggested that Bean-Bayog might be overinvolved with Paul Lozano, Adler was one of the three psychiatrists who were consulted and one of the two who praised her treatment.

Later, Adler, who was the director of student education and psychiatry for Harvard Medical School at the Massachusetts General Hospital, had Lozano as a student. On February 26, 1990, Lozano began a thirty-day psychiatric rotation, a core requirement for graduation, under Adler's supervision. Adler had no idea that Paul Lozano was the patient about whom he had been a consultant for Bean-Bayog, because she told me that in consultations she never identifies the patient by name.

Adler said that he taught his students by example. They would observe him interview psychiatric patients in order to learn how to take a patient's history and work up a provisional diagnosis. In mid-March 1990, as Adler was interviewing a woman who claimed to have had an incestuous relationship as a child,

Lozano became visibly upset. According to Adler, Lozano told him immediately afterwards: "You know, I really have to talk with you because that patient upset me very much because I have had a relationship like that, an incestuous relationship, with a member of my family and I am really, really upset."

Adler told Lozano that if he was in therapy, he should discuss it with his therapist. Later, Blau cited this anecdote as an independent confirmation of Lozano's childhood sexual abuse.

It was not necessarily an independent confirmation, however. Lozano had broken into Bean-Bayog's Cambridge office at least once in November 1987, and stolen his own McLean Hospital records. He may have stumbled across and photocopied Bean-Bayog's sexual fantasies at that time. Apparently, he also read her Process Notes. In those notes, Adler is mentioned as one of the psychiatrists with whom she consulted as to her possible overinvolvement with Paul Lozano. Hence, Adler's report of Lozano's incest claim is not necessarily an independent confirmation but may be yet another attempt by Lozano to enlist someone else as a sympathetic ally. If so, he was willing to act out the part to great extreme.

Immediately after Adler's interview of the incestuous female patient, Lozano dropped out of his psychiatric rotation—and once again, out of medical school—and was committed for a second time to the psychiatric ward of the Faulkner Hospital. He left a message on Adler's answering machine, explaining that he'd been hospitalized for a gastrointestinal disturbance and would miss the final half of his psychiatric rotation. Out of compassion, Adler gave Lozano a passing grade.

Adler, still under oath, expressed a formulation—a psychological autopsy—on why Paul Lozano killed himself. First, though Gault may have legally had no choice, his reporting Bean-Bayog to the medical board set into motion forces very deleterious to Paul Lozano. Second, Stromsten's decision to inform him "that his therapist or former therapist had been talking about her sexual fantasies about [Lozano] at seminars . . . was a very destructive and undermining thing . . . a serious error."

Indeed, in her affidavit, Stromsten revealed that: "I told him

that he had been sexually abused by Dr. Bean-Bayog and what
Dr. Bean-Bayog was doing was wrong. I also told him I knew
what he was saying [sic] true because Dr. Bean-Bayog had discussed her sexual attraction to him in the supervision group."

An irony of Amy Stromsten's involvement—or perhaps overinvolvement—is that, according to Adler, her zeal to help
Lozano may have contributed to his possible suicide.

One thing Stromsten did not mention in her April 1 affidavit
was the key and pivotal role she played seven months earlier. It
was she who engineered one of the crucial elements in Bean-
Bayog's catastrophic downfall. In a long distance call, Stromsten
induced Pilar Williams, a woman she had never met or spoken
to, to replace Thomas O'Hare with Drew Meyer, an attorney
that Stromsten did not know. O'Hare had just filed the lawsuit
about two weeks earlier on September 17, 1991.

Stromsten must have been persuasive because Williams took
her advice. The man who suggested to Stromsten that the Lozanos hire Meyer must have been persuasive too. His name was
Harrison G. Pope, M.D.

In January 1991, Tom O'Hare, the lawyer Williams hired at
Gault's suggestion, asked Lozano how he had managed to find
so much to talk about with his therapist three to five times a week
across a nearly four-year span. O'Hare told me he couldn't believe that his client, who was somewhat shy and introverted,
could keep the conversation going for so many years.

According to O'Hare, Lozano said, "I just made things up."

This revelation should have raised doubts about Lozano's
credibility. Why couldn't he also be making things up about
having sex with Bean-Bayog?[1] But what intrigued me more was
that O'Hare had questioned how a patient could talk at such
length to a psychiatrist, because O'Hare—he happened to mention it in passing—is married to one.

---

1. LATER, IN EARLY 1993, O'HARE TOLD THE PSYCHIATRIC TIMES, "WE WILL NEVER
KNOW (WHETHER THEY HAD SEX). THERE'S ONLY ONE PERSON WHO KNOWS. THAT'S
DR. BEAN-BAYOG. WITH PAUL'S DEATH, WE LOST THE CHANCE TO EVER GET TO THE
POINT WHERE HE WOULD HAVE BEEN A COMPLETELY RELIABLE REPORTER."

I had a hunch that there was something O'Hare, who, incidentally, used to be the in-house counsel at McLean Hospital, wasn't sharing with me. A few days later, I discovered an amazing irony. At the very moment O'Hare was exploring a lawsuit against Bean-Bayog, a lawsuit for malpractice and wrongful death was pending against his wife, Dr. Prudence "Penny" Allen.

Allen was being sued for allegedly causing the death of Judith Krasnow, a patient who had been sexually abused as a child by a parent and who committed suicide while still under Allen's care.

Krasnow's widower hired an attorney and sued Allen. The attorney he hired was none other than Drew Meyer. The expert witness that Meyer hired was none other than Dr. Harrison Pope, who declined to be interviewed for this book. Pope criticized Allen, among other things, for sloppy record keeping.

But on February 20, 1991, ninety-nine days after O'Hare first met Lozano and forty-one days before he killed himself, the lawsuit against O'Hare's wife was dismissed in appellate court.

Pope, who is thin, intense, and balding, stated under oath that in McLean Hospital he ministered to Lozano at least seventeen times between October 14, 1986 and June 5, 1987, but had apparently misplaced some of his notes. "My memory is that I wrote a note, but upon examining the chart carefully I cannot find one either in the McLean's chart or in my own records."

Pope did admit that he made it clear that his involvement in Lozano's treatment need not stop simply because the patient was being transferred to Faulkner Hospital. "Although after Paul was discharged from McLean Hospital, both after his first admission and again after his second admission, I made it clear that I was available should he or Dr. Bean-Bayog want me if they had any questions with which I could help."

Pope was then asked if either Lozano or Bean-Bayog called him with any questions. Pope replied: "I do not specifically remember such questions."

According to Pope's testimony, based on his notes and recollection, he did not see Paul Lozano after June 5, 1987 until:

April of 1988, a year after his second McLean's admission (when) Paul came to see me because he was doing work with relationship to his area of concentration . . . He was aware that I was doing work in a related area, namely the neuroleptic malignant syndrome, a dangerous side effect of antipsychotic drugs . . . He discussed his work with me, and he and I thought that we could collaborate on a study linking the two areas of knowledge that we were exploring. Specifically, Paul had developed a test . . . (which Lozano believed) could correctly identify malignant hyperthermia victims . . . If this test were successful, it would become an invaluable tool for subsequent psychiatrists because it would help to determine who might be vulnerable to this dangerous and potentially fatal side effect of antipsychotic drugs.

Then Pope said something extraordinary:

I confess that Paul and I had visions of patenting the test and making a million dollars from doing it . . . (Emphasis added.) At that time, I told Paul that Prozac was now on the market and that he might want to consider trying it, in place of the Desipramine, which had stood him well in the past two years because Prozac has fewer side effects. Accordingly, I gave him a prescription for a small supply of Prozac for him to try and he tried it, but it proved to be ineffective and he experienced a recurrence of the depression as soon as he shifted off of the Desipramine and onto the Prozac. So that we abandoned the Prozac and resumed the Desipramine and that was the end of it.

Pope then explained that the experiments failed and the collaboration was abandoned in April 1988 or "thereabouts." He was asked when was the next time, if any, he had contact with Paul Lozano or with anyone concerning Paul Lozano. Pope replied: "When I got a call from Amy Stromsten in October or November of 1991."

Pope's claim that he did not recall treating or having contact with Paul Lozano between June 5, 1987 and April 1988 is not reflected in the patient's hospital records and in Bean-Bayogs's Process Notes. According to those records, Pope was consulted over a dozen times about Lozano's medication. Perhaps this is a reflection of Pope's sloppy record keeping.

For example, after Lozano's discharge from McLean and transfer to the Faulkner Hospital, a psychiatric resident wrote on June 30 in Lozano's hospital records:

> The psychopharmacologist is Dr. Pope at McLean (page him there). Until recently we did not consider changing his medications; because he has become so depressed in the past 24 hours (with Dr. Pope's help) some additional medication trial . . . of Lithium.

Again, on July 14:

> Dr. Osser suggested lithium for both mood swings and possibility that patient has paranoid ideation . . . may benefit from Ativan for evening anxiety . . . start lithium per discussion with Dr. Harrison Pope.

And again on July 28:

> Discharged to home today. Follow up with Dr. Bean-Bayog for outpatient psychotherapy and Dr. Alexander (sic) Pope for pharmacotherapy.

In the Process Notes, for example on July 28, it appeared that Pope continued to be actively involved in Lozano's psychopharmacology: "Re: Lithium. Dr. Pope plans to (discontinue) Li[thium] when he starts fluoxetine [Prozac] in September and decrease Desipramine.

This seemed to contradict Pope's claim that he suggested Prozac to Lozano nine months later. Pope's name is mentioned seven more times in the notes between July 28 and April 2.

For example, on April 2:

> (Patient) called with questionable distonic reaction. What (should he) take? Gave (him) benadryl. Pope hadn't. Ativan, called him back . . . Still having reaction, myoclonic jerks, cogwheeling etc. Pope said double-drug effect.

On April 15, Bean-Bayog made the following observations:

> Patient used Dr. Pope for psychopharmacology problems initially. Patient maintained the split, repeatedly telling Dr. Pope I was taking him off his medications. But able to feel supported. Patient working on research project on Halothane-induced hyperthermia. Began to collaborate with Dr. Pope on developing a blood test to screen patients for malignant hyperthermia from phenothiazines. Dr. Pope asked patient to call him Skip. Suggested that the three of them (Dr. Pope, assistant, and the patient contact a patent lawyer, and not mention the project to anyone) Patient got intensely anxious: "He was my doctor and now he's telling me to call him Skip, talking about making $500,000/year on this test. We don't even know if it works. I can't feel comfortable calling him about my own medications any more. I don't know if he's my doctor or business partner."

Lozano also told her: "[Pope] said if I dropped by [his] house he'd let me use his daughter's pony. [He said,] "People from [the] Southwest like horses."

Here, at least, there was at minimum a grain of truth in what Lozano said. Pope's daughter does indeed have a white pony that is wintered in a private barn on upper Monument Street, just down the road from Pope's residence.

It seemed odd to me—and questionable at best—that a physician would entertain a business venture with his own current or former patient. However, it certainly did not appear that Pope was exploiting Paul Lozano for financial gain. On the contrary, Pope was generous enough to be willing to share the potential credit and a large sum of money from the profits of an important, lifesaving test with an impoverished minority medical student. It is the psychological implications of a psychiatrist entering a commercial venture with his mentally ill patient that may raise concerns among Pope's colleagues. In fact, when I queried psychodynamically oriented psychiatrists, they called it a "clear border violation." When I queried biologically oriented psychiatrists, they called it an "error in judgment."[2]

As noted, Lozano's tests did not produce the desired results and Pope said that after April 1988, he had no contact with or discussions about Paul Lozano until Stromsten called him in the fall of 1991. Bean-Bayog was under the impression, however, that Pope was still Lozano's psychopharmacologist. She said that Lozano continued to claim to be speaking to Pope about medications. For example, in the notes for September 5, 1989, five months after the end of the Pope-Lozano business collaboration, she wrote:

Wants to stop desipramine. Decreases sexual functioning. Dr. Pope suggested Bethanechol,

---

2. REGARDING BEAN-BAYOG'S USE OF THE "NONABUSIVE MOM" IN THE FALL OF 1987, PSYCHODYNAMIC PSYCHIATRISTS FAMILIAR WITH THE EVIDENCE CALLED IT A POSSIBLE "ERROR IN JUDGMENT." BIOLOGIC PSYCHIATRISTS CALLED IT "A CLEAR BORDER VIOLATION."

other suggestions. Will discuss with Dr. Pope
again.

Two months later, she wrote:

Off desipramine 24 hours. Getting drunk
more . . . Plan 1) start different drug, 2) Consult
with Dr. Pope—re: what to start . . . wants to try
antidepressants with less sedation, less sexual
problems.

The final time Pope's name appeared in Lozano's hospital
records was on April 12, 1990. Lozano told Dr. John Vara, an
evaluator at the Massachusetts Mental Health Center, that he
had been "referred by Dr. Skip Pope at McLean [Hospital] for
[a] psychopharmacological consult and treatment."

Lozano may have been lying to Vara. From April 1988, he
may have been lying whenever he told Bean-Bayog that Pope
was still advising him on his medications. Pope also stated that
he can't recall if he ever spoke to or met Bean-Bayog. Her recol-
lection is different:

"I would call up Pope and consult, because the medication
problems with him [Lozano] were extremely technically difficult.
He was on more medicine than I had ever seen, and whenever
there was a side effect or something, I called Pope, or there was
information that the patient would like to see Pope about this,
and so Pope was giving instructions on how to do stuff right
through to the final hospitalization, but what he says in his
deposition is that he wasn't his doctor, that he'd done a consultation briefly . . . 'Oh yeah, we collaborated on a research project that might have generated a million dollars a year in royal-
ties,' but he denies that he was continuing to serve as Lozano's
doctor."

In fact, Pope was asked if he ever covered for Bean-Bayog's
practice. He responded very carefully:

I do not believe that I ever formally covered for
her practice, although it is possible that I may

have said to Paul that I would be available if she was not available, if he wanted to call me for something.

When asked about Amy Stromsten, Pope said:

I hardly knew her. She remembered me because she had been a social work intern (during Paul's two McLean hospitalizations) and had apparently admired my consultation work with Paul, and hence, had called me because I guess I was the person she remembered best from that time.

Pope contended that Stromsten remembered him better than Frankenburg, the on-site chief of the unit and overseer of Lozano's care. In fact, Stromsten and her supervisor reported to Frankenburg for whom Stromsten worked.

Pope was then asked if he heard from Stromsten again.

One more time. *She followed my suggestion and called a lawyer. The lawyer who I suggested was attorney Meyer of this firm,* (emphasis added) because I knew him from his having purchased my house many years ago.[3]

However, Meyer told me that his participation came about because "a number of doctors had ... wanted me to get involved in the case."

---

3. IN 1982, AFTER SETTLING A SIZABLE LAWSUIT, MEYER MOVED UP FROM A SMALL TWO-BEDROOM DUPLEX TO A MAGNIFICENT COLONIAL-STYLE STUCCO MANSION WITH ANTEBELLUM COLUMNS SITUATED ON 12.8 ACRES OF PARTIALLY WOODED LAND SLOPING DOWN, SOMEWHAT TERRACED, TO 544 FEET OF FRONTAGE ON THE SUDBURY RIVER IN CONCORD, A WEALTHY BOSTON SUBURB. POPE SOLD HIM THE ESTATE FOR $410,000. TODAY, IT IS VALUED AT $1.6 MILLION. THE MANSION'S MOST STRIKING FEATURE IS THE FRONT ENTRY'S DOUBLE STAIRCASE, SWEEPING LEFT AND RIGHT, WHICH RISES TO A SMALL LANDING ON THE SECOND FLOOR WHERE THE BEDROOMS ARE LOCATED.

In his deposition Pope neglected to mention that he also knew Meyer from serving as his paid expert witness in the lawsuit against the wife of the first attorney handling the Lozano case.

> (Stromsten) said that she had talked to attorney Meyer, who felt that a potential malpractice case existed (actually, the lawsuit had already been filed) and that attorney Meyer wanted to contact someone in Paul's family to discuss the matter. She said she had no way of ascertaining the address or telephone number of Paul's family, and was there any way that I could produce it. I inquired at McLean Hospital and was told that this would not be within the range of McLean's policy and I called her back and told her that I was not permitted to assist her on that matter. And that was the last conversation.

It was very accommodating for a busy, world-renowned psychopharmacologist, who is notorious for working at a frenetic pace, to accommodate a former social-work intern, whom he could hardly recall.

A few days after Pope suggested the name of attorney Drew Meyer to Stromsten, she telephoned Williams at the Providence Memorial Hospital in El Paso. Williams told me that she had no idea how Stromsten had tracked down her phone number.

"This better be good," Williams remembered saying when she took the call during a typically busy day in the intensive care unit. She had been receiving a spate of dunning phone calls, because Lozano had died with unpaid bills to credit card companies, department stores, and student loan services, totalling over $15,000.

" 'It is very good,' " Williams recalled Stomsten replying.

Williams told me that Stromsten called her "Polara," which Williams and I thought was the first name of Pablo Picasso's daughter. (Actually, his daughter's name is Paloma.) When I got back to Boston, I had a vague memory of that name. I checked the records of Lozano's first admission to McLean. Sure enough, Stromsten had written "meet with [the] patient regularly to establish rapport and encourage patient to give permission to contact sister (Polara)." Had Stromsten somehow gotten a peak at Lozano's McLean records, which contain the home address of Marcos and Epifania Lozano? The Lozanos, whose phone number could have been obtained from directory assistance, may have given Stromsten Williams's work number.

Williams told Fabiano that Stromsten called her about three months after her brother died. But Williams later told me she must have been mistaken. Stromsten had first called her about two weeks before Williams fired O'Hare and hired Meyer at Stromsten's suggestion. Stromsten called Williams at the end of September, approximately the same time that Pope recalled that Stromsten had called him in "October or November." Lew stated that Stromsten called him on September 25 and said that "she and Skip Pope . . . were pursuing a malpractice suit" against Bean-Bayog.

By this time, O'Hare had already filed the lawsuit in Middlesex Superior Court on September 17.

Stromsten, who apparently believed that the lawsuit was not being pursued vigorously enough, did speak to Meyer before contacting Williams, because Pope had mentioned it. Pope reported that "[Stromsten] said that she had talked to attorney Meyer, who felt that a potential malpractice case existed and that attorney Meyer wanted to contact someone in Paul's family to discuss the matter."

Stromsten, who definitely knew that the Lozanos had already retained O'Hare, may have mentioned O'Hare's name to Meyer.

If Meyer wished to contact the Lozanos, he could have done so himself by checking the plaintiff's index in Middlesex Superior Court and then contacting the lawyer listed on file. Perhaps, Meyer's interest was also sparked because he had lost the lawsuit against O'Hare's wife seven months earlier, which had cost Meyer's firm a considerable sum. Meyer not only failed to recover any of his legal costs but forfeited the bond he had posted when the lawsuit against Allen was initially rejected by the medical malpractice tribunal.

Stromsten knew that O'Hare was the Lozano's attorney, because she had spoken to him shortly after Lozano's death.

Though Stromsten reported in her affidavit that she learned of Lozano's suicide from Dr. Levy in May 1991, O'Hare told me that a few days after Lozano's death, Williams found Stromsten's phone number in his address book and gave it to O'Hare.[4] O'Hare said he presently telephoned Stromsten, whom he described as hostile:

"Well, she began interrogating me about my experience and she wouldn't answer any questions . . . I told her that I'd much prefer to talk to her here than with a stenographer, but we can do it that way if we had to. And I never heard from her again . . . I did warn your colleague [Alison Bass] to check anything she said three ways before she printed it . . . I think [Stromsten's] a loose cannon."

In early October, 1991, O'Hare got a startling call from Drew Meyer, from whom O'Hare did not relish any communication whatsoever. "[Meyer asked] for copies of all the files," said O'Hare. "I said, 'Excuse me? I'm not gonna give you anything until I hear from the family.'"

The next day, Meyer faxed O'Hare a letter from Williams authorizing his replacement. O'Hare was stunned. He immediately called her in El Paso.

"She did not say why," O'Hare said quietly. "I asked her and all she would say is that it was a 'family decision.'"

Before the interview ended, I asked him another question. It was an academic one. I knew that Paul Lozano had departed for El Paso before O'Hare received a copy of the Process Notes that he had requested from Bean-Bayog. But I asked O'Hare anyway.

"When were they handed over? In other words, what was the time between [your] request and [your] receiving the treatment notes?"

"It was actually fairly quick . . . They were not requested as part of the lawsuit but rather pursuant to the patient's rights

---

4. I TOO SAW STROMSTEN'S PHONE NUMBER IN LOZANO'S ADDRESS BOOK WHEN I WAS BROWSING THROUGH A BOX OF PAUL MEMORABILIA THAT WILLIAMS KEEPS ON A SHELF IN ONE OF HER BEDROOM CLOSETS.

under the mental health bill . . . I would say it was probably within a month when I got them. I understood why," said O'Hare.

". . . And [Lozano] did not see them?"

"No."

"Did [Bean-Bayog] say anything about his seeing them?"

"She wrote a note to me. It *may* have been on that cover sending those notes, something to the effect of 'consider very carefully whether you allow Paul to see [them] . . .'"

"So Paul never saw the treatment notes?"

"The Process Notes?"

"The Process Notes, yeah."

"Not to my knowledge," said O'Hare.

21

SITTING IN PAUL LOZANO'S CHAIR

In mid-October, Bean-Bayog finally called me again. She had decided to meet with me. So I began a series of clandestine interviews with her. These conversations, by phone or in person, continue, from time to time, even as I complete this book.

Why did she choose me to confide in?[1] I'm not sure. Neither is she. I think she needed someone independent to talk to. I had written a pivotal story about her and established a good relationship with Michael Blau. I don't know if my father's reputation in alcoholism helped or not.

Bean-Bayog had good reason to worry about secrecy. If her lawyers—Blau, Mone, and Barry—had discovered their client was not only speaking to a reporter, but even allowing him to tape her comments, they would have been furious, because the civil suit was still pending. She might have jeopardized the terms of her own malpractice insurance, which would have left her completely without coverage when and if the suit went to trial. But she must have felt that the benefits outweighed the risks in meeting with me. She told me not only about her feelings and her potential defense against her accusers, but also shared the part of her life she most wanted to protect, the adoption of her infant son.

There were other legal risks for Bean-Bayog. If Drew Meyer, the Lozano family attorney, had learned of my tapes, he would surely have subpoenaed me. I had no desire to become part of

---

1. "MY BLIND, STUPID TRUST IN PEOPLE BORDERS ON THE PSYCHOTIC," BEAN-BAYOG LATER TOLD ME.

this story by going to jail for contempt of court. As a reporter, I enjoy only a limited shield in revealing confidential sources if compelled to testify. Yet, I felt bound to keep Bean-Bayog's secrets until their revelation could no longer be harmful to her and her family in court.

Part of my amateurish attempts to maintain secrecy included using a rented car to drive to her home. My own car, a battered 1939 Chevrolet, was far too conspicuous. It had already more than once become a target for people displeased with my reporting. I was worried that if I drove my wife's car someone would trace it through the license plate, and I took the precaution of asking employees of the car rental company to alert me if anyone, including someone claiming to be from the police, inquired about my activities.

Except for the first two meetings, controlled by Blau in his law office, the secret interviews were always held in Bean-Bayog's private office.

Three years after moving into her husband's Lexington home, Bean-Bayog filed a permit with the city of Lexington to construct an addition to the family home for office use. Completed in 1988, it featured a small outdoor lift, required by law at a cost of $10,000 for handicapped patients, which, she said, had never been used.

I felt lightheaded the first time I sat in the chair that Paul Lozano had usually occupied, although I learned later that he was often so agitated that he moved around, sometimes apparently helpless, sometimes intimidating and threatening. At other times, he sat in the waiting room next to her potted spathiphyllum plant and spoke to her from there. Sometimes, he sprinkled small pieces of paper around his chair, symbolically establishing a boundary between himself and his psychiatrist.

Once, Bean-Bayog took out from a drawer a wrinkled plastic bag from a bookstore in Harvard Square. She said it was Lozano's hyperventilation bag. Whenever he became too agitated, he would put the bag over his mouth and inhale his own breath to stop himself from passing out. She also showed me a gift from Lozano, a coffee mug with pithy aphorisms about medicine and healing. She said someday she is going to burn the bag and smash the cup.

At our meetings, Bean-Bayog always wore plain dresses or skirts that fell well below her knees. She usually sat with her feet on a small white ottoman and often brushed her bangs away from her forehead when she spoke.

In her office, there were two brown vinyl chairs, the obligatory couch, and one beige fabric chair, some wooden file cabinets, an antique secretary, a tapestry on the wall, a few awards, and a collection of books and journals.

At first, these interviews made me uncomfortable. I couldn't formulate my problem then, but in some inarticulate way I realized that I would have to be careful not to allow our meetings to become therapeutic sessions for myself. I was beginning to realize that my job was not merely to assemble facts, but to try to understand the emotional complexities of the people who acted in this story. I could not hope to remain entirely outside it. It was a job made all the more intriguing by the fact that I had entered a territory where "facts" are often not concrete at all.

As our relationship evolved, Bean-Bayog labelled me, at times, her savior, one of her therapists, and a callous inquisitor.

"I know this isn't how you intend it," she once said to me, "but there are times when you are asking me questions and I feel like a woman holding her dead child and you sticking a microphone in my face asking me how I feel."

There were no preconditions to our interviews. Bean-Bayog never saw a single word of this manuscript prior to publication, never received any remuneration or consideration from me or anyone else for allowing the interviews, and fully understood that as a "detective reporter" I would follow the evidence wherever it led. Even if that meant finding her guilty or liable of any or all of the charges against her.

Who is Margaret Bean-Bayog? I suppose I will truly never know, just as I will never know with absolute certainty whether she and Lozano were lovers. For me, one mystery is how she survived this ordeal, the public destruction of her reputation and career, and survived it so well.

Once, when I asked her how she was managing to cope, she paused and looked away. I felt she'd fallen into a black hole from which escape was impossible. Often, I could hear despair in her voice or see it in her eyes. Only once in my presence did she cry. Often, she refused to meet with me for several weeks; occasionally, she would agree and then cancel. At times, she accused me of exploiting her so that I could make money by writing this book.

What kept her alive, I believe, and prevented her from drinking again was her family, in particular John, her newly adopted infant son. He was her reason to endure. At almost every meeting, she had new photos to show me.

"The baby has been lifesaving, because he's been a safe place. You see the baby doesn't feel contaminated with the rest of this stuff. He will if it hits the papers about the adoption. He will also be in danger . . . But at the moment, I have a face that's separate, that doesn't kick up this stuff. My time with him is cozy and pedestrian and full of the stuff of life. You can change his diaper or you can read to him. It's not anything I can't handle."

As noted, she went back on Antabuse and resumed seeing her analyst. She also used "avoidance and denial" by reading few of the newspaper accounts and by watching none of the TV newscasts. She said she skimmed some of the *Globe* stories, "looking for personal attacks." She avoided the news about herself because she did "not want to feed into the abuse cycle." She could not bear to meet the false persona created by Meyer and the press.

Finally she responded to my question.

"Sometimes I feel kind of like the whole thing is a tempest in a teacup. I feel like I'm not this important. And what you do is you withdraw and examine the areas of your life that are not affected. And there aren't many, because my family, of course, is affected. Parts of my life are massively affected, but you begin to go back to things that you did before. I mean I've been a doctor for so long. I can't remember what I used to have as hobbies before I went to medical school. I used to take modern dance and I had interests in history, and I did various athletic kinds of things like canoeing and hiking. And part of it is that I really live in a swirling little community, which is full of people. My extended family has a lot going on. Like yesterday, I saw patients in the morning, I spent the afternoon taking the au pair to the hospital to deal with her dislocated jaw, and I came back to a birthday party that was full of everything that you hoped for in a birthday party. It was wonderful. And I had been afraid. I had got my daughter a present that would be special to her, that I knew would be special to her, and I was afraid that she was going to reject it.

"When I first [became her stepmother], when she was five or six—her name is Ruby, by the way—well, she and I fell in love. I fell in love with the boy too, but, it was different. She was younger. And I took her out one day and we were in some fancy mall, and I found an antique jewelry store with a beautiful ruby ring, which was a child's ring but from some estate. And I spent more money than I should have. I couldn't really afford it. And she loved it. And she tended to lose things she loved, the way she lost her mother. And so love as possessions were at risk at times of loss or trauma to her. And the day her uncle, who had lived with us for three years and who adored her, went back to the Philippines, she lost the ruby ring in the grass out in the back yard and we never saw it again. I bought her another ruby ring yesterday."

Near the end of one interview she said something that stayed with me, as a sort of warning. She said, "When you're a victim of abuse like Paul Lozano was, you believe that everyone is out to get you. That's what's fascinating is that he succeeded in getting me into a situation where my life felt like his."

I knew I had to keep a balance, that I had to remain partly outside Bean-Bayog's newly narrowed life as I became more involved in it, not dissimilar to her balancing act in treating Paul Lozano. I was more comfortable as Joe Friday, just wanting the facts, ma'am, than as a confidant, but I also knew that the "facts" were not the whole story here. I was dividing my time between poring over all the documents, trying to uncover the "facts" about Bean-Bayog's relationship to Paul Lozano, and listening to a woman whose professional and personal life had been shattered. I was attempting to "get the goods" on someone while I was listening sympathetically to her distress. What unsettled me more than the fear of falling off my tightrope was that I was finding it so easy to switch roles. The context created by my sessions in Bean-Bayog's office did not seem to enter the context of my work outside it. I wondered whether this peculiar dissociation was itself a parody of the psychotherapeutic process. I had no good answer, however.

22
CONVERSATIONS
WITH
BEAN-BAYOG

My interviews with Bean-Bayog continued throughout the fall, winter and into spring. In the following chapters, I have grouped her comments so that her views on matters related to Paul Lozano and her own understanding of psychotherapy can be "heard." Her comments are the raw, spontaneous answers to my questions. They are barely edited. I think they provide an unusual insight into the thoughts and feelings of someone who has been the subject of so much public controversy, the voice that was missing from the opening scene, because the chief actor in the drama was not allowed to speak her lines.

As November 10 loomed, the day Bean-Bayog's resignation would go into effect, I asked her to describe how she felt about the prospect of never practicing medicine again.

"Where I am right now is that I'm in a peculiar state. Part of me is really happy that I'm not going to be a doctor and that I could not be subjected to this kind of thing again . . . But there's a kind of retrospective bitterness or negativity, which is really not my style.

Talk about how you saw yourself in medicine, your mission in medicine.

"Well, I really believed that it was a dream that I actually participated in at some point in what the medical community is supposed to stand for, and I don't feel like I do anymore, I don't feel like there's much left to that community, and this whole case hasn't helped it very much, but . . . [When I taught medical students I'd say] 'Come on in. The water's fine. This is fun and exciting, working with alcoholics. You can be elegant, you can be sophisticated, you can be rigorous and you can be kind and you can be a grown-up, and you can have a good time,' and I was a very popular teacher . . . the experience with this guy was that what you do is you break down your expectations into little bitty steps and you stop expecting him to turn into a movie star and [what] you want him to do at the beginning is like going home and taking his pills instead of getting drunk and jumping in front of a car. You're looking for little things. You're looking for the ability to delay a half an hour before he calls you at three in the morning, and later he doesn't have to call you at all. You break things down into tiny steps and you look at them and then you keep feeding back to him his successes. Every situation I'm in, most of them don't make these kinds of demands on me. I like to be pushed. I think it's amusing to find out whether I'm capable of rising to the occasion."

Why did you get so much training?
"I loved to be in school, I really liked studying about things and just a lot of work. And so I did my child residency after my adult residency, did school of public health, and I did analytic training, and I did an advanced psychotherapy fellowship because I could afford it. I didn't have kids. And I didn't have to make a huge amount of money because when you're in training you don't make any and you have time to see patients for nothing and paying for supervision, you basically have lost a handle on your income and that goes on for years. And so that was very satisfactory and I gradually built up stamina for doing clinical work . . . And at that point I made a decision that I really didn't want to do academic medicine. I knew I didn't want to become a professor, because my father was a professor and I could never see it being done any other way. He was never available to the family as a result of his being very absorbed with what he was doing. He basically disappeared into the hospital when I was five

and was never seen again. He came home for meals and stuff. He was in love. I mean he really was wildly in love with medicine and so I sort of followed him into the hospital . . . so that by the time I was seeing this patient [Paul Lozano] I had had a ton of training. I had also seen, oh, I don't know, sixteen medical students with a variety of problems, mainly addiction related."

Were you obsessed by Paul Lozano? Why did you devote so much time and energy to him?

"Let me tell you what else was going on when I took on Paul Lozano. I was seeing thirty hours of patients a week. I had no household help, because I really wanted these kids to be Americanized, which meant that I was your cook and bottle washer and the shopper and the child schlepper to soccer and that whole thing. I was also at that time the president of the American Society of Addiction Medicine. I was one of about a dozen people who transformed it from a sleepy little outfit of four hundred members with a budget of about $70,000 a year into a thriving operation of $1,500,000 budget a year with 3,400 members and twenty-six standing committees, which has had a major impact on the teaching of addiction and basically we are responsible for the fact that addiction is now a medical specialty. Not only that, but my father got metastasis from his colon cancer and it began to be clear that my mother had Alzheimer's, I was flying back and forth to Iowa where they lived, I was coping with their finances. So that during the period that this guy was most out of control, he was not all I was doing."

There are many horrid memories from this experience. What's one that immediately comes to mind.

"One of the worst things was having a friend that I had discussed this case with need to get the hell away from me."

Why?

"Well, I think she felt I had mismanaged him and that she was tainted and she was going to look terrible if her name somehow got involved. I haven't spoken to her since March . . . So I don't know where her thinking was, but I think she felt simply that she would have been assaulted too. In fact, a lot of people around town did. I mean, a lot of people who had consulted with me were screamed at by their patients. 'How could you be associated with this terrible woman?' So that was one of the most painful experiences, because she was someone I had turned to for help and she abandoned me."

How did your patients put up with all of this?

"My patients have been remarkable, but there's been absolutely terrible trauma. In fact, one person panicked because he was afraid of being photographed on 'Hard Copy' . . . Oh, they were so upset. 'I feel like I'm watching my mother being raped' was a common one. Or, 'I can't believe this is happening to my therapist.' Or 'You were the one who always gave me hope when I said things were hopeless, and now I'm worried that you're not going to survive.' Or, 'I can't believe that these people are doing this stuff to you.' One of them said that they would kill themselves if they had to watch me go through the hearing."

What was your husband's reaction to the sexual fantasies you wrote about another man.

"I mean Roger understood what the sexual fantasies were all about. He's a psychiatrist too. He was dismayed not that I would have the feelings, but that we would be vulnerable. It's a hell of a story, isn't it? It's such a soap, such a complete soap . . . but the effect on my husband was just heartbreaking to me. You know what it's like for an Asian man to lose face, to be accused of being cuckolded by his wife supposedly sleeping with a patient who is psychotic and who had severe acne? . . . He was a hero at first. He supported me. And I needed him. And he came through like a trooper, and the kids soldiered through it. And then I left [to adopt the baby]. And he got so angry with me, that he was barely speaking to me for the whole time I was away. I made him come out and meet the baby and bring Ruby, because I wanted her in on this. And the two of them nearly killed each other on the plane. They had a real set-to which had to do with the fact that my daughter was accommodating to the fact that she wasn't the baby anymore, and he was accommodating to the fact that she was having a tantrum, because I, her mom, was gone . . . So everyone who took care of Ruby disappeared. And there are these people beating her mother up in the press every day, and she doesn't know what the hell her friends are saying."

Why did Roger get angry at you?
"For leaving. I left him for six weeks to adopt John. And so I didn't know if he was ready to leave me over this, because the whole time I was in California I couldn't tell whether he was angry, because he was ready to go, which would've been understandable. Most men, really, would have, I suppose. But I didn't expect he would because I knew what he's made of. And I knew how good the marriage was, but you never know, and I got back and within twenty-four hours, I knew that he was just furious that I had left. He always hates it when I leave. But once I got back and I knew that that was what he was mad at, then I was relieved, because I could not have endured his leaving me . . . And the trauma continues. For example, I got a call from a Filipino woman who is a friend of my husband's in California, who I know really well, who was inviting us to her wedding. And she said that she had heard a rumor that my husband and I were breaking up from people in the Filipino community in Boston. And I said that I hadn't heard that."

After the news first broke, how did you cope?
"I went charging back to see my old analyst [Dr. Gerald Adler]. I hadn't seen him for a while. And my husband and I had been to see somebody about the adoption issues and the miscarriages. We had been ready to terminate [the therapy], but we stayed. She was very helpful. She was really proud of how well we were handling the impossible."

How did this affect your stepchildren, Franz and Ruby?
"We had to decide whether we were going to take Ruby out of school or whether we were going to put her in boarding school. That week we also had to be in touch with Franz in college. My husband had to decide whether he was going to quit his job and disappear . . . Well, my kids protected me. But the first day this

appeared on TV somebody came up to my daughter at school and said, 'Do you know that woman?' And she said, 'Yeah, that's my mother.' But mostly, the advantage is that my kids are a different color and their last name is Bayog."

How are you feeling as a result of this experience?
"I think I'm still pretty brutalized. I'm also in the process of nearly winding up my practice. I feel like I've just gone over Niagara in a barrel, and I'm bobbing around underneath the falls. I'll wash up on the shore and find out how many broken bones I've got. And I think it's going to be a long time 'til I find out how much damage there's actually been, and that's part of the difficulty is that I sort of don't know who believes what and who's read what, and I feel I have this enormous existence in the public mind that has nothing to do with who I am, and I'm kind of alone, I mean people are projecting everything they say they've got on me, and so I'm not really sure what I'm going to do . . . I've had heart palpitations. I've never had them before. I have nightmares. I am paranoid about opening the mail, answering the phone, returning phone calls. You never know when you are talking to somebody what they really think or if they would tell you if they did. You know they have an opinion, but you don't know what it truly is . . . Every day there are four or five body blows."

Give an example. [She explained that she had recently gone to a local hospital because her au pair's jaw became dislocated.]
"So I've got the baby and [the au pair's] jaw is out and there were doctors floating in and out because there were various things happening, and they were moving up the ranks to get somebody, and they called in an ENT [Ear, Nose, and Throat] resident, and by this time several people had come to make friends with the baby who was engaging in the extreme.[1] And so

---

1. "HAVING JOHN WITH ME CUTS DOWN ON MY RECOGNITION. PEOPLE DON'T HAVE A VISION OF THE WITCH DOCTOR WITH A BABY. FEWER PEOPLE RECOGNIZE ME WHEN I'M WITH HIM," SAID BEAN-BAYOG.

there was an internist and I said, 'Can I watch. I want to see how this is done.' And she was playing with the baby. So at this point there were five people in the room besides me and [the au pair]. And she's getting her jaw hauled down on and there's been a lot of chatter and the internist has found out that I am a doctor . . . and she says, 'Maybe I'll go into pediatrics.' And I said, 'Don't do it too quickly. I did it for a year and sick babies are not the same as well babies, and working with babies is a tiring experience. Having babies and taking care of healthy ones is one thing, but if you have a family who has a dying child,' and so forth. And so she and I were chatting about that and this guy—the ENT who had walked into the room—he's overhearing all this stuff and working on the jaw. And I asked him if I could watch and he said, 'I don't think you should try and do this yourself.' And the internist said, 'Oh, she's a doctor.' And he said, 'Oh, do I know you from somewhere?' And I said, 'I don't know.' And he said, 'You look really familiar to me.' And I said, 'I'm Margaret Bean-Bayog, the wicked witch of the west. You know, who is accused of screwing a patient.' You know, I could've said nothing. 'Oh,' he said, 'you really look pretty good for someone who's gone through all of that.' And then there was this dead silence when no one has any idea what the conversation should do. I mean, I don't know how you handle this. It's not my habit to hide or pretend to be something other than I am. I knew where he'd seen my face. I could've said nothing, 'Gee no, I must look like someone you know.' I don't know whether I do it out of hostility. I don't know whether I do it because I want reassurance. But the ongoing exposure where I am in a circumstance where people know me, or where someone is breaking into our garage and writing graffiti on all the cars is more than I can bear."

What do people say to you? That they are sorry? That they believe in you?

"I am very ambivalent about how much I want to hear about how other people feel. I just got a call yesterday. It's another one of those things where somebody said, 'Look, I really wanted to call you and I am feeling very guilty. I wanted to write a letter the very first day the media coverage came out.' And this is a colleague. She works in alcoholism and has done research with me and she's outraged about this because I'm a woman. And she said, 'I haven't. I've been so ashamed because I never wrote the letter because I was afraid.' But she's actually braver than most, because most people don't write the letter because they're afraid and don't know it. Or they don't even think of writing the letter. Or the commoner one is that they disassociate themselves from me by saying, 'She must have done something to deserve this. I'm not like that. This couldn't happen to me.' And the reason this woman was afraid was that she was afraid that she would draw the fire of the public—the forces out there of the witch-hunt atmosphere, which is very characteristic. It's not crazy. It's not totally cowardly. It may be self-protective. But when you are in the midst of a witch-hunt and you say, 'That's not a witch. That's good neighbor Jessie or Sally or somebody,' people are likely to go after you next . . . You know what used to get to me? When somebody was nice to me. Like saying, 'I'm really sorry about what's happened to you or I believe you.' I would begin to cry. Or when I had to think about someone else. When Michael [Blau] would talk to me and say, 'Hey, how's your husband doing? How are your patients?' I didn't cry for myself for a long time, but the effect on my husband was just heartbreaking to me."

When I first met you, you seemed in pretty good shape. What happened?

"My mood was great for the first three or four months of this whole disaster because I just thought, you know [that no one would believe it]. I mean, they knew me. The whole damn [psychiatric] community knows me and it's that I've taught and taught and taught and that I give talks that are taped and the tapes are sold and Harvard has a continuing medical school education program and I've taught every year, and that's about $600 just to come to each one and I've lectured at thirty of them and so thousands of physicians have heard me discussing how you do this kind of work, so it's an enormous exposure and I had a symbolic role in the community. I was the person who represented the idea that working with alcoholics was fun and that it could be elegant and that it required skill and discipline . . . Part of my problem is that I think of myself as so emotionally resilient. I think of myself as someone who is so solidly constructed and so durable and so able to tolerate various kinds of stress and trauma. I like a lot of stress. I tend to choose very challenging situations. When I got married I married a widower with two small children who were not in very good condition. And I thought it was easy. It barely gave me exercise. I mean this was very demanding. And having a newborn is very much easier than dealing with two kids that don't trust you, that think you're the wrong person, who are furious at their pain [because of their mother's death from cancer], who are very bruised, are quite developmentally impaired because of what they've been through. So I like the idea of thinking of myself as somebody where this experience would just kind of slide off like teflon. So when this all started, I thought that was what was going to happen. In March, April, May, and June, that's the way I felt. When you met me in June, I was cheerful and I told you that I saw no reason why I couldn't turn this into a positive event. I was optimistic that, I mean I really saw what was written in the newspapers about me as—they're lying. So what. They can destroy my reputation, but they can't touch my belief in myself and my integrity."

What happened?
"I think it was cumulative. I think my defenses began to get frayed around the edges because the battering continued and the ante went up."

What effect do you think this has had on psychiatry?
"This case has had a terrorizing effect on the psychiatric community, so that lots and lots of people are practicing defensive psychiatry, avoiding the really difficult patients, transferring all their assets into their spouse's name, burning their journals,

because my private fantasies were stolen and used as an example of malpractice in the most horrifying public crucifixion that you could ever imagine. So that people that used to keep dream notes or personal journals, because one of the ways you worked with very crazy, primitive people, was that you paid attention to your own dreams and fantasies, [but now you shouldn't keep them anymore]. And now, the question is whether, in fact, the climate for doing serious exploratory psychotherapy with very sick, crazy, damaged, and traumatized people is now impossible.

Describe the way people have reacted to your situation.
"It's the kind of thing where you will see a woman attacked in New York City and raped or killed or beaten with a large crowd [watching], almost none of whom raises a hand and how does that happen? Why is it that my colleagues who knew me, why is it that there are people out there who knew my whole twenty-five years of life of teaching and public contact and said nothing. I mean I wasn't a big, big figure, but I wasn't a quiet one either. I wasn't somebody who never went in public and spoke. I wasn't somebody whose ideas were not contagiously useful. And why was it that when this happened to me, it was as though that whole other part of me had to be denied. It stopped existing."

Were you dumb to take on such a sick patient?
"I believed that physicians have to work with sick patients if they're really physicians, and I've struggled with this question myself, before this happened, of taking on another very sick patient and thinking about the difference between internists who work with AIDS who have to go in there and draw that patient's blood and we absolutely require that of them as part of the membership of the profession, something they bought when they got their M.D. We expect them to endanger their own lives in the pursuit of the welfare of their patient . . . I remember understanding that this was like father Damien, the guy who went out to the leper colony, and that this was something I bought. It came with the territory. And I believed it and I believed it for psychiatry. And I question whether one reason why psychiatrists

don't get the respect that other physicians get is because they don't put their lives on the line. They don't want to treat sick or dangerous patients. There is a large group of them who behave in a way that I don't believe qualifies them as members of this profession . . . The people who work with the sick patients, the people who do the dangerous work, the people who are brave, are now considered crazy. They are now considered self-destructive. They are now considered to have 'poor judgment.' "

Describe the role of Harvard, which you've been affiliated with since you were an undergraduate, during all of this mess.

"Harvard University, which first accepted this guy, positioned me to believe that I had a responsibility to take care of him. I pick him up from treatment. He turns out not to be able to pay me. I work with him and hold him together. The medical school knows all about his mental illness. They know that I am working to hold him together . . . They knew all about the work I was doing with him. I remember I met the dean of students at a banquet. He said, 'I'm not supposed to know about this stuff but there's something I have to thank you for.' And he was basically making it clear that he was referring to the fact that I was taking this guy pro bono, because he was in our medical school . . . Part of my decision to terminate came from the fact that I can't work with somebody who's gonna hurt patients and who doesn't give a goddamn whether he does or not as long as he can graduate, and I am then accused by this guy of doing these various things and then the letters Harvard sent me presuming my guilt . . . One was written saying basically, 'We suspend you immediately.' This was sent to me by courier with the request that I never return anymore to the sites of my teaching. I wasn't allowed to go back to say good-bye to people I'd worked with for the last fifteen years. I believe it's what their lawyers tell them to do. But the language that was used and the tone were not friendly or polite. One would think that if you've had a faculty member for twenty years you might deserve a phone call. You might deserve somebody saying, 'This isn't like you. Why don't you come in and explain what happened . . .' And the other real ironic thing was [that one of] the person[s] who did telephone me to tell me that I was suspended is somebody who is known to have had sex with a patient. I think the medical school made him agree that he would stop seeing patients for psychotherapy and it moved him from the medical school [to another position] but retained him at full professorship and kept everything private and quiet. He called me up and said to me, 'I'm sorry to have to do this to you, but we don't care what you did; we love you anyway.' I said, 'You bastard, you think I slept with this guy.' But he didn't care because he thinks I just did what he did. 'We don't care, we love you anyway, but, of course, we do have to suspend you.' "

Why have you decided to settle the civil suit?
"Jim Barry and Michael Mone both recommended that I settle. They said that eight out of ten juries would convict me because of the publicity and because I had resigned my license. And if I were to insist on going to trial they would have no liability because they had recommended that I not go to trial. They were willing to settle for the limit of my insurance policy, for $1 million, but any amount above my policy limit, suppose they got a $10-million-dollar judgment from one of these eight out of ten juries, then I would owe the difference. They said their exposure is $1 million and anything above that if I insist on going to trial and I lose, that I would have to pay the difference."

23

FURTHER CONVERSATIONS WITH BEAN-BAYOG

You've been criticized for not terminating when Lozano told you he had broken into your office. Why didn't you?

"I didn't terminate because frankly I was preoccupied with the risk [that] he was going to kill his previous doctor [Frances Frankenburg], but the other thing is that I probably used a kind of denial. I mean my hierarchy when working with a patient like this is this. Is he going to kill himself or somebody else? Breaking into somebody's office is a minor crime when you're dealing with the potential of suicide and murder . . . So at the point he broke into my office, the issue for me was whether he was going to be alive between sessions and, frankly I didn't think in terms of reporting him to the police. I got back the [McLean Hospital] files he stole, but I didn't know that he had gone through everything else in my office."

Didn't you commit a boundary violation by telling Lozano that you were his mom?

"Well, I was exhausted when all this lunacy was going on and you know the whole period when I was preparing him to my going to the Philippines, when I was doing all of these transitional objects, and all of these mom things, and all of these flash cards, and all of these stories in all these children's books, I mean you can make a case that it was a boundary violation, that the cumulative effect of that was a boundary violation, but

I thought that it would keep him quiet and alive. So did he. And it did."

But don't you agree that many of your colleagues would look at this and raise some serious questions about what you did in the fall of 1987?

"I agree that there are some real serious questions that people have raised about the way I went at the psychotherapy. I guess when you get past the sensationalism, the big question technically in the psychotherapy was what I was doing with this guy leading him toward a psychotic conviction [also called a psychotic transference] that I was his mother, which would have been very bad for him, or was what I did simply a life-saving, short-term device so that he could stay alive until the next session after my three-week vacation, at which point we could discuss his confusion about whether or not I was his real mother or not. That's a perfectly legitimate argument and there are tons of very reputable psychiatrists that will tell you that I was off the wall and that what I was doing is way out of the normal and that it is not in the books. Well, it is in some books, but it's just that it's in a particular school; it's an empathic, exploratory, supportive approach opposed to the reality-testing, limit-setting school that says you've got to teach them that they can't get what they want and they have to give up those ideas, that they cannot ever have a mother that can make up to them for what they didn't get when they were babies, and they'd better just stub their toes and wipe their tears and go out there and cook . . . But the people who do the stuff that I do are also perfectly respectable, they're out of style at the moment, the analytic empathic people are losing ground to the behavioral psychoforum reality-oriented school. So part of this thing over me is wars within psychiatry. But the point that Fabiano would have made is that you don't write somebody letters saying you're his mom and that's an absolutely legitimate question. And if the community of psychiatrists decided at some point that that was wrong, I would be willing to consider. I would just recommend that they try working with a patient like this one, without the refuge of his mom.[1] I have no question that the idea of his mom kept this guy alive and I'm very sorry if they don't like it, but I think he would have been dead a lot sooner and so I'm willing to listen, if they want to consider this malpractice. I'll listen to them in a way that I won't listen to Fabiano when he says that it's malpractice for me to treat a medical student without charging him."

Talk about Lozano's sadomasochistic fantasies toward you. What were they like? What was it like hearing them directed at you?

"It felt like he was vomiting out all this stuff. He was pissing out this garbage. There was pus and blood all over the room and that's what happens . . . I think he started spewing out the sexual fantasies about me in July 1987 and I started writing mine down in August or September, and I think that I couldn't take notes in the sessions. I found myself so shocked at the content. I would write down that he was having these fantasies. I did not write down the details. I just couldn't break through my own horror and I was so agitated by being subjected to these assaults, and so that's why I started writing down those fantasies. I mean I just couldn't write them down during sessions because I was too freaked out and so I wrote them down either right afterwards or at some point when I had an hour free . . . I would write those countertransference things as fast as my hand would move . . . Even though they seem to be my erotic responses to him, and in a sense they are, they are a map of the patient's relationship with his mother, and what was shocking about them were not that they were sexual or sadistic . . . but . . . that they depicted interaction between an adult and an infant and I didn't get it at first, because what you're getting is the detail of the sexual event and the assault of the event and the powerlessness . . . and then what I did was I studied them and I thought about them and

---

1. IN BEAN-BAYOG'S DEPOSITION, SHE TOLD MEYER THAT LOZANO "USED THE WORD 'MOM' AS A CONDENSATION FOR 'MOM WHO WOULD NEVER TOUCH ME.' "

talked to people about the feelings I was having and then I realized that what was going on was a perversion, that this is what had happened to him . . . I was freaked by the experience. I knew how you had to act. I knew the rules. I knew that it would be violent both to me and to him to act on these feelings. I thought that people who slept with patients were the scum of the earth, absolutely the scum of the earth, the bottom of the pit, and I remember thinking, 'Oh my God, so this is how it happens!' They start to feel this stuff and they just do it, and I talked to all kinds of people and I had one friend, who later said, 'Margaret, you yakked about that guy all the time, and you yakked about your feelings, and I knew you hadn't slept with him because nobody would have talked about it if they had . . .' Basically what those countertransference fantasies are is a depiction of a perverse relationship, filtered through my own psychodynamics, between a mother and a little boy . . . Actually, the most powerful thing you do in therapy is you feel with the patient. It is not a spectator sport . . . I've never seen anything like this before. Never. I have never been expected to withstand anything that was as assaultive as this guy's transference and every time I thought, 'I can't stand this,' I would think how the hell did he stand it, he was only a baby! . . . One of the ways I stood it was that I wrote down my reactions—my countertransference feelings. I am extremely fluent and extremely verbal and it relieves my feelings enormously and I thought it was a great idea, but it was stupid."

He apparently got your sexual fantasies when he broke into your office just before the November 2 therapy session. By having them, did he, in effect, take control of therapy without your knowing it?

"If that's when he got them, then he may have. He used to talk about it. He used to say, 'Sometimes I don't think you realize what you've gotten yourself into.' Or he would say, 'You know I'm really afraid because my relationships always end up a disaster. I always end up hurting you and you don't have that coming.' Or he would say, 'I'm afraid that I'm going to turn out to be the sort of sociopath or monster that they thought I was at

McLean and I'll hurt you, and you don't deserve that . . .' I cannot imagine his having this stuff [the written sexual fantasies] and not killing himself . . . I thought he might have stolen them at the end of the treatment, because it just didn't make any sense to me that he could have possessed this and done the kind of work that he did with me. I don't really know when he stole them. Michael Blau thinks he stole them right around the time of the break in. There was another break in. Our house was burglarized in 1990 around the time he was psychotic, and I didn't make the connection at the time, but it was a very strange burglary. There was no evidence of forceable entry. It was considered an inside job by the police."

How could he have done it?
"God only knows, but he had done enough breaking and entering in other circumstances. He was very accomplished. He stole all of his text books from the Countway Library, which has excellent security. He took all of his medical school textbooks from there. He routinely shoplifted his food . . . He routinely falsified research data. He stole exam cartridges when he was taking exams in high school. He routinely got into places he wasn't ever supposed to be, and when you asked him how he did it, he always said that it was easy."

How did you feel in the spring of 1991 when you learned that he had a copy of your sexual fantasies?
"I was pissed at him. I could not believe that he had taken those things and I could not believe that he had broken into my office with me eating my heart over his self-hatred and he was in possession of those things that he was keeping in reserve to harm me, should he decide he wanted to at some later point."

How suicidal was Lozano compared to other suicidal patients you've treated?
"He was the scariest guy I had ever seen in terms of suicide risk. I don't know when I realized that but I know that by the time I had admitted him to Faulkner, I wrote a ten-page disquisi-

tion on this guy's suicide risk in his Faulkner admission chart. The reason I wrote that was I thought he was going to kill himself during that admission and his psychiatry resident had just begun July 1 and he was this guy's first patient and I was partly writing that to help protect the psych resident so that he wouldn't be too thrown off course when this guy killed himself. And I was probably doing it to indicate how many things made it more likely that this guy was going to end up dead rather than alive."

Was he the toughest patient you've ever taken on?
"Paul was the most difficult and frightening patient I've ever worked with."

Why didn't you run for the hills?
"Well, he was in pain. What I ran for was the 'mom,' because she calmed him down and that was the reason that she was invoked. We tried the normal routine. We tried setting limits. We tried screaming at him, telling him to shape up, but none of that stuff worked . . . What calmed him down was the idea that somewhere there was an island of safety in which there was a mother who would not run her hands on his genitals, that there was a mom who would quote 'Never, never touch me . . .' What would calm him down was not a reality check, but the fact that his doctor is not raping him but taking him back to the experience he was grappling with, which was a memory. He was grappling with memories of his childhood abuse, and what was coherent about it was that every single piece of detail—there are millions and millions of corroborating and reverberating systems here—and everything corroborates the idea the he was raped sexually.

How so?
"First was the way he expected everyone to act toward him, Dr. Frankenburg, Dr. Pope, me, and others; then the way he projected all this sexual stuff onto me; the stories that he told about his family and the amount of detail and the amount of reluctance that he had towards them; and the fact that once he

had vomited out all this stuff about sex for about a year and a half or two years, he got better. He stopped being so homicidal, and he wasn't scary anymore, and I stopped taking notes, because he basically wasn't going to kill himself. He was basically much, much better and he stopped being paranoid about people. And he would begin to say things—like when he would start to flip out and he wanted to hurt somebody because he thought they had hurt him, he would say, 'Dr. Bean, I can see it's craziness and I think that sometimes my anger isn't merited.' So that was the way he could begin to tell that the real source of his problem was the memories he was experiencing—he was putting them on to everybody, including me . . . I think that a lot of people have taken a look at the fact that it's got a lot of sexual content and assumed that something was going on between him and me. That's naive. They don't understand the psychotherapeutic process. I mean when a child is sexually abused, they aren't happy about it. That doesn't mean they don't experience sexual stimulation and there certainly was that, but the experience they have is that they've been had, and they tend to be very depressed and often suicidal and furious, and sexually provocative."

Were you too caught up in the therapy, too blind to see how dangerous this guy was? One psychotherapist told me that Lozano sounded like a borderline psychopath, the most dangerous kind of patient of all. Why didn't you realize it?

"A lot of people have talked about how come I was so blind to how dangerous Paul was. Part of the answer is that if I had grasped how dangerous he was, I wouldn't have been able to stay in the room with him. But I was in it. I was committed. And I wasn't thinking about myself. It's one of the things that people don't realize. Doctors don't think about themselves when they are in the middle of doing treatment. They take risks. They get into boundary crossings . . . [L]et's say you're about to leave town at three Friday afternoon and at five of three, you get a page from the answering service and you call the patient back and he says, 'Give me one good reason why I should stay alive until Monday when you're scheduled to see me again. What do you do? Get on the plane? So when you're working with patients who will die according to how you act, you think differently about things. And I think one of the ways I dealt with this guy's sadistic, homicidal perverse nature was by having a relationship with a tiny little piece of him that wanted to be a good doctor, and the tiny little piece of him that was an abused baby. And that's what I locked onto."

Given what has happened, doesn't this say something about your own judgment in taking on this particular patient?

"I know there are people who think that the fact I took this guy in for treatment is evidence of my poor judgment and the way I feel is, I mean it's one of the reasons I'm so relieved that I've turned in my license. I didn't realize how scary it is to practice medicine until I got into the position where I didn't have to do it. How frightening it is to have that much responsibility and to be that vulnerable to how sick somebody may be and I don't mean just the litigation aspect. I mean the human responsibility. I mean from time to time I would take on the toughest patients. I should say that probably in the last twenty years I've done maybe five or six of what's called heroic treatments like this. I mean people with at least three major illnesses, people who were definitely, I mean without question, going to be dead, who decided they were not going to be [dead] after three or four years of treatment with me. I mean like major league. A man who was burning the word 'God' on the inside of his thigh with a lighted cigarette. I started seeing him about sixteen, seventeen years ago. He just finished law school and passed the bar. He was a border-line and his parents are alcoholic and they sexually abused him as a baby, physically and emotionally and he was horribly, horribly abused and he was a zoo. And when this thing [with Lozano] broke, he called me and said, 'I can't believe what they're doing to you, because I know what this guy is saying, because it's like what happened with you and me, and it saved my life, and if you hadn't done what you did with me I wouldn't be alive and you're the best person I know and they're pillorying you . . .' I had to hospitalize him every single time I left town for a weekend for over two and a half years, I was seeing him five times a week, he was calling in the middle of the night, he was the one who would call when you were in the airport and have you paged right before you're plane left and say, 'Give me one good reason why I should stay alive till you get back.'"[2]

How did you feel when you saw that your therapy was working, that a patient was actually getting better?

"Oh sheer joy, watching somebody let go of that stuff and stop tripping over themselves and helping them feel better both short-term and long-term and it's like watching a little kid get bigger and learn and get stronger and flower and stop kicking themselves in the shin and shooting themselves in the foot at the same time and I think there's something really powerfully healing for me in proving to myself that people don't have to stay stuck in horrible grim depression . . . so every single time I have a patient who comes to me hopeless and demoralized and in agony and furious and arguing with me about how bad it is, it's like, 'Let's roll up our sleeves.' "

Were you trying to save Paul Lozano?

"I thought maybe I could help him save himself. I tried to help him stop himself from destroying himself. I'm not God. I never was. All I could do was say to him that there is a chance, because of a misunderstanding he had with himself. And there is a chance that if you know yourself better, you will be able to tolerate what you find and have a productive life. I can't guarantee it. That's all I've got to offer. I've got a relationship and a chance for you to look at yourself. I can want you not to kill yourself, but if you want to I can't stop you. I remember one time where I said it was a chess game and he said, 'I hope you win.' And I said, 'It doesn't work that way. I hope we both win, but I can't do this without you."

Why the 3-year-old? Why did he want to be 3 again?

"He wanted to be 3 again because he knew that he had to go back there to get at the trauma, to tell the story, and once he got

---

2. I HAVE ALTERED DETAILS TO PROTECT THIS PATIENT'S PRIVACY.

back there he was obsessed with finding a mom who would not screw him."

Some therapists hug patients. Did you ever hug Lozano?
"I never hugged him. I high-fived him in the parking lot after he had stayed alive when I was in the Philippines for three weeks. I think that was the only time we ever had physical contact."

You seemed so determined to help him. What made you give up on him?
"What defeated me was my realization that he was breaking the alliance with me, that he was going to make it impossible for me to work with him, because of two things: He went back to medical school and . . . he refused to be supervised. Basically up until that time I had believed that he was my colleague, and that he was going to be a physician, or that he might become a physician and I had also believed that he shared the value system of the physician. I had believed that he really cared about a patient's welfare. What I found out was that he didn't. He didn't care whether his patients died if his judgment was bad because he stopped his med[ication]s. He only cared if he graduated. He only cared if he got through his rotation and graduated."

What did you see in this guy that was so important to save, that was worth the effort?
"I saw this guy as a lot of things. First of all there were two parts of him that I liked. One was the baby that didn't want to be abused, and the other was the part of him that didn't want to grow up to be a child molester, the part that wanted him to go to West Point, and if he was going to kill and be killed and do the things that soldiers do, then he might as well get a medal, rather than taking an AK-47 into a parking lot of McDonald's and sexually abusing children or something like that and then the part of him that wanted to be a doctor and save lives and coping with his murderous and homicidal symptoms.

Without stopping to think, what is the first thing that comes to mind that is most loathsome about this whole experience?

"Walking into Meyer's office [for a deposition], it's like a Kurd going to see Saddam Hussein. It's a negative event. A deposition is something where you can only lose. What they want is for you to say things that they can use against you. So your goal is to cut the damage. Your goal is to say as little as possible, which is constitutionally impossible for me, as you can see from the way I talk."

If Lozano hadn't killed himself, how would you have felt listening to him on the witness stand accusing you of psychiatric sexual misconduct?

"There was no way he [Lozano] could face me on the stand. I had kept him alive, and I had fought for him, and I had gone the extra mile for him a thousand times. And he said so. I mean when he was talking about suing me, and I said, 'We have to talk about the fact that you're talking about suing me.' He said, 'After all you've done for me? I would take an eye out first before I'd sue you.' Well, he took his life out first."

24

THE BONFIRE OF
THE VANITIES[1]

For nearly a month, Bean-Bayog did not reveal to me the most compelling reason behind her decision to negotiate a settlement, and when that failed, to resign.

She had alluded to tensions between Blau and herself but I had no inkling that she felt rancor toward him and that it ran so deep. In mid-November, it began to gush out.

"[M]y decision to try for a settlement was financially motivated. The money issue is what started the negotiations . . . [and] the major reason I did not go to the hearing was financial," said Bean-Bayog.

"Michael Blau and his financial assault was genuinely threatening to me in a way that the newspapers were not. I think that the idea that my family's financial stability, my kids' college education, my baby's college fund, my husband's sense of security in the universe, which because he came from a poor background and had made it. I mean he was talking to me about what it would be like if we had to go back to renting an apartment, to an apartment in Reading or wherever it was that he lived when he first came to Boston. And what it would be like if we lost everything. Blau was talking about us paying money that amounts to more than our net worth. Our house, both of our retirements, the inheritance from my mother, and the book rights. So that any future income that I would have, if there were

---

1. THAT FALL, BEAN-BAYOG READ *BONFIRE OF THE VANITIES* BY TOM WOLFE AND SAID SHE CLOSELY IDENTIFIED WITH THE PROTAGONIST, SHERMAN MCCOY. "ONE SMALL MISTAKE AND HIS LIFE BLOWS UP," SHE SAID.

income to come from the book, would also be taken. And this was somebody that I had laid my trust in. Somebody that I believed was going to take care of me and protect me, who had told me not to worry about the money, who had told me that he would see to it that this was not going to be a problem, who couldn't keep his promise, and who then freaked out and was threatening to jump off the case."

What is surprising is that Blau, who was aware of her emotional turmoil, had no idea how deeply upset his client was with him, because she concealed it so well. Their relationship had remained extremely cordial at all times. Blau had been on a tightrope, balancing his client's interests and his firm's, while dealing with his own insecurities. Nevertheless, he knew something was bothering her.

Finally, several weeks after her resignation, she and Blau met with ABC's Diane Sawyer in his office,[2] and after the meeting, Blau confronted Bean-Bayog alone.

"[Blau] said [to me], 'You know, there's something not right between us and we have to discuss it . . . I said, there are some things that you did that were deeply hurtful to me. And one of them was about the money.' And he said, 'I know, but I always made it clear to you that there would be a cap.' . . . He fails to remember that I had to hire two different lawyers to get him to do that . . . And I said, 'The thing that upset me was when I first got that letter from you and you had promised me that there would be an amount and that not to worry about the money. And then I got this [June 24] letter from you.' [He said], 'It was a draft, not a letter, a draft.' I said, 'I know but it came from

---

2. BEAN-BAYOG, WHO MET WITH SAWYER TWICE, DECIDED NOT TO APPEAR ON HER SHOW, "PRIME TIME." SHE WAS ALSO APPROACHED BY CBS'S MIKE WALLACE OF "60 MINUTES" AND CONNIE CHUNG, WHO WAS WITH NBC AT THE TIME. BEAN-BAYOG DECLINED THEIR INVITATIONS AS WELL.

ACCORDING TO BEAN-BAYOG, SAWYER SAID: " 'I DON'T THINK THE OTHER SIDE OF THE STORY HAS BEEN HEARD . . . I REALLY THINK I CAN HELP YOU. I'VE SEEN THESE STORIES TURN AROUND. I THINK THIS STORY WILL TURN AROUND, AND THERE'S TWO THINGS I'LL PROMISE YOU. ONE IS THAT I THINK I COULD MAKE YOU LOOK GOOD, AND THE OTHER IS THAT I THINK YOU WON'T BE DISAPPOINTED. THE PEOPLE THAT I DO THIS FOR USUALLY END UP MY FRIENDS.' "

you . . . You have to remember, I'm a trauma victim and that I was very upset . . . Up until that time, I was very comfortable. I didn't feel very guilty and I felt like we would get our story out and I didn't feel very traumatized. And the way I was doing that was that I was very dependent on you to protect me. And it's like what happened in Vietnam when your buddy was blown up. I felt, when you did that, like my buddy had been blown up. And in fact, between you and me, I felt more than that. I felt like I had been attacked by my buddy.' "

Bean-Bayog handed me a copy of the June 24 "draft" from Blau:

> **As we have discussed, legal fees for these matters could reach $500,000 . . . (W)e understand that you have approximately $140,000 in retirement funds . . . and that you have more than $250,000 of equity in your home . . . Moreover . . . you expect to receive an inheritance of approximately $250,000 within the next year . . .**

Blau's letter then went on to suggest that Bean-Bayog assign to Blau's law firm other potential assets, such as book, television, and film rights until her legal obligations were met. However, in the meantime, all "out-of-pocket expenses," including expert witness fees, court costs, and other office expenses would have to be paid by her directly.

She had been under the impression that Blau and his firm were going to "eat most of the costs." In fact, that is essentially what Blau had told Janie James and me. "Most of the costs" can mean one thing to Bean-Bayog and another to a major law firm, however. Misunderstandings over money between client and counsel are very common.

"[Blau said to me], 'Don't worry about the money. If it goes above a quarter of a million, we'll eat it. If you can't pay it, we'll eat it. I don't care about money. I am called Robin Hood around here because of the cases I take on. My partners are furious because they know that I could be making much more money for them if I were, you know, charging more, because I'm worth more than I charge. I am not charging you for all of my hours by a long shot. I'm working nights and weekends but I'm not putting in billable time, just like you did with Paul Lozano. A lot of this is pro bono.' So he told me that stuff. So then I get this [June 24] letter which freaks me out completely . . . So I typed this [July 3] letter and took it in with me and gave it to Michael Blau:"

> This is . . . in response to . . . the costs of your representing me . . . I want to confirm our conversation after I returned from California on June 3rd and found that you had massively expanded the level of investment in the work of this case without my knowledge while I was away. At that time you told me that had there been no media coverage of this event, the costs for my Board of Registration legal representation would have been in the range of $20,000 to $30,000 but that in this situation the cost of the case had escalated to $250,000. I said that I wasn't this important enough to justify the huge legal campaign, and you acknowledged that the case was "no longer about Margaret Bean-Bayog," . . . It was for these reasons you felt the case had to be managed with the massive infusion of manpower and resources you were now mobilizing and which you now say may surpass $500,000. You indicated verbally that you would not expect me to pay all of the costs of your very skilled efforts. It was not until I received the bill[3] and read the draft of the letter about what you did want me to pay that I realized that I had better clarify to you the limits of what I can and will (pay) . . .

---

3. ON JUNE 22, SHE GOT A BILL FROM BLAU FOR $169,569.36.

What I am able to guarantee to pay you is a total of $50,000 cash from my own pocket, some of which you have already received. I will also guarantee a contingent payment of $100,000 from payments received by me for rights to my story, including book rights, publication rights, movie rights, TV rights, and other media rights relative to this case. $150,000 is the maximum total liability I can assume.

. . . I want to make sure that if we go forward from here that you understand the limits of my ability to serve as the sole financial resource of this massive legal juggernaut . . . (and) . . . please don't ask me to demolish my family's finances and mortgage all my children's futures; that I cannot do . . .

However, Blau declined to accept her letter.

"He said, 'Actually, I'm very uncomfortable dealing with you because I am so invested in this case. So my senior partner has offered to help me out. So you no longer will be discussing finances with me. And would you like to go meet Harvey [W. Freishtat]?' And he walked me upstairs and the two of them sat down and discussed finances with me. And they said, 'We don't understand why you're playing such hardball about this. We have made a major commitment to your case, and we need to know from you if you share our commitment. We really can't understand why you would not relinquish your publication rights. We are willing to cap our demands on your personal equity. We will cap it at $250,000 cash from your assets if we can get from you a statement that the balance, should there ever be any value from any publicity that should result from this case for you, should come out of publicity rights and any other rights which are related to this case. This is what we want from you.' And I tried to give the letter to Michael Blau and he said, 'No, no, no. You should give that to Harvey.' And I tried to give the letter to Harvey and he said, 'No, I don't want to take it because I think it would impair our ability to have a relationship.' [But]

I had basically told them what was in it . . . And the next thing I got in the mail was a [August 4] letter from Blau:

> . . . As we have discussed, on the basis of our normal hourly rates, legal fees for these matters currently exceed $350,000 and could reach as high as $1 million. Our current estimate for completion of these matters, on the basis of our normal hourly rates, including fees incurred since March of 1992, is approximately $750,000–850,000.
>
> . . . (W)e have agreed to cap your financial liability for our legal fees (incurred since March 26, 1992) at $250,000 (excluding disbursements), with no financial responsibility for invoices already rendered by us in excess of $250,000 unless . . . you were to receive payments for . . . (book rights, movie rights, TV rights or other media rights relating to this case), merchandising rights, or consulting fees, royalties, honoraria or other payments made to you for matters relating to this case (hereinafter referred to as "Payments"). We would receive a mutually agreed portion of any Payments as you receive them . . .

At the bottom of the letter was "cc: Michael Mone, Esq." Why did you hire Mone? I asked her.

"Basically I ended up hiring Mike Mone as a lawyer to protect me against my own law firm. And he acted like a hero . . . He is a good negotiator, very warm and very personable and his manners are good, but he gets things done. He writes one sentence letters. He skips everything but the central point . . . And let me tell you how angry [Blau] was about my bringing Mone in."

So later, I asked Blau, who spoke to me with Bean-Bayog's permission, about Mone. Why had he become involved in the case?

"Mone got involved for [several] reasons," said Blau. "He is past president of the Massachuetts Bar Association. He is an excellent trial attorney. He is principally a personal injury attorney . . . One was because he has a wealth of insurance-related expertise. Secondly, he has, or he had the respect of Drew Meyer. Third, that he battles from the same side of the fence as Drew Meyer . . . You know, he is honest, he's ethical . . . and he's a complete straight shooter . . . And as they got deeper into the malpractice case, it was clear that if there was going to be discussions of settlement that a person like Mike Mone could have the role, a significant role, in dealing effectively with Drew Meyer. And so that was one of the reasons. And that was probably the principal reason why he was brought in . . . And he became sort of another personal adviser to her. He became a trusted personal adviser, because of who he is and because he is a very bright and capable guy. And he's got a practical sense of justice and judgment. He knows the system well. And you know, he helped her through in the areas . . . [of] financial relations with our firm. He helped her to think that through and to work that through with us a little bit. He worked in go-between situations where it would be appropriate for him to do so. Sort of trouble shooting here and there. And he played a very constructive role, I thought, from everyone's perspective."

Then, Bean-Bayog said, Blau sent her another letter on August 18, which she also handed me. It read in part:

> **And that I will, on or after August 31, 1992, withdraw as your trial counsel in this case . . . (and) you will need either to (1) engage other counsel to try this case or (2) pursue other alternatives to hearings (e.g., resignation of your license) . . .**

But Blau changed his mind. He was prepared to go to the hearing, and at the last minute wrote an impressive document, the Respondent's Evidentiary Submission.

Later, I asked Blau how his partners felt about Bean-Bayog's bill:

"My partners, I can't say were happy with it, but I would say that . . . I got them reconciled to it. We are, it's a difficult trade-off for them to take an attorney like myself, who can work 60 hours a week, every week of the year and get paid 100 to 110 percent of the value of my time, and then take essentially, what up to that point had been a half a year of my time and of my work and put, no, I wouldn't say put no value on it, but receive no compensation for it. And it's not your typical pro bono type of arrangement. We do pro bono work . . ."

"Well, this woman wasn't exactly destitute," I said.

"Exactly. She would not meet our firm's profile for a pro bono client."

"What her definition . . . of what she can afford, is not necessarily what another person's definition might be."

"Exactly. So those kinds of cases present dilemmas for organizations such as ours because it's not a pro bono case, yet we realized that we have made a commitment to the case. We have to see it through," he said.

Eventually, Mone worked out an agreement with Blau that called for two caps, one if the case settled, another if it went to the hearing.

If Bean-Bayog settled with the board, her legal costs would be $175,000 to Blau and about $45,000 in costs. If her case went to hearing, she would pay $250,000 to Blau and about $150,000 in costs.[4]

"To me there is an enormous difference between $210,000 and $400,000. Mone didn't see it. Two hundred thousand dollars was not enough to make a major decision about. But by this time I also knew that my practice was falling apart and that I had no future source of income. So for me the $200,000 difference was a major factor."

I asked her how she thought the hearing would have worked, if she had not resigned.

"The way it would've worked is that eventually I would have been put on the stand and been able to testify. But for the first [two] weeks, Fabiano would've had himself a prosecu-

---

4. IF BEAN-BAYOG'S ACTUAL LEGAL BILLS WERE APPROACHING $1 MILLION, BLAU DID INDEED "EAT MOST OF THE COSTS," NAMELY, ABOUT $750,000.

tion case with nationwide international TV and they were not
going to let me testify during that part of the process. And
then there would have been a hiatus [of several weeks] while
we are allowed to prepare our defense. And at that point, I'd
finally be allowed to testify and rebut the charges after the entire scene of last spring [March 26] had been repeated. But the
way it was going to be done was the first two witnesses
[Fabiano] was planning to call were the grieving parents. He
knew that if I was allowed out of my cage that I would not be
good for his case. I am very credible, and I don't look like the
kind of person I have been depicted to be. I have a midwestern accent and my manner is also midwestern. And so they
were planning to keep me from testifying. They would not let
me answer any questions. So that part of the media rape
would have been to see to it that the entire public was poisoned against me on a scale that made last spring look like a
Sunday-school picnic, this time with nightly TV coverage . . .
And one of the major reasons for me not to go to the hearing
was because I didn't know who my enemy was. My own lawyer? Fabiano? It's not clear to me yet which one was more
dangerous and damaging to me. I mean I spent such an enormous amount of warlike energy protecting myself from Michael Blau's [financial] attacks on my family and me that by
the time we got to the point of me thinking of trying to mount
[a defense at the hearing, there was no point] . . . the experience that I had was that the major emotional task for me for
the summer was to keep myself from being destroyed by my
lawyer—after Mone told me I was stuck with this bastard.
And the fact that my husband doesn't want me to go to [the
hearing]."

"Why not?" I asked.

"Don't you think he'd had enough? Just exactly how much
abuse do you think he should've been subjected to? Just exactly
how much public shaming do you want him to have gone
through? Just exactly how much voyeuristic exposure do you
think our kids should have been subjected to? I mean what is in
it? Why would you back that kind of treatment for a family. One

thing that Judy Herman[5] did say was that my getting out of there when I did was the only sensible thing I did. She said, 'You could not have. It's absolutely the only way you could stop the abuse. And it was a very sensible move . . .' And so I'm in a situation where my finances have been blown up. My career has been blown up. My lawyer is attacking me. I'm about to be burned at the stake on nationwide TV every night for several weeks. And people who hear that I'm considering not doing this are telling me, "Gee, you should do it." . . . You should continue to trust the legal process. You should believe that justice will prevail. You should believe that if you tell your story, people will listen and the truth will come out. You should believe that if you are innocent, it will be discovered."

"Do you still believe those things?"

"Are you kidding?"

"Then why are you meeting with me?"

"I don't really know . . . But what I'm saying to you is that the major trauma of the last six months for me was not the media assault. It was Michael Blau . . .

"But anyway just to finish the story with Blau. So . . . when he realizes that I am dead serious about resigning, he gets clever. He wants to save his ass. He wants to look like he did something for his quarter of a million dollars. He wants to show something for the five months of his life that he invested in the show he was about to put on. And what he succeeds in doing is thinking of a way to have me resign with a submission of documents, which of course throws Fabiano into a frenzy . . .

"[After September 21], Blau was sort of off the hook, because now my personal attorney is Mone. And Mone is negotiating with the various people and so forth. And Blau does a couple of things. One, is that he makes phone calls every week or so to ask

---

5. TO DEAL WITH HER OWN TRAUMA, DR. BEAN-BAYOG MET WITH, AMONG OTHERS, DR. JUDITH M. HERMAN, AUTHOR OF *TRAUMA AND RECOVERY: THE AFTERMATH OF VIOLENCE,* WHICH THE *NEW YORK TIMES* CALLED, "ONE OF THE MOST IMPORTANT PSYCHIATRIC WORKS TO BE PUBLISHED SINCE FREUD." DR. HERMAN TOLD HER THAT BECAUSE SHE WAS SUFFERING FROM POST TRAUMATIC STRESS DISORDER, SHE SHOULD WAIT AT LEAST A YEAR BEFORE TRYING TO WRITE A BOOK.

me whether I really don't want to renege on my resignation and say I want my license back."

Blau was suggesting that although her resignation was irrevocable, it could be rescinded before it went into effect on November 10!

Later, I asked Blau to explain.

"I think we had an argument that until it was in effect that it was potentially rescindable. We also had arguments that she was under unconscionable pressure and was doing this against legal advice. And once, in a sense, she 'came to her senses,' I think we would have had grounds for arguing that under the circumstances she should be allowed to rescind. Whether the board would've permitted her or not, I don't know . . . In any event, it would've been absolutely Fabiano's worst nightmare."

"Why?" I asked.

"Because he would've had to gear up for this case again on a pro bono basis. He would've had to actually try this case with all the risks that he had. He did not have a strong case. He was going to have a dramatic opening to his case with the testimony of Pilar and the mother, but other than that he did not, other than the drama of the first couple of days which I think would've been effectively negated by a good cross examination of those witnesses. His case was going to quickly fall apart."

Blau and Mone had strongly advised her against resigning her license, because it was a permanent and irrevocable act, far worse than any outcome the board could have imposed. But Bean-Bayog disagreed.

"[T]here isn't any legal outcome that is worse than what you have to go through for it. But that one of the major issues that I had as an experience, besides being massively assaulted and having my family massively assaulted and being financially demolished by this case, was that I had an enemy at my side. Someone who would turn on me in a split second if it would make his career better. Someone who would lie to me shamelessly. Someone who really would have no compunction and then would pretend that it was all for my own good."

"Do you have any reservations about what you've just said

about Michael Blau appearing in this book?"

"Sure. There are parts of him I liked. There were things that I am grateful to him for. I mean he's not all bad. He's simply a limited human being with a cruel streak, and a selfish streak, who did not have the equipment, which would've required an extraordinary kind of equipment, to stick to his own integrity given the forces that were acting . . . I think he was a small man in a very big pond.

Later, I asked Blau if he wished to respond to Bean-Bayog's tirade against him. He said that he felt very good about the defense he had prepared to mount on her behalf, had charged her a fraction of what his firm had spent on her, and understood the trauma from which she was suffering.

"I really have no response. Let people draw their own conclusions," he said quietly.

Several months later, Bean-Bayog softened her criticism of Blau.

"I've considerably calmed down about Blau. I'm in less pain. I feel less like he deliberately betrayed me," she said. "It was not his fault that I was clinging to him like a spar. I had no room for him to be less than perfect and he wasn't."

In the meantime, she had received her mother's inheritance but was thinking about not paying her bill to McDermott, Will & Emery.

Michael Blau was also traumatized by the experience and particularly its outcome. Although we chatted on the phone from time to time, he did not sit down for a series of formal taped interviews until seven months after her resignation.

I asked him if there were traumas other than her decision to resign.

"Well, yes, there were."

"I know you had to deal with some heavy duty people. You had to deal with the medical board. You had to deal with tough guy Fabiano," I said.

"But those aren't, those things didn't matter to me. Dealing with Fabiano was no problem. Dealing with the board was no problem. In a sense, dealing with the press, although it was very anxiety-provoking because they're just all over you at all times, and you always wonder what it's going to look like in the paper the next day, even that was OK. What was difficult . . . were Dr. Bean-Bayog's emotional ups and downs, and dealing with her. That was where the real hard issues were over the summer . . . following her up and down emotional spirals, both up and down as she went through her decision-making process of what she wanted to do, was agonizing. It was just agonizing. I would not want to put anyone through that."

I asked Blau if he had personally been affected by the whole experience.

"Oh, my lord, it affected me in so many ways . . . I was enormously disappointed when Dr. Bean-Bayog decided against our advice, and against Mike Mone's advice and against the advice of others, to resign her license. We had put in a monumental effort to prepare this case for what was going to be a very public hearing, a very unfortunate and very public hearing. But then, there it was . . . And as a human being, and a lawyer, you always wonder whether you can rise to the challenge and perform well under those circumstances. This was a unique kind of challenge. The Alan Dershowitzes[6] of the world get to see these kinds of cases and have these kinds of opportunities all the time. I didn't invite it. I wasn't looking for it. I'm not a glory seeker, publicity hound. This was a case that just happened to be thrown out into the public light . . .

"I wasn't looking for the limelight, just the opposite. But once the spotlight is turned on you, you have to reach down deep into your soul and you have to kind of question whether you have what it takes to do the job which needs to be done. And it

---

6. IN FACT, LATER THAT FALL, BEAN-BAYOG MET WITH HARVARD LAW SCHOOL PRO-FESSOR ALAN DERSHOWITZ FOR ADVICE ON WHAT LEGAL ACTION, IF ANY, TO TAKE AGAINST BLAU. "ONE OF THE ADVANTAGES OF MY NOTORIETY IS THAT THERE ARE VERY FEW PEOPLE AROUND TOWN WHO, WHEN I CALL THEM UP, CAN'T FIND TIME FOR ME. I MEAN, I CALLED (DERSHOWITZ). HE WAS ON HIS WAY OUT THE DOOR FOR TWO DAYS. I HAD AN APPOINTMENT WITHIN 48 HOURS," SHE SAID. BEAN-BAYOG DECIDED NOT TO SUE BLAU.

involves a lot of soul searching . . . When she finally resigned her
license, it left me with a huge lingering question which was . . .
why had we gone through all of this work? But secondly, if it had
come to fruition and we had gotten finally into the hearing
context, where I was confident she would have been largely, if
not wholly, vindicated, whether I personally would've risen to
the challenge and given the kind of performance as an attorney
that one would hope and expect . . . It really plagued me
throughout the fall. And I was, I think, in a sense, paralyzed. Dr.
Bean-Bayog says that we were both in a state of shock."

To resolve this pain, Blau said he realized he had to face a
terrifying challenge and "see it through to completion." In the
spring of 1993, Blau and his wife went to Jamaica on vacation.

"On the far end of the [island] . . . where all the happy hippies
went in the late '70s to watch the sun set . . . [is] a bar up there.
And they also have the highest cliffs in Jamaica there. And
people go cliff jumping," he said.

"Bungee jumping?" I asked.

"No, it's just into the water. Cliff jumping into the water. Not
cliff jumping to one's gory death in a ravine . . ."

"How high are the cliffs?"

"Fifty-five feet. The place is also sort of known as lovers'
leap . . . I fixated on those cliffs. And I said I knew that it would
take very bit of gumption that I had to get myself up to the top
of that cliff, to look down. It would be absolutely terrifying to
me, terrifying in the same way, in some sense, that facing this
unbelievable public ordeal would've been with Dr. Bean-Bayog.
And then see whether I could successfully pull it off without
killing myself . . . We got there . . . and I hadn't said a word to
my wife yet about the cliff diving. And . . . I said to her, 'I've got
to do this.' And she looked at me with terror and she said, 'You
have two children . . .' I told her I was going to do this. And she
realized that I was going to . . .'"

"Were you planning to do it feet first or head first?"

"Feet first. I'm not that foolish. This was not an attempt to
commit suicide . . . About five people a year break their necks,
and every day someone gets injured, and the question is would

I get injured . . . But anyway, I knew it would be terrifying. And there's this spit of land that goes out . . . to a little jumping area. This jumping area is no larger than the size of a dinner plate, just big enough to put your feet on before you jump. And it extends out a little bit over the water so you don't have to worry about jumping out over the cliff. If you just jump straight down from the cliff you're going to get into the water . . ."

"Was your wife watching?"

"Yeah, my wife was watching . . . And I got to the jumping platform, and once having gotten there, I was resolved. I was going to go through this . . . and I jumped . . . So you know, it wasn't until I did that that I felt like I could begin to put this whole ordeal behind me. It was my symbolic rite. I didn't get the chance to face up to the challenge [of the hearing]. Now, I've done something terrifying. I've faced up to the challenge. I've taken the risk. I've gotten it over with. At least it was completed. It wasn't Greg Louganis.[7] I didn't do a triple somersault and split the water evenly. But I did it. And I got it done. And it was over with."

"Your dad's a shrink?"

"Yeah."

"Did you discuss it with him?"

"Oh no, I've never, I would never tell him this story . . . I've told very few people this story."

My father said that Blau's cliff jump was a quasi-suicidal gesture. Bean-Bayog thought so too.

On December 16, 1992, the civil suit was settled out of court for $1,000,000. James J. Barry, Bean-Bayog's malpractice insurance lawyer, filed a terse and uninformative document in Middlesex Superior Court:

The Plaintiff Maria Pilar Williams, Adm'x and the defendant, Margaret H. Bean-Bayog, M.D., stip-

---

7. GREG LOUGANIS, AN AMERICAN, WON THE OLYMPIC GOLD MEDAL FOR PLATFORM DIVING IN 1984 AND 1988.

ulate that . . . this action is dismissed with prejudice and without costs as to the defendant . . .

Barry sent a copy to Meyer and Mone, but none to Blau.
The next day both the *Globe* and *Herald* ran their final front-
page stories on Margaret Bean-Bayog.

The *Globe* reported,

> The settlement, which contains no admission
> of guilt on Bean-Bayog's part, will be paid by
> Bean-Bayog's insurance company and repre-
> sents the full amount of her annual malpractice
> insurance . . .
> Attorneys who represent plaintiffs say that $1
> million is a substantial sum for cases involving
> either sexual misconduct by psychotherapists
> or inappropriate treatment. Recent settlements
> in cases involving sexual misconduct of psy-
> chotherapists have ranged from as low as $15,-
> 000 (in cases where there is no malpractice
> insurance) to a high of $2 million.
> . . . Neither Bean-Bayog nor the Lozano family
> responded to requests for interviews.

Pilar Williams, however, did grant interviews to newspapers
that she felt had shown more sympathy to the Lozanos' claims.
She told the *Herald,*

> "That was the resolution for me. As far as the
> settlement goes, this was for my parents. All the
> expenses—his funeral expenses and pursuing
> the case—was coming out of their pocket. This
> will give them a chance to get on with the griev-
> ing and be able to heal now."
> Williams said the "bulk" of the settlement will
> be put toward a scholarship for Hispanic medi-
> cal students . . .

Andrew Meyer, the Lozano family's attorney, said the settlement shows Bean-Bayog's insurance company "made a decision that this case should not be defended" . . . The family is totally satisfied that justice has been served and full compensation has been given.

Williams told *New York Times* reporter Fox Butterfield, who in his article referred to the defendant as "Ms. Bean-Bayog,"[8] that:

The family had agreed to settle the civil suit because they saw no need to proceed further against Ms. Bean-Bayog after she gave up her license.

"This was not about money for us," Ms. Williams said. "What we wanted was to get the truth out. That was done by the medical board."

Part of the settlement will reimburse the family for therapy bills and for funeral expenses, Mr. Meyer said, but most of the money will go toward establishing a scholarship fund for Hispanic medical students.

On the late news, Williams, who gave a telephone interview to WCVB-TV5, said:

We did everything we could to stop her from harming anyone else and hopefully to leave an impact on the profession and use that as a deterrent to hopefully keep from anyone else

---

8. THE RESIGNATION OF A MEDICAL LICENSE DOES NOT INVALIDATE THE MEDICAL DEGREE EARNED FROM MEDICAL SCHOOL. HENCE, SHE OFFICIALLY REMAINS MARGARET BEAN-BAYOG, M.D.

being hurt the way my family and my brother was.

Bean-Bayog told me that she "authorized a settlement [because] . . . the whole prospect of waiting two years for another public hanging was more than I could bear."

25

THE DEATH OF PAUL LOZANO

Throughout the case, the most sensational questions were: Did Bean-Bayog cause Lozano's death? and Did they copulate? As to the sex, the only living witness, Bean-Bayog, adamantly denies it. Tom O'Hare told me he did not include it in his lawsuit because it was unprovable. The medical board did not bring an allegation of sexual misconduct. Both Meyer and Fabiano told me that they didn't know with absolute certainty either. In other words, had this case gone to court, the Lozanos probably could not have mustered enough evidence to substantiate that Bean-Bayog had sex with Paul Lozano. She may have, but I don't think so.[1]

How did Lozano die? Did Bean-Bayog cause his death? Was

---

1. DURING HIS FOUR YEARS' OF THERAPY WITH BEAN-BAYOG, LOZANO WAS HOSPITALIZED FIVE TIMES. AT LEAST 117 MENTAL HEALTH PROFESSIONALS (PSYCHIATRIC NURSES, SOCIAL WORKERS, PSYCHIATRIC AIDES, PSYCHOLOGISTS, AND PSYCHIATRISTS) WERE ENGAGED WITH HIM. LOZANO NEVER MENTIONED OR HINTED TO THEM OR TO HIS ROOMMATE, VICTOR GONZALEZ, THAT HE HAD BEEN SEXUALLY INVOLVED WITH BEAN-BAYOG. DR. GONZALEZ, WHO IS CURRENTLY AN OPHTHAMOLOGIST IN BOSTON AND DECLINED TO BE INTERVIEWED, WAS BRIEFLY INTERVIEWED BY THE MEDICAL BOARD:

> Q. What did Mr. Lozano tell you regarding his relationship with Dr. Bean-Bayog?
> A. He never discussed his interaction with Dr. Bean-Bayog in detail with me. He had only positive comments about the treatment he was receiving from her.
> Q. If Mr. Lozano discussed his relationship with Dr. Bean-Bayog with you, when did these conversations take place?
> A. The few times Mr. Lozano talked about Dr. Bean-Bayog were scattered throughout the two years I lived with him.

his death, in fact, a suicide? Ten months had elapsed between the end of Bean-Bayog's therapy and Lozano's cocaine overdose. Was her therapy a factor in his death at all? These are questions that would have to be satisfactorily answered to prove the charges of wrongful death against her in court. To do so, Lozano's last ten months would have to be assiduously revisited. What exactly did go on in those final months? What was going on in Lozano's mind?

Bean-Bayog had predicted his death. She maintains that without her "heroic" therapy, he would have killed himself long before.[2] She had implicitly warned Tom O'Hare in her February 4, 1991, letter that apparently accompanied a copy of the Process Notes she mailed to him.

But Paul Lozano wanted to live as much as he wished to die. In Lozano's final assault on his own life, he cried out for help, as he had done so often before.

Faulkner Hospital's Dr. Jerome Rogoff wrote: "[Patient] has always stopped himself or called in help to help him from suicide attempts."

Bean-Bayog told me that the reason she took such voluminous notes, which she often reread, was to be certain not to miss an imminent, subtle suicide attempt. His final cry for help, however, went unheard.

The Lozanos are a devout Roman Catholic family. Immediately after Lozano's death, his body was prepared for burial by the Martin Funeral Home. Four days later, he was buried at the Evergreen East Cemetery following a eulogy, spoken by father Ricardo Rodriquez in Maria de Guadalupe Church. A rosary Mass is said for Paul Lozano on every anniversary of his death and birth.

---

2. DR. JOHN T. MALTSBERGER, A PROMINENT HARVARD PSYCHIATRIST, WHO RE-VIEWED THE EXTENSIVE RECORDS IN THE CASE, AGREED. IN A SPEECH GIVEN IN SAN FRANCISCO ON APRIL 15, 1993, TO THE AMERICAN ASSOCIATION OF SUICIDOLOGY, HE SAID, "THERE IS LITTLE DOUBT IN MY MIND THE PATIENT WOULD HAVE COMMITTED SUICIDE LONG BEFORE HE DID WITHOUT DR. BEAN-BAYOG'S EXTRAORDINARY DEDI-CATION AND TENACITY."

In most cases, a Catholic ceremony would have been impossible had the family confessed that his was a suicide. The death certificate stated the cause of death was "accidental cocaine intoxication."

For God, Lozano's death was accidental; for a lawsuit, suicide.

El Paso police officer Juan Esparza, Jr., said that Lozano's father, Marcos Lozano, who discovered his son's body, reported to him: "It was possible that his son had taken his own life, since he was taking medication for depression (for approximately three years) and that he had attempted to take his life twice before."

Officer Esparza later told me that he recalled Lozano's father saying that they had been keeping an eye on him because of his previous suicide attempts. Esparza also said that Lozano's sister said, "I know it's not his fault. He was driven to do it." The El Paso police report stated: "The sister, Pilar Williams, told me that her brother had attempted suicide in Boston while attending Harvard and he had used the same method of injection with sodium chloride but had failed in his attempt."

In her July 1992 deposition, however, when asked: "Are you aware that he ever attempted suicide during his life?," Williams answered, "No."

Nonetheless, the cause of Lozano's death was officially listed as "accidental." The notion of suicide lay dormant for seven months. Tom O'Hare did not raise it when the lawsuit was initially filed. It was resurrected when the Lozanos replaced him with Drew Meyer.

Paul Lozano was a risk taker. He liked to toy with death. He was a sky diver and a scuba diver. He remarked once how when deep underwater, he could simply turn off the air. As noted, he once went jogging at night in a marginal neighborhood of Boston. Also, he mixed his potent antidepressant and antipsychotic medications with alcohol, a risky business. Lozano's ambition was to be a pediatric anesthesiologist, but he told Bean-Bayog that he was afraid he would sexually molest his young patients.

"That was the thing he said he hated the most about his

mother, that he knew he was capable of sexually abusing babies and that he was going to do that if something happened and he talked about that. He threatened to sexually abuse a baby just to get back at his parents. 'My M.D. would stand for Monster Doc, the child pornographer. I would set up a child pornography and prostitution practice, a prostitution ring in my pediatric practice.' No wonder he wanted to be dead. He was terrified he would end up doing that and yet he was terrified of not being a doctor." said Bean-Bayog.

Lozano was knowledgeable about drugs, contraindications, and antagonists. He had become an expert on how close to the edge he could venture with quantities and mixtures of medications. His Faulkner Hospital medical records stated:

> He reports that he wants to be an anesthesiologist and has been starting IVs on himself and injecting himself with ketamine and lidocaine at home in order to observe their effects . . . Patient began experimenting with injections of lidocaine/ketamine combo to take self near death and then add reversal agent.

Bean-Bayog wrote in the Process Notes:

> Paul injects himself with ketamine and fentanyl and then takes narcan, a reversal agent, to prevent himself from dying.

At the beginning of his second McLean hospitalization, she wrote about a conversation he had with a staff nurse:

> He felt terrible shame about: (his recent) IV injection. (His) nurse discussed his actually maybe could've gotten laryngospasm and died and he knew it. If he keep(s) getting close, sometime it'll work.

Although he spoke of leaving a suicide note in an earlier attempt, he apparently did not on the day he died. However, two notes were found, one on his bed, the other on his desk. Police officer Dale F. Fernandez reported that "a note [was] found on [Lozano's] bed. Apparently, the note is written by a friend of [his]. A second note was found on the desk, apparently, written by the same person." Both notes are signed by "me." One of the notes apologizes for being a "neurotic nag" and pleads with Lozano to "take care of yourself." Williams later told me they were written by Maura Thomas[3], an older woman, the wife of a doctor with whom Lozano was friendly. Williams said that Thomas visits Lozano's grave often.

Although the press repeatedly reported that in killing himself he had "injected himself 75 times with cocaine," the autopsy report did not state that. It reported seventy-five fresh needle marks.

It takes only one potent injection of cocaine to kill oneself. Perhaps Lozano was "skin popping," a technique used by some addicts who inject cocaine. Skin poppers inject a series of small amounts just under the skin, to extend the euphoria.

As we've seen, El Paso Country Medical Examiner Juan U. Contin wrote: "Innumerable needle marks are noted both ante-cubital fossae [the crook of the elbows], both forearms and both hands, estimated to be approximately 75. They all appear fresh."

But officer Fernandez reported there were also needle marks on Lozano's feet, typical of habitual users. "Fresh" means that if the mark were squeezed, blood would ooze out. From the thirty-eight photographs—including close-ups of his arms and hands—taken by police after his body was discovered, most of the marks do appear bloody—as if Lozano had just jabbed himself repeatedly. And in the photographs, needle marks do appear on Lozano's feet, though not noted in the autopsy report.

Lidocaine, which was found in his syringe, is a topical anesthetic that can be used to adulterate street cocaine. Perhaps he was frantically trying to inject Lidocaine in order to counteract

---

3. HER NAME WAS CHANGED TO PROTECT PRIVACY.

the effect of a cocaine-induced arrhythmia[4] in a desperate, but futile, last-minute bid to save his life. This could explain the seventy-five needle marks over his arms and hands, in his attempt to locate a vein.[5]

For a medical student, medicinal cocaine is very difficult, though not impossible, to obtain. Otolaryngologists and ophthalmologists often use it in their practices, but it is kept in locked cabinets. Lozano could have stolen it on the last day of his rotation at the hospital, the day before he died. But Williams said a cocaine bottle was not discovered at the scene. None was noted in the police report either. It is possible that Lozano used street cocaine, or the ampules were removed before the police arrived.

If Lozano had been a habitual user of cocaine, the amount found in his system may or may not have been sufficient to kill him. Cocaine can kill in high toxic amounts but also in minute ones as well, especially if there is cocaine-induced damage to the heart muscle, producing the fatal arrhythmia. According to the autopsy, his cocaine level was 36 nanograms. Standard analytical toxicology texts state that the lethal dose of cocaine can range between zero and about 26 nanograms. Some heavy users, however, can tolerate as much as 200 nanograms.

I did examine all the police photographs with a powerful magnifying glass to determine if Lozano had any older "marks" from previous injections. I couldn't find any, which would somewhat support the family's claim that he was not a habitual intravenous drug user.[6]

Further supporting the family's vigorous claim was a mysteri-

---

4. AN ALTERATION IN RHYTHM OF THE HEARTBEAT EITHER IN TIME OR FORCE.
5. IT IS OFTEN REPORTED IN THE PSYCHIATRIC LITERATURE AND BY MANY FORENSIC PATHOLOGISTS THAT MANY SUICIDES HAD MUTILATED THEMSELVES EXCESSIVELY PRIOR TO THE FINAL ACT, WHICH LED TO THEIR DEATH. ALSO, THESE ''HESITATION MARKS'' WERE THE ONLY WAY THEY COULD FIND TO RELIEVE TENSION.
6. MARKS ARE SCARS FROM PREVIOUS INJECTIONS THAT BECAME INFLAMED. A MEDICAL STUDENT WOULD PROBABLY USE STERILE NEEDLES, BUT WOULD ALSO HAVE BETTER ACCESS TO THE TUBERCULLIN-TYPE SYRINGES WHICH ARE CAPPED WITH MINUTE NEEDLES THAT RARELY LEAVE SCARS. ALSO, THE REASON JUNKIES INJECT THEMSELVES IN THEIR FEET IS THEY CAN NO LONGER FIND ANY USABLE VEINS IN THEIR ARMS.

ous April 1 letter written by Dr. Kevin T. Allen to Dr. Gault[7] found on Lozano's bed. It was the original letter, signed in blue ink, stating that Lozano's urine toxicology showed no evidence of illicit drugs. I was unable to verify the letter's authenticity because Allen did not return phone calls. I wondered what Allen's original letter—not a photocopy—was doing in Lozano's possession.[8]

For many students, the third year of medical school is particularly stressful. It is the beginning of clinical training. Medical students begin hands-on responsibility for live patients. A number of studies have suggested that the third year of medical school can activate a student's dormant psychological problems.

It was at the onset of Lozano's third year, July 1986, when he decided to seek psychotherapy. About a year later, he began what would be a nearly three-year leave of absence from medical school. He was working on a doctorate in pediatric anesthesiology. After Bean-Bayog's return from her three-week vacation in the Philippines, Lozano's condition improved. However, in the fall of 1989, when he made the decision to return to medical school against Bean-Bayog's advice, his illness rekindled.

Bean-Bayog said that if he had stuck to pure research, Lozano would not have killed himself. But research doesn't pay well and Lozano felt compelled to become a doctor so he could help support his parents.

---

7. SPEAKING OF MYSTERY, GAULT'S FATHER, WILLIAM CAMPBELL GAULT, IS A NOTED DETECTIVE WRITER WHO PUBLISHED HIS SIXTY-FOURTH BOOK, *DEAD PIGEON,* IN 1992, AND IS THE CREATOR OF PRIVATE EYE BROCK CALLAHAN. IN A REVIEW, THE *NEW YORK TIMES* ONCE CALLED GAULT'S CALLAHAN ''SURELY ONE OF THE MAJOR DETECTIVES SINCE CHANDLER'S PHILIP MARLOWE.''

8. DR. COLLINS, AN ANESTHESIOLOGIST, WHO WORKED WITH LOZANO BETWEEN 1986 AND 1988 IN A LOCAL RESEARCH LAB, TOLD THE MEDICAL BOARD'S PROSECUTOR THAT HE BELIEVED LOZANO WAS ABUSING DRUGS, BECAUSE HE ALWAYS WORE SUNGLASSES, HAD ''A TREMOR IN HIS HANDS, A LETHARGIC DISPOSITION, AND A CERTAIN LACK OF COORDINATION IN HIS MOVEMENTS.'' LOZANO EXPLAINED TO COLLINS THAT THESE SYMPTOMS WERE SIDE EFFECTS OF THE ANTIDEPRESSANTS HE WAS TAKING, BUT COLLINS, WHO DESCRIBED LOZANO AS ''A LONER AND A CLEARLY TROUBLED INDIVIDUAL,'' SAID THE SIDE EFFECTS COULD NOT BE FROM THE MEDICATION BUT WERE FROM ILLICIT DRUG ABUSE.

"Invariably when he went back to medical school to a clinical rotation he stopped taking his antidepressants . . . When he was in a clinical situation where you have to interact with human beings, you're not just dealing with test tubes. You're expected to perform. You're supposed to be able to tolerate the stress and the long hours. People get angry with you. They humiliate you. All the things that he most couldn't stand. The way medical students are treated is unbelievably horrible. They feel stupid and incompetent because they don't know anything yet," she said.

Even Williams acknowledged that she too noticed Lozano's decline whenever he came into contact with patients. She said she raised these concerns with his therapists in his later hospitalizations in 1990, though there is no mention in Lozano's voluminous hospital records. When I told Williams that in the spring of 1990, Lozano had shot himself up with Ketamine, she was astonished. As a nurse, she knew how potent the hallucinogen was. Williams expressed disbelief that his care-givers allowed him to continue medical school—indeed, that Harvard Medical School itself would have permitted his return as a student. He was not only a danger to himself but to his patients as well, a concern Bean-Bayog had expressed. Dr. Gerald Adler and his colleagues gave Lozano a passing grade after he dropped out half way through his psychiatric rotation. Adler's motivations may have been sincere, but his leniency may also have jeopardized the best interests of both Lozano and the community he wished to serve. Bean-Bayog expressed such strong reservations about Lozano's becoming a physician, that she urged him to join the impaired physician's committee. Had he done as she suggested, Lozano would have been closely monitored and tested for drug use. As we've seen, he refused her recommendations, so she refused to keep treating him.

After discussing the termination of therapy, on and off, for seven months, Bean-Bayog finally ended therapy in June 1990, while Lozano was hospitalized, because she thought it was the safest place to do so. She even provided him with two flash cards to keep with him and, she hoped, comfort him. The first one read:

We've done an incredible piece of work. I want you to get well. I want you to take good care of yourself and not hurt yourself. I still love you and always will care what happens to you. You've been stuck feeling either you would get rejected or get too close. The choice I had was either to let you in close or inflict pain. It will be easier in a new therapy to understand what happened and to have more life besides therapy. I will miss you too. Love, Dr. Bean-Bayog.

The second one continued.

I love you. I loved working with you. I want you to stay alive and get well. I'll miss you too. Sometimes we had a wonderful time. Sometimes it hurt. We both got angry too. You know how to use help to get well. I want you to get all the way well so you can take what I gave you and fly. Things you wish you hadn't done or said weren't your fault. Or mine. Take care of yourself. Let me know from time to time what has become of you.
Love, Dr. B.

But Lozano did not bond with his subsequent therapists. After terminating with Bean-Bayog, Lozano was hospitalized at Malden Hospital and Carney Hospital. He was also seen on an out-patient basis at the Massachusetts Mental Health Center, the Massachusetts General Hospital, the Human Resource Institute, and Harvard University's Stillman Infirmary.

In his final Boston-area hospitalization, however, he did seem to bond with William Barry Gault, a doctor at the Newton-Wellesley hospital. The relationship began on October 19, 1990. With Williams's permission, Gault gave Lozano nine ECTs during his five-week admission. His final shock treatment was on November 14. According to Gault and Williams, Lozano's condition improved dramatically.

Two weeks after Lozano's final ECT, Dr. José Saporta, one of Gault's partner's in "Newton-Wellesley Psychiatry," described Lozano's current condition somewhat differently:

> (Lozano) floated in an out of the—I believe that this patient had transient periods of psychosis where he would lose the ability to test reality, and at other times gain it. And there were times when he would say, "You know, I really believed she (Bean-Bayog) was my mom." At times he believed it and at times he didn't.

When deeply depressed patients who have been paralyzed by their depression begin to recover, ironically their risk of suicide may increase, because they have more physical and emotional strength to carry out the act. If Gault's ECTs diminished Lozano's depression, they may have provided him with just enough strength to kill himself.

Finally, the short-term memory loss associated with ECTs would not have favored Lozano's preparation for the second part of the Medical Boards.

Even Pope, also a biologically oriented psychiatrist, was reluctant to use ECTs. In a November 1986 consultation note, Pope wrote:

> If . . . also fails, the choice would be ECT or fluoxetine (Prozac). I'd be inclined to exhaust medications with TCA's and MAGI's before considering ECT. I suppose the memory loss from ECT would be quite a nuisance for a medical student, given the large amounts of memorization required in medical school.

Lozano himself also expressed doubts about ECTs during the same hospitalization: "To feel well, I would do whatever the Docs say except ECT, which really freaks me."

Williams persuaded her brother to try it, however.

After nine ECTs, he wanted to resume his clinical rotations.

Harvard Medical School gave Lozano permission to do two rotations in El Paso. The first rotation began on February 4, 1991. It seemed like a good idea to be physically close to the support and comfort of his family. Bean-Bayog, however, had much earlier noted that whenever he was home on vacation, his agony and thoughts of suicide increased.

Sure enough, the minute Lozano landed in El Paso, he began suffering severe anxiety attacks and was admitted to the psychiatric ward of the Sun Valley Hospital.

During Paul Lozano's final two months of life, multiple apprehensions weighed down on him. He had returned to a clinical rotation. He was living with his parents in a rundown section of El Paso. He was taking two powerful drugs, an antidepressant and an antipsychotic. He was, at least on one occasion, experimenting with intravenous drugs. The hearing on the complaint against Bean-Bayog was looming. He would have to meet with and be interrogated by lawyers and investigators upon his return to Boston. Eventually, he would have to provide testimony against her in open court. But more immediately, he would have to take the grueling second part of the National Boards, testing his clinical competency. He could not graduate without passing this exam.

Among the documents released by the medical board, I stumbled across an obscure, but significant, letter. On December 11, 1990, Gault had written to Dr. Edward M. Hundert, Harvard Medical School's associate dean for student affairs, four months before Lozano's death:

> Mr. Lozano has been my patient since October 19, 1990. In my opinion he is ready to take Part II of the National Board Examination in April, 1991 and to resume his clinical rotations in June, 1991.

Although Lozano had been on a nearly four-year and very troubled leave of absence from clinical studies at medical school,

Gault concluded that Paul Lozano[9] was ready to take his National Boards.

In January 1993, when I mentioned to Williams that her brother was supposed to take the National Boards,[10] she gasped. "You're right. I had completely forgotten about that. He was supposed to take that exam back in Boston." Did she know the exact date of the exam? She shook her head. I did, however.

Gault's partner, Dr. José Saporta, was the last Boston-area psychotherapist to see Lozano before he died. In Saporta's notes from a November 28, 1990 therapy session, he wrote that Lozano was "terrified of failing upcoming boards." Saporta also noted that Lozano "was so frightened about the report to the medical board [accusing Bean-Bayog of unethical behavior] and felt so bad about it and so guilty."

During his brief hospital admission after landing in El Paso, he was seen and evaluated by Dr. Francisco Marquez.

In a *Herald* story, Williams said, "Dr. Marquez told me Paul said he was going to kill himself, that he was feeling really badly about what was in the documents (relating to his therapy with Bean-Bayog)."

But that is not what Marquez wrote in Lozano's medical records:

> This patient . . . (was admitted) indicating that he wanted to shoot himself with a gun that his father kept at home . . . Once he was admitted to the hospital, his sister came over here and indicated that the patient sometimes got those

---

9. HE WAS ABSENT FROM MEDICAL SCHOOL FROM MAY 3, 1987 TO JANUARY 29, 1990, AND FROM MARCH 15, 1990, TO FEBRUARY 4, 1991.

10. THE NATIONAL BOARDS PART II IS A TWO-DAY, MULTIPLE-CHOICE EXAM AND A PREREQUISITE TO GRADUATION. THE EXAM—COVERING LOZANO'S WEAKEST AREA, CLINICAL COMPETENCY—CONTAINS AN EQUAL NUMBER OF QUESTIONS IN INTERNAL MEDICINE, OBSTETRICS AND GYNECOLOGY, PEDIATRICS, PREVENTIVE MEDICINE AND PUBLIC HEALTH, PSYCHIATRY, AND SURGERY, EACH WITH RELATED SUBSPECIALTIES. THE TEST MEASURES A MEDICAL STUDENT'S ABILITY TO DIAGNOSE AND TREAT PATIENTS, THE VERY ACTIVITY THAT SEEMED TO TRIGGER LOZANO'S MENTAL ILLNESS. HOWEVER, FEW AT HARVARD FAIL THIS EXAM.

anxiety attacks in which he felt under a lot of pressure, and he was prone to say he was suicidal ... On (the next day), I called his psychiatrist in Boston ... Dr. José Saporta stated that Mr. Lozano was a patient in chronic suicide risk, overconcerned about his performance at school and about his clinical expectations in the new rotation ... Additionally, the sister informed us that the gun (at) the patient's parents' home had been removed. Furthermore, the patient was not going to stay with his parents but was going to stay with his sister, who is a very energetic and assertive R(egistered) N(urse) in one of the local hospitals in El Paso ... Recommendations: *The patient is to stay with his sister.* (emphasis added)

Lozano's Sun Valley medical records do mention that "[Lozano] was treated by a female psychiatrist, with whom apparently the patient had sex, and he says there is a lawsuit going on about this." But this statement was not mentioned in connection with Marquez's explanation of why Lozano was admitted to Sun Valley Hospital.

On March 1, 1991, a month before Lozano's death, his hospital medical records stated that the legal action against Bean-Bayog was weighing on the patient's mind:

(Patient) states (that he) got anxious last week after getting a letter that an expert witness will investigate his previous doctor and also that Board of Medical Examiners is getting involved. *He doesn't want to give his permission* (emphasis added) ... Then (he) says (he) doesn't think his sister likes him ...

I found no evidence in Lozano's Sun Valley records supporting Williams's claims that her brother had become suicidally despondent over his relationship with Bean-Bayog.

More than a year after Williams told El Paso police officer Esparza that her brother had attempted suicide before, she claimed otherwise in her July 1992 deposition:

> Q. Paul ever threaten suicide?
> A. Never.
> Q. To the date of his death, he never threatened suicide to you?
> A. No.
> Q. Did Paul ever tell you that he had suicidal ideations?
> A. No.
> Q. That's at any point in his life. He never told you he had a suicidal ideation, correct?
> A. That's correct.
> Q. Are you aware that Paul attempted suicide as a child?
> A. No.
> Q. Are you aware that he ever attempted suicide during his life?
> A. No.

Later in her deposition, Williams was asked again under oath:

> Q. Did Paul ever report to you that he attempted suicide?
> A. Which stage are we talking now?
> Q. At any point in time, did your brother ever tell you that he attempted suicide.
> A. No.

Later, Williams was asked if she had ever discussed his suicidal thoughts or attempts with any of the mental health professionals who treated him.

> Q. Just so I understand, with any medical practitioner that treated Paul, you never discussed

the issue of suicide, suicidal ideations, suicide attempts, correct?

A. That's correct.

Q. That would include Dr. Gault?

A. I guess after Newton-Wellesley, we did speak
about that.

Q. So now it's your memory that you did, in fact,
speak to somebody about suicide and your
brother?

A. That his depression was making him feel suicidal, yes.

Q. When was the first time that anybody ever
told you?

A. Dr. Gault.

In addition to the police report, there were many places in Lozano's medical records that suggest Williams was well aware of his suicidal thoughts and attempts.

For example, in the handwritten records of Lozano's second hospitalization at McLean Hospital, a nurse wrote:

Paul . . . called his sister to tell her of (his) hospitalization and precipitating incident on rooftop.
She was initially shocked . . . able to express
relief he's safe . . . He said his sister had asked if
he had thought what it would do to the family to
have him "splatter himself all over the side-
walk." He wondered that that hadn't occurred
to him. He also said he guessed he "needed to
hear that."

His McLean Hospital social worker, Roberta Goldwyn, wrote,

(I) met with patient on 5/20 to discuss the possibility of a family meeting when his mother and
sister come to Boston. He had agreed to this

plan by the end of the week but stipulated that
he have control over the information given
them. He did not want his mother to know about
his suicidality (he did tell sister over the telephone) and wanted neither of them to know
about his previous admission.

The Process Notes indicated that Williams was quite familiar with her brother's suicidal tendencies. Here are just two examples:

"My sister called yesterday . . . I guess Mrs.
Goldwyn (McLean Hospital social worker)
called her. She wonders why I'm still here too . . .
(Williams said,) 'I can't understand why they're
hounding you, spending thousands of dollars
(on you). (It's) not like you were (a) cardiologist
or Nobel Prize winner. You just go out and do it,
(and they could just) hose it away.' . . . "My
sister can be remarkably frank sometimes. (She
has a) refreshing sense of humor."
(Bean-Bayog replied), "I don't think (it's) too
hilarious."
"(It) put things in perspective. She goes, '(It)
wouldn't be first time. Thousands of students do
it a year.' She's just a little frustrated. (It) does put
in perspective though. She just thinks you all are
a little too concerned. You aren't saying much."
"(I was) just thinking if you did kill (your)self,
she'd kick (her)self for (the) rest of (her) life."

Four days after he was transferred to the Faulkner Hospital,
Lozano said to Bean-Bayog:

(The) social worker from McLean talked to her
(Williams) and told her about my being on 13th
floor. My sister was mad at me. "Why were you

doing that. (You) must've made them (the hospital staff) mad. You're gonna end up in those places all rest of your life." I was mad, but I kept my temper. "(I) guess you're right." Then she got even madder, so I let her have it. "No I won't. I won't be in places like this the rest of my life. I won't put up with it. There won't be a rest of my life. You think I'm playing games." (I) told her how it felt to be up there leaning out. "Just take your hands off. I've had these feelings a long time. As a kid, (I remember) running up the stairs (chasing my brothers) with the butcher knife. (I was) miserable after school." Pilar said, "I love you, but I can't remember anything that would've made you feel that." "I must've been born that way." She apologized. (Lozano then said he was) mad at (the) social worker. "(I) wonder why they did that (called Pilar) after (my) discharge (from McLean Hospital.)"

When I interviewed Williams, she confirmed the story about Paul chasing his brothers with a butcher's knife when he was four or five years old.

In February 1991, during his final hospitalization in El Paso, the records indicate that her brother was released into Williams's care on the condition that he reside with her.

But Lozano did not go home and live with his sister. I wondered why Williams had not met that crucial condition for her brother's release. In her deposition, Williams stated that he was taken to his own apartment where he lived alone in the retirement complex managed by his parents. His parents were the resident managers of Pilot House, a motel that had been converted into a retirement home. Lozano resided in a room about a hundred feet from his parents' unit.

Despite the many discrepancies in her deposition, I found Williams persuasive, charming, very quick witted, and spontaneous. I interviewed her in person and by phone for over twenty hours. She readily admitted when she was wrong and was willing to accept new information and amend, though not radically, her deeply held convictions about Bean-Bayog's culpability in her brother's death.

Williams told me something I already knew. She said that half way through her deposition her own lawyer interrupted her to inform her that she lacked a key bit of information. Williams had testified that she visited her brother during his first McLean hospitalization almost immediately after he had begun therapy with Bean-Bayog. Williams was, of course, mistaken. Williams visited him at McLean Hospital nearly a year, not immediately, after his therapy began. During that visit, in May 1987, she believed it was her brother's first hospitalization for mental illness, because Lozano refused to allow Bean-Bayog or the McLean staff to inform his family of his previous one. However, when Williams gave her deposition on July 7, 1992, it was fifteen months after her brother's death. The Process Notes had been handed to the Lozano's first attorney, Tom O'Hare, in early 1991. Subsequently, virtually all of Lozano's hospitalization records were amassed by O'Hare's replacement, Drew Meyer. Those hospitalization records, including Lozano's first stay at McLean Hospital, were included in the Offer of Proof. Pilar Williams had more than ample time to educate herself about the facts in her brother's case so that her opinions and convictions could be informed ones. However, at the time of her deposition, she still had no idea that her brother's first psychiatric hospitalization was in September 1986.

For me, this was a crucial bit of information. I began to realize that her unequivocal denunciations of Bean-Bayog were based on a sliver of information and an imprecise memory. She knew almost nothing about the documentary evidence. Her accusations were emotionally, not factually, based.

When I read to Williams some of the gentler excerpts from the Process Notes in which her brother recalled anecdotes of his childhood, Williams repeatedly exhorted, "What a liar, what a liar!" I was tempted to ask her if her brother was such a liar, couldn't he have been lying about having sex with Bean-Bayog? Also, she did not know that Dr. Harrison Pope, Lozano's world-renowned psychopharmacologist at McLean Hospital, had gone into business with her brother. When I told her, she exclaimed over and over, "What an idiot!"

Perhaps Williams's many discrepancies and confused temporal memory resulted from the need to suppress the possibility of her own or her family's part in her brother's suffering and death.

Williams told me that in the final two weeks of his life she had reached the breaking point with her brother's mental illness. She believed he could use the cold shower of reality. She claimed she was tired of hearing him repeat "Margaret, Margaret . . . I thought Margaret loved me . . . I just need my blankie and my Pound Puppy and I just need to curl up."

When I told her that Gault had reported in his deposition that on the day before her brother died, Lozano said that he had "stopped communicating with his family." Pained, Williams said, "Paul meant that he had stopped talking to me."

In the final two weeks of Lozano's life, an estrangement, borne of frustration, had developed between her and her brother. Nearly a year later, Williams admitted, she was having trouble visiting his grave, located several minutes from her home. She thinks of him when it snows. She sees frost on his subterranean face and it makes her shudder.

In the evening of April 1, 1991, Gault called Lozano in response to the many beeper messages from him earlier in the day. "Paul sounded revved up . . . admitted he had stopped taking his antidepressant medication . . . referred to his family as 'a bunch of jerks,' and denied being on cocaine," said Gault. Reading from his notes, Gault also reported that Paul:

> sounded manic, with pressured speech and a
> disinhibited expansive tone . . . he told me that
> he wasn't communicating with his family. I
> urged him to resume his lithium and his thora-
> zine, get back in touch with his psychiatrist and

resume contact with the family, particularly his
sister, Pilar. He did not sound at all depressed
when I spoke with him and certainly did not
raise the subject of suicide.

He didn't sound depressed or suicidal for a very simple reason:
Lozano was lethally high on cocaine. Gault admitted that: "I was
worried about his condition. In fact, I had the plan that I'd
probably try to reach Pilar Williams the next day, just to make
sure he was okay." The next day, of course, was too late. The
next day it was Williams who called Gault to report that her
brother was dead. Williams said she now understood why Gault
had sounded almost hysterical and so apologetic. Gault declined
to be interviewed for this book.

The night before Lozano died, he dined on Mexican stew with
his family and told them he'd be sleeping late. Then he returned
to his studio apartment at 7:30 P.M. Earlier that day, he had given
a sample for a urine toxicology to prove he was drug free.
Lozano had paged Gault all day. Finally, Gault returned the call.
Lozano, who had an appointment with him on April 2, probably
told him he would have to cancel the appointment because he
was staying in El Paso another month. Soon after talking to
Gault, Lozano took a shower. Then he spritzed himself with
Calvin Klein cologne.
Several years earlier, Bean-Bayog had recorded the following:

He then associated (his suicide) to his parents'
reaction. Furious, vengeful, chilling joy it would
mean to him to show all the people who had
admired him and told him he had it made who
had accepted the surface and ignored what it
cost him to produce it . . . (He would enjoy)
having the last laugh.

On the day Lozano injected himself seventy-five times with
cocaine, he chose to do so in the small complex where his parents

served as caretakers, in his own dingy room. Near the body, the police found a blood-stained bandage, a blood-stained rubber strap, and blood-stained gauze on the carpet and on his desk. While Lozano was in the middle of this rite of self-injection, there was a knock at the door at 9 P.M. It was Marcos. He had filled a prescription for his son, who, without opening the door, instructed his father to leave the package by the door. Lozano did not say good-bye.

Marcos discovered his son's body the following day at 1 P.M. When officer Esparza arrived at 1:40 P.M., emergency medical personnel were already on the scene, but could not revive Lozano. The police report stated, apparently without intending humor, that "The deceased showed no signs of life."

On the first day of the news coverage, the *Herald* had reported that Lozano "put on his best clothes and injected himself with a fatal dose of cocaine." That description is contradicted by the police color photos. They show Lozano, with his eyes and mouth half open, clad only in white blood-splattered jockey shorts. His right arm, from elbow to hand, was also covered with blood. There were drops of blood on the carpeted floor.

A couple of days later, the *Herald* quoted Williams: "He had everything (needle, injection bottles) laid out perfectly on his desk, just like a physician would. All of his medical books were lined up on his desk."

That too is contradicted by the police photographs, which show Lozano sitting dead in front of his desk. The desk is a mess, covered with bloody scrub brushes, bloody gauze, two open containers of blood, several syringes, several open and unopened ampules, and two molded styrofoam sections from a "double-decker anesthesia tray with epinephrine and lidocaine/epinephrine." Buried under the debris on the desk are two hard-bound volumes of *Internal Medicine*. There are three test tubes with Paul Lozano's name on them. One of them is filled with blood. There is a splotch of diluted blood on the wall above the desk, shot from a syringe. Lying scattered on the floor to the right of Lozano's body, seated at his desk, are several medical texts, an uneaten banana, and a Sony Walkman. One of the medical books is open; some of the text is highlighted in blue. Next to that is a brand-new Precor 614 rowing machine. Several years before, Lozano had told Bean-Bayog: "I have always used exercise to get myself out of depression and usually run up to twenty-four miles a week."

At 3:20 P.M., medical examiner Danny Flores pronounced Paul Anthony Lozano dead. His body was removed in a Ziegler bag. In a dresser drawer in Lozano's apartment, the family claimed to have found a baby "security" blanket and a stuffed bear in hospital garb, the same bear that Bean-Bayog is holding in one of the six photographs that Lozano took of her in her home office. The blanket or stuffed animal is not mentioned in any of the police reports or by any of the responding police officers that I interviewed.

Large quantities of Lithium and Haldol, two powerful psychotropic drugs prescribed by Lozano's local psychiatrist, were found in Lozano's bloodstream during his autopsy. The two are used in combination when a patient is out of control and truly a danger to himself. The levels of Haldol and Lithium in Lozano's bloodstream were near the maximum of their suggested therapeutic range. Also, when these drugs are used in combination, they can produce severe side effects, including irreversible brain damage and even death. Perhaps these prescribed drugs are what killed him. However, this is impossible to determine.

If Lozano was not bent on suicide, but was merely toying with injecting cocaine for the thrill of it, it is hardly likely that he could have accurately calculated the effect cocaine would have in combination with the massive doses of medication he was taking.

On the other hand, maybe it was suicide, but not for the reasons the family claimed. Perhaps the two powerful drugs swimming in Lozano's bloodstream conspired with the memory loss often associated with shock treatments to diminish his intellectual capacity.

When all of the drugs, the ECTs, the pressures of the administrative complaint and civil lawsuit, and his problems with clinical work are factored in, in the final analysis, it may have become impossible for Lozano ever to pass the National Boards. He may have sustained too much damage to function well in any demanding role.

Lozano was slated to take the two-day exam in Boston, from 8 A.M. to 5 P.M., on two consecutive days. He may have realized that he could not pass the exam, and would never become a doctor. In locations across the country, the two-day exam began on April 2, the very day Lozano killed himself[11]

Williams said that her mother, Epifania, viewed the $1 million dollar settlement the family later won as "a gift from my son. I feel at peace now. I know I will be safe and secure 'til I can be with him."

Yet the final blow may not have been that Lozano realized he would never pass the National Boards and hence never become a physician. Nor was it the prospect of facing Bean-Bayog, whom he may have falsely accused, at the medical board hearing or in civil court.

By chance, I discovered something else. It was something that made Lozano realize that his family's darkest secrets or his own most outrageous lies were about to go on public display.

---

11. ON THE OTHER HAND, LOZANO MAY HAVE DECIDED TO DELAY TAKING THE EXAM, WHICH WAS GIVEN AGAIN IN SEPTEMBER, 1991.

26

THE FINAL BLOW

In late January 1993, I was sitting in the lobby of the Marriott Hotel near the El Paso airport. Kareem Abdul Jabaar had just walked by. Pilar Williams and I hardly noticed him. She had just said something that stunned me.

If there was one theme that had recurred throughout Lozano's four years of psychotherapy with Bean-Bayog, it was that he was very protective of his parents. He wanted to buy them a house. He was going to be a doctor, not a lab researcher, because he would earn more and could then afford to support his parents in comfort. He told her repeatedly, "I didn't want to see my mom hurt. You'd have to be some sort of animal. I don't wanna see things hurt them, or [see them] ashamed."

Public exposure of the Process Notes would hurt and shame them profoundly. If the Process Notes became a court document, openly discussed in an investigation by the medical board and/or in the discovery process of civil litigation, Lozano's graphic descriptions of his mother's alleged sexual abuse would become public record. His family would be publicly humiliated, openly ridiculed, dishonored, and viewed with contempt—all because of him. Lozano could vehemently deny it. The family could vehemently deny it, too, claiming he fabricated it all or that Bean-Bayog had invented it. But there would be a cloud of doubt cast over the family's reputation. Had Lozano read the Notes?

I asked Williams again if she were absolutely certain. Williams insisted that in a phone call from Boston her brother said he had spent several hours reading them: "I know for a fact that O'Hare showed him the Process Notes. As soon as he got back to his apartment, Paul called me right after he saw those things. He was hysterical. He said, 'I read the notes. I'm so ashamed. I feel so dirty. It's very ugly, very ugly. I feel like I've been rolling around in mud.' He said, 'They're pretty horrible. I can't believe I'm the same person in those notes.' I kept telling him what's in there isn't important. 'Let's drop it,' I said."

Williams also claimed that after her brother's call, she contacted O'Hare right away and asked him, " 'What was it that you showed Paul that upset him so?' O'Hare said he showed him the records."

When I told Williams that O'Hare told me that he had never shown Lozano the Process Notes, she said, "He's lying. O'Hare's lying. That why the kid's dead . . . The greatest mistake was Mr. O'Hare showing him those Notes."

Someone is mistaken.

The first thing I did when I returned to Boston was to check the records. Bean-Bayog's letter to O'Hare warning him about showing Lozano his medical records is dated February 4, 1991. The letter reads:

> **Exposure of Mr. Lozano to the psychiatric material contained in his record may be harmful to his condition. It may increase his risk of harming himself or others. I would advise against disclosing this material to the client.**

Since Lozano flew back to El Paso on February 1, it seemed that Williams must have been mistaken. Lozano's Sun Valley Hospital records confirmed that the same day, February 1, he was hospitalized in the Sun Valley Regional Hospital. It would have been impossible for O'Hare to have shown Lozano the Process Notes, because he had received them after his client departed Boston for El Paso.

Bean-Bayog's letter did not sound like a cover letter, however. There was no notation in the letter of any "enclosures." Was this letter possibly sent as an afterthought?

I called Bean-Bayog immediately. She said she believed she had sent the letter after she sent the Process Notes to O'Hare, but wasn't sure. So, I called Blau. He said that the letter went out after she sent the Process Notes to O'Hare. In fact, Blau remembered asking her if she had sent the warning in a cover letter they had discussed. He said that Bean-Bayog said she had not. Then Bean-Bayog called me back. She checked her income-tax records and located a $357 receipt for photocopying. The receipt was dated January 26, 1991. She said, "Now I remember. I wanted to get rid of that stuff right away so I went to the post office and mailed it the same day to O'Hare." She said she mailed the Process Notes "priority mail" and paid cash. January 26 was a Saturday. O'Hare could have received it on Monday, January 28. Four days later, Lozano departed for El Paso.

Hence, if Williams's account is accurate, then her brother read the Process Notes just before his departure from Boston. This might explain why he was hospitalized in a psychiatric ward moments after he landed in El Paso. He would have read his own graphic descriptions of his mother having sex with him. Either those descriptions were true and Lozano was confessing a horrid family secret, or he was falsely accusing the woman who had nurtured and raised him. In either case, these passages would become part of the public court record. His parents would be exposed to ridicule. What's more, he may have falsely accused Bean-Bayog, his "nonabusive mom," of sexual abuse. And finally, he knew he would never become a physician. Lozano may have felt boxed in with no way out but one.

It didn't seem to me that Meyer or Fabiano could have proven that Bean-Bayog was responsible for Paul Lozano's death.

27

LINGERING DOUBTS

Notwithstanding Meyer's manipulations, Williams's contradictions, and Lozano's prevarications, I still had serious reservations about several claims of Bean-Bayog's.

The first was her 1984 drunk driving conviction.

In June 1984, she was stopped and arrested for drunk driving. She pled guilty and lost her license for thirty days. But there were extenuating circumstances, she told me, the press was never apprised of.

In 1984, she had just gotten married for the first time at the age of 41. Soon thereafter, several students were helping her move from her home in Brookline to her new home with her new husband and her new stepchildren in Lexington. It was a hot summer's day. She'd been perspiring a lot. One of the students went to get something to drink and returned with a refreshment. None of her students knew she was a recovering alcoholic. The student returned with several bottles of California Cooler. Bean-Bayog said she had never heard of the product. She had no idea it contained alcohol. Thirsty, she started drinking. She was thirstier than she realized. She had drunk a lot when she climbed into her heavily laden white Volkswagen Rabbit and headed to her new home in Lexington on the evening of June 22, 1984. Even though her blood alcohol was 1.9, she wasn't weaving. In what would be one of many mishaps of fate that would soon plague her, she was stopped by the Newton police for a minor infraction: failure to drive in the right-hand lane when available for travel, one of the most obscure and rarely enforced violations on the books. Realizing she was drunk, Patrolman Kenneth B. Donovan arrested her for driv-

ing while intoxicated. She said she decided not to fight the
case, because "nobody believes the stories that drunks tell."
As noted, she was fined $15, her license was automatically sus-
pended for thirty days, she was automatically assigned to a
Driver Alcohol Education Program, and she was placed on
two years' probation. She claimed that her lawyer told her the
conviction would be sealed, equivalent to a deletion from her
record. Obviously, a drunk driving conviction for an expert in
the field of alcoholism is an embarrassment, so she was delighted not to have to admit it on her medical license renewal
applications. Consequently, when she renewed her license to
practice medicine with the state medical board, she did not
check "yes" to the question, "Have you, at any time, been a
defendant in any criminal proceeding other than minor traffic
offenses?" Meyer cited this omission to impeach her credibility. The medical board had included this minor infraction
among its allegations against her. Bean-Bayog said that she
thought the case had been sealed and therefore did not have to
report it.

A blood-alcohol level of 1.9 is extremely high, nearly double
the legal limit. At some point, Bean-Bayog must have realized
she was becoming inebriated but kept drinking. In other words,
she was on a binge, then got into her car and began to drive, a
serious error in judgment. I suspect she was very anxious about
moving her belongings into her new home in which her two
young stepchildren considered her a usurper.

My father also had his doubts about her story. "I find it hard
to believe that someone so involved in alcohol problems would
not know that wine coolers contain alcohol," he said.

Earlier, while I was still covering the story for the *Globe,*
Meyer had advanced the theory that Bean-Bayog was not a
recovering alcoholic but an active one, prone to "alcoholic
blackouts," and that her drinking had "clouded her judgment"
in her treatment of Lozano. Her drunk-driving conviction was
one example. Meyer cited two others.

The first was a 1989 traffic accident for which she was at fault.
The second were the six photographs that Lozano shot of Bean-

Bayog in her office.[1] In two of them, she is posing "unprofession-ally."

First, I checked out the traffic accident.

In the early afternoon of June 5, 1989, Denise Dwelling and her 79-year-old friend, Hilda, were in a 1986 Nissan Stanza station wagon, returning from the high school graduation of Hilda's grandchild in Winchester. They were driving down Maple Street, the street that Bean-Bayog lives on, in Lexington. Coming from the opposite direction was Bean-Bayog in her white Toyota station wagon. She slowed down to turn into her driveway.

"Suddenly, she did a bizarre thing. Out of nowhere, she turned in front of me. I had one second," said Dwelling.

Dwelling's companion was not wearing her seat belt and she cracked the windshield with her head. She was bleeding badly from her forehead and elbow. All three were taken to the hospital for minor injuries. There was nearly $10,000 damage to Dwell-ing's and Bean-Bayog's vehicles.

"She said, 'I'm so sorry. I just didn't see you. I had a client I was late for and I just turned in.' I didn't think she was drinking. I would have been aware of it," Dwelling said, adding she is currently suing Bean-Bayog for whiplash.

Next, I looked into the six photographs. Meyer had told me that in her deposition, Bean-Bayog stated that she had no recol-lection of these controversial photographs, several of which had been shown in the original news broadcasts. It was one of the areas that Meyer covered in her deposition:

> Q. I show you a picture and ask you whether you recognize that picture?
> A. Yes.

---

1. THERE WAS A SEVENTH PHOTOGRAPH, INCLUDED AS AN "EXHIBIT" IN HER DEPOSI-TION, WHICH DID NOT FIND ITS WAY INTO THE RECORDS RELEASED BY THE MEDICAL BOARD. IT WAS A PHOTOGRAPH OF A BRUNETTE BEAN-BAYOG IN HER MID-20S. WITH OAR IN HAND, SHE IS SEATED IN THE BOW OF A CANOE LOOKING BACK SMILING AT THE PERSON TAKING THE PHOTOGRAPH. I CAME ACROSS THE PHOTOGRAPH IN THE BOX OF PAUL LOZANO MEMORABILIA THAT WILLIAMS KEEPS IN HER CLOSET. BEAN-BAYOG SAID THAT LOZANO MUST HAVE STOLEN IT TOO. WILLIAMS SAID THAT BEAN-BAYOG GAVE IT TO HIM.

Q. Tell me is that you in the picture?

A. Yes.

Q. Who took that picture?

A. I don't know.

Q. Do you know when it was taken?

A. No, I don't.

Q. Do you know where it was taken?

A. It's in my (home) office.

Q. Do you recognize the bear in the picture?

A. Yes.

Q. What do you recognize about this bear?

A. The bear is the bear that he had given me for Christmas . . .

Q. Do you take medication, by the way, Doctor?

A. I beg your pardon?

Q. Do you take medication?

A. No . . .

Q. Do you have any problems with your memory? . . . Did you use to have a memory problem?

A. No . . .

Q. Just so we're clear for the record. You have no memory of these pictures that have been marked ever having been taken at any time, is that right, by anybody?

A. That's right.

Of the six photographs, two of the poses appear unsettling. In one, Bean-Bayog is cuddling a teddy bear dressed in a doctor's garb. In another, she has her thumbs in her ears with her fingers splayed and is playfully sticking her tongue out.[2]

Later, Meyer asked Bean-Bayog,

---

2. I THINK IF THIS PARTICULAR PHOTOGRAPH HAD BEEN PUBLISHED IN THE FIRST DAY OR TWO OF MEDIA COVERAGE, IT WOULD HAVE DAMAGED BEAN-BAYOG EVEN MORE. PERHAPS IN AN UNCONSCIOUS AND COLLECTIVE DISPLAY OF RESTRAINT, NO LOCAL NEWSPAPER OR TV STATION EVER RAN IT. THE LOS ANGELES TIMES, HOWEVER, DID ON APRIL 8.

> Q. Would you consider the demeanor as por-
> trayed in that photograph appropriate de-
> meanor for a therapist during a therapy
> session?
> A. No.

Bean-Bayog, who has an exuberant and animated personality, said she was horsing around because Lozano had shown her that the camera was empty.

"The question that Meyer asked was do I remember [Lozano] taking my picture? What I did not say to them, because my lawyers told me to answer the questions precisely and not do anything more than that, was that he came in with a camera, showed me that it had no film in it. And was playing around with it. So when Meyer asked me if I remember his taking my picture, the answer is 'no.' So if he's says I'm lying or I must have been drunk at the time, he's wrong. There's another explanation that Meyer didn't think of or asked me about."

She said that after Lozano showed her that the camera had no film in it, he pretended to be taking her photo, clicking the shutter, advancing the film. She playfully posed. She said that either he switched cameras or when she got up to get a drink of water (which she sometimes did whenever I interviewed her), he slipped a roll of film into the camera.

In the turbulent fall of 1987, Lozano did express a desire to take her photograph and record her voice. About a month before her three-week Christmas vacation to the Philippines, she recorded in the Process Notes:

> Also expressed some terrible sadness about my going (on vacation) . . . (He) wanted a tape of (my) voice. "You wouldn't approve. (I) have to bring in small recorder or bring camera." "Psychiatrists don't do that," (Bean-Bayog said). We discuss taping (the children's story) *Goodnight Moon.*"

But the photographs were definitely not taken just before her Christmas vacation but had to have been shot between the months of May and September, because in one of them the trees outside her office window have green leaves. Nonetheless, the poses in the photographs, even if Bean-Bayog thought there was no film in the camera, are inappropriate and unprofessional.

In preparation for her 1987 vacation, she composed six short stories: "Restless," "Morning," "Cookies," "Fishing," "Pie," and "Shots." Each was handwritten by a "mother" to her "baby." Their intention was to comfort Lozano, if he became suicidal, during her absence. She wrote out seventeen letters in advance to be opened one day at a time. I find some of their content a little provocative.

For example, in "Restless," she wrote:

> You can't sleep. You are restless. I come. I never hit you. I pick you up and hold you. We walk up and down in the moonlight. You have a drink of water . . . You have your legs around my waist. Your head is on my shoulder. You can feel my body, smell me . . . You can hear me breathing, and my heartbeat. My body is soft and warm against yours. You like the feeling. You are calmer but you don't want to go to sleep . . .

One of the letters, dated December 21, is also a bit unsettling:

> This drives me *nuts*. I miss you. I want everything to be fine, but I also want to *know* what's happening. I miss all of you. I want to protect you in case your parents are tricky. Try this: think of them as if *they* are 3-years-old. it makes it easier to tolerate them, and they're less threatening . . .

But then she wrote in a December 27 letter:

And I hope you aren't hurting and hating yourself. I hope Pilar is on your side. When she is I
always want to send her love too. And here's
some for you. Love, Dr. B.

Though tremendous controversy swirls around whether
"recovered memories" of childhood incest need to be unlocked
by therapists or have been induced by them, Bean-Bayog said she
believed that Lozano's already existing state of regression and
his sadomasochistic sexual fantasies toward her suggested
strongly that he had been abused by his mother.[3] Perhaps Bean-
Bayog is correct or perhaps there were other causes for this
behavior. The first time Bean-Bayog advanced this theory to
Lozano was when she shared with him the Dr. Alayne Yates
article on childhood incest. In fact, Bean-Bayog told me she used
this article as a "road map" in his treatment. Many aspects of
this story resonate in Yates's article: an intense relationship did
develop between doctor and patient; Bean-Bayog's countertransferences were fierce; she did not suppress them but instead ven-
tilated them by writing them down; Lozano tried every strategy
to seduce her; he did indeed eventually accuse her of sexual
misconduct; and finally, millions of people believed him.

Yates, who had read news accounts of the lawsuit against
Bean-Bayog but didn't know her and had never spoken to her,
told me that the hypothesis of childhood sexual abuse bore more

---

3. AT THE THIRTY-SEVENTH ANNUAL MEETING OF THE AMERICAN ACADEMY OF PSY-
CHOANALYSIS IN SAN FRANCISCO IN 1993, A SEMINAR WAS HELD ON "THE EROTI-
CIZED TRANSFERENCE: TOOL FOR THE RECONSTRUCTION OF CHILDHOOD SEXUAL
TRAUMA." DR. TERESA BERNARDEZ, THE FACULTY AND SUPERVISING ANALYST WITH
THE MICHIGAN PSYCHOANALYTIC COUNCIL, STATED THAT EROTICIZED TRANSFER-
ENCE SHOULD BE SEEN AS AN INDICATION OF POSSIBLE SEXUAL TRAUMA. "THE
ANALYST HAS TO NEITHER DISCOURAGE NOR SATISFY THE PATIENT'S DESIRES WHILE
MAINTAINING A CLOSE CHECK ON HIS OR HER REACTIONS AND FANTASIES," SHE
SAID. "THE ABILITY OF THE ANALYST TO STAY IN CONNECTION WITH THE PATIENT
WITHOUT FEARING THE INVOLVEMENT AND WITHOUT REJECTING IN HERSELF OR THE
PATIENT THE MATERIAL THAT TELLS THE STORY OF THE ASSAULT IS REWARDED WITH THE
RECAPTURE OF THE PAST."

validity if first advanced by the patient, less so if advanced by the therapist. On the other hand, Bean-Bayog's hypothesis was predicated on her expert understanding of emotional disorders, fifteen years' experience with troubled patients, and a thorough knowledge of the patient. She did not contact the Lozanos directly because her patient expressly forbade her to.

Then, in passing, Yates mentioned something startling: It is common for rural Mexican mothers to pacify their infant sons by massaging the penis. Lozano's mother, Epifania, comes from a rural Mexican background. Her parents were migrant farm workers. I related this bit of cultural arcana to my father who, in turn, related it to a colleague working with patients suffering from deep psychological conflicts. The colleague said he was not surprised to hear it. He had recently taken into treatment a Mexican-American woman who, for reasons she could not yet articulate, would never allow her own Mexican mother to be alone with her child. As a matter of fact, this patient said her feelings were so powerful that she had advised her sister not to leave her young children alone with their grandmother either.

The infusion of American standards on rural Mexican practices may have complicated Lozano's response, because there is absolutely no evidence to suggest that the rural Mexican male population has a higher rate of deep psychological disturbances than others.

It is possible that Lozano was indeed sexually abused by his mother. Or, in the migration from one culture (Mexican) to another (American), Lozano may have concluded on his own or with Bean-Bayog's encouragement that he had been sexually abused by his mother. Or his mother may have continued the rural Mexican practice of penis pacification longer—perhaps much longer—than culturally appropriate. Or none of the above.

Did Bean-Bayog's speculations about Lozano's childhood incest ferret out these memories or create them? No one will ever know.

I also had misgivings over several ambiguous passages in the Process Notes. So I read to Bean-Bayog the following passage from August 21, 1987:

"Only three year olds get to play like this with their moms."

"Sexual games?"

"—" (He began) hyperventilating.

Gave (him) bag to rebreathe. Explained what was going on. Made sense out of my experience. He and I were in the middle of a perversion, like how the love between him or a baby and his mother got distorted, destroyed, twisted, poisoned by her molesting and abusing him. That was what he felt was happening and I had parallel experience, raw, overwhelming, him molesting me, *me molesting him* (emphasis added); shared mother-child incest fantasy: pretty raw, but that's what (I) think she did; Patient agitated, aroused, furious, regressed. "I don't remember. I don't want to remember." (He) fell *asleep.* (I) woke him: too much to deal with at once, but this is the stuff that's making you suicidal, that got you into McLean, that repeated the abuse by his mother. As much as he can stand, we have to understand it. Hyperventilation. "I don't remember. I don't remember what you said." Maybe just as well. "Don't leave me." Panicky. Hard to end session. Took several transitional objects. Planned check ins.

I asked her if she ever discussed her own countertransference fantasies with Lozano. She said she would never commit such a therapeutic blunder.

"I think a lot of the time the stuff I am writing down is my countertransference experience, but is not the stuff I am actually verbalizing, so just because I wrote it down, doesn't mean I said it to him . . . Sometimes what I put in parentheses is something I've said, sometimes it isn't. Sometimes I don't put parentheses, sometimes I do. I was writing down this stuff as fast as I could. But there are a couple of times I write down that I am very angry with him, but I'm not telling him that . . . I can't imagine ever saying anything like that to him, just writing it down and thinking it. But there was a lot of stuff that I was explaining to him with the mother-child fantasy."

"Who wrote the mother-child fantasy?" I asked.

"I wrote a chart for him of the parallels. The mother-child fantasy was about the fact that there was a similar experience in every single one of these projected transference experiences—the one he had toward Frankenburg, the one he had toward one of his teachers in the third grade, the one he had toward me, the one he reported toward a series of teachers in college, the one he had toward this person, toward that person. What I did was pick out the situations where he used language that was similar to what he eventually described was going on in his relationship with his mother. And so the mother-child fantasy I don't exactly remember exactly what was in it, but what it said was, 'Look, there's a parallel going on here. What you're coming on to me with comes from someplace and you have it with a lot of other people.'"

Next, I asked Bean-Bayog the question that had most troubled me and others, including members of her own defense team. How was it possible for Lozano to steal her sexual fantasies in early November 1987 and for her not to know it.

On April 15, the *Herald* ran a story, claiming that Bean-Bayog's Notes from the November 27, 1987, suggested that she knew Paul Lozano had stolen her sexual fantasies and implied that she was lying. The *Herald* article reported:

> But when Bean-Bayog realized Lozano had taken at least one of her fantasies, she wrote that the two discussed it: "Proceeded as in fantasy . . . would have me in a device like stirrups . . . reveled in control. Cold sadistic pleasure in turning me on and then hurting me. Sometimes in restraints on the floor as in fantasy."
>
> In the therapy notes Bean-Bayog also wrote, "spent last part of session reviewing the fan-

tasy . . . with the *alternation between torturing
me and turning me on."* (Emphasis added.)

At the *Globe* we wondered if we should run the story too, but
decided not to, because there was too much ambiguity about
which fantasy she was referring to. Nevertheless, it gnawed at me
for a long time. I later realized the *Herald* may have missed a key
correspondence between the recitation of Lozano's fantasy during the November 20 therapy session and Bean-Bayog's own
sexual fantasies.

She recorded that he stated: "I'd touch you everywhere, running my hands all over, turning you on again and then I'd just
enter you thrusting you against the wall, and explosively come."

Her sexual fantasies conclude: "Then, at last, not caring, you
begin to move in and out fast, hard, hurling yourself against me,
harder and harder, until finally both of us explosively come and
come and come."

I asked her if the coincidence of this phrase "explosively
come" suggested that he had possession of her sexual fantasies.

Bean-Bayog said it did not suggest to her that Lozano had her
fantasies because "explosively coming was something he talked
about all the time . . . When he started with this stuff, it was
overwhelming to me and I did not write the details down . . .
Then I got more comfortable with [hearing] it and that's when I
started taking more notes on it and I had thought about it and
I was much more oriented about it and I was talking to people
about it and all that, so the other thing is that . . . his mother . . .
does the same thing, I mean, she alternately hurts him and loves
him. That's what was getting transferred on to me . . . This kind
of talk is not a part of my shtick. I don't talk like this."

I listened and pondered what she had said. Her sexual fantasies were a reflection of his. Therefore, images, such as alternat-
ing between torture and arousal, and phrases, such as
"explosively come," would appear in both. True, the psychiatric
literature supported her claim that a psychotherapist does have
reciprocal countertransferences, including love, hate, and jeal-
ousy, toward a patient, which are reactions to the patient's transference, hence "countertransference."

I concluded that I was entering a realm where the evidence was becoming impossibly muddled—and certainly not provable in court. If Bean-Bayog's countertransference fantasies were a reflection of Lozano's sadomasochistic fantasies, her language and images would naturally be similar to his. Therefore, the one he expressed on November 20, after the break-in, would naturally be expected to sound like hers, whether he had stolen her fantasies or not earlier that month. For it to be clear and convincing that Lozano's theft of her sexual fantasies is reflected in the fantasy he spouted out on November 20, there would have to be astounding similarities in language and image; and Bean-Bayog would have to recognize those similarities enough to realize that he was, in effect, mimicking her own fantasies.

When she heard and wrote down "alternation between torturing and turning me on," she said she was simply referring to his archetypical fantasy that she had heard him repeat over the past several months.

"What would you have done if you had discovered he had stolen your countertransference fantasies?"

"Oh, I almost certainly would have had to terminate with him. I would have to have hospitalized him and gotten consultations, but I can't imagine—. See, the other possibility that is in my mind is that he got the fantasies later; there's a chance that he's the one who could have burglarized our house in the spring of '90 and that in a way makes more sense to me."

"Except how could he have made copies? He would have had to break in twice."

"The same way he did everything. He was very smooth with that stuff. It would have been easy to break in. He knew when I was out of town. He knew when we were away, because he was told. And he knew how to reach me. So he could have easily called to confirm I wasn't home. Called me where I was to make sure I was away."

"Just to repeat, if you had known that he had stolen your sexual fantasies in the fall of 1987, you would have terminated with him.

"I can't imagine that he could have worked with me. If he had them, then I don't understand why he didn't kill me. Because if he had gotten his hands on that stuff, to him what it would have been would be the most profound betrayal. It would have meant that everything I had told him during the whole therapy, which was there was a safe mom who would never, ever do anything abusive to him, and that he saw me as representing it [would be false]. It would mean that once he had begun to trust me that this person he had begun to trust, who had said she would never abuse him, had turned out to be just like his mom and would have raped him—in fantasy, but definitely on paper and he would have been enraged. If he had that stuff, I don't see how he could have worked with me . . . When I found out he had that stuff, I said, 'Oh, my God. I'm lucky I wasn't killed. I may be killed now.' Seriously, I called the Lexington police and tried to get a restraining order when I found out, because I knew when he was talking about suing people he was also homicidal. I am incredibly lucky he didn't kill me. Incredibly lucky. He had reasons. That stuff is a rape, that's a verbal rape from the one person he believed was never going to rape him. So what makes sense to me clinically is that he stole it in the spring of '90, when he was being hospitalized and discharged a lot. I mean, we didn't know the date of the break-in, because there was no evidence of it. It wasn't like we came home and the window was broken and there were dirty footprints over the floor. There was a bunch of jewelry missing from three different places in the house from three different people's rooms.

"And where was all the Paul Lozano stuff?"

"In my office."

"He had the discharge summary and the mother-child fantasy for a whole year?"

"Yup."

"That's a long time. Wow."

"Yup"

"How did you feel about that? Why'd you tolerate that?"

"I had given him the mother-child fantasy earlier, and he could have gotten the discharge summaries legally from McLean. I didn't know it was going to be such a big deal."

28

REFLECTIONS

There were times when Bean-Bayog doubted herself. During our interviews she occasionally wondered about the degree to which she might actually be responsible for Paul Lozano's disastrous end and her own misfortunes. She wondered whether her character or background, or some unanalyzed aspect of her behavior, had affected Lozano badly and, at the same time, created in her an unconscious desire to destroy herself. She even wondered whether she had indeed provoked Lozano sexually, however unintentionally. She knew that he had tried his best to sexualize their therapy sessions, and she acknowledged the powerful countertransference that she had expressed in her sexual fantasies. She seemed to worry most, however, about things that might have escaped her notice. The nearly thousand pages of Process Notes, which she had scribbled down to prevent just such an oversight, may not have been sufficient. The many formal and informal consultations, Lozano's admissions to hospitals, the extra time and energy may not have been enough. On the other hand, perhaps the very fact that she committed herself to extraordinary efforts on Lozano's behalf may have been too much, may have reached obsessional proportions. As my father had told her, she may have been guilty of trying too hard, hardly a reprehensible sin, but one with appalling consequences for her.

She had risked unusual, creative, and therefore controversial tactics. Her admittedly chancy use of the flash cards, her decision to stick with her patient even though she knew he was dangerous and manipulative, her struggle with her own countertransferences, in which she internalized the language and structure of Lozano's sexual obsessions, all left questions, not only for her accusers, but for her as well. Removed from the heat of the lurid context crafted by Drew Meyer, these might be approached rationally, but never fully resolved in her own mind and in others.

One thing is clear. Paul Lozano remained alive while in her care. He did not survive a year after he left it.

Nonetheless, there could be no definitive answers. Lozano had allegedly committed suicide ten months after leaving Dr. Bean-Bayog's care, after he had come under the supposedly scientific eyes of biological psychiatrists, one of whom favored repeated electroconvulsive treatments, several hospital admissions, and a return to his family environment. Meyer and Williams had condemned Bean-Bayog both for her therapeutic involvement and for its termination. While Bean-Bayog did not accept the substance of these charges, she compulsively reviewed her fatal entanglement with Lozano looking for subtler reasons for their mutual mischance and for the faint possibility that another course of action might have led to happier results.

There were no evil players in this drama, only fallible ones. Drew Meyer may appear in this book as particularly aggressive but actually he was just "doing his job." He was in the business of winning dollars for himself and his client. His reputation and financial well-being depend on victories, not high-minded scruples. Meyer acted in a sleazy moral climate, exploited the media and even took advantage of the all too easily accepted, ritual of hiring well-paid "experts" to support whatever position the task-master-of-the-moment wishes them to promote. What fuels the whole circus is profit, not truth seeking. Competition for dollars and status—one that exists as much among the contending factions within psychiatry as it does in the newspaper, TV, and legal professions—is the great engine that drives the spectacles that entertain millions of people in their living rooms and bedrooms. The watchwords for those who want to avoid trouble and controversy have to be "Keep your head down" and "Cover your ass." Bean-Bayog did neither, especially the latter.

Although I was astonished to learn that Williams, who spoke so assertively and eloquently to reporters, knew next to nothing about the details of her brother's therapy, and was, in the end, not really all that interested in learning more. I no longer wonder why. The lawsuit gave Williams a wide platform to express her family's honor. An unmarried pregnancy, the financial failure and penury of her parents, Lozano's failure at West Point and his multiple admissions in mental hospitals provoked shame and humiliation in a Mexican-American family. Her indignation and the million-dollar settlement that "proved" the family was right allowed Williams to bring the trophy of family honor home again. Williams struck out at Bean-Bayog to win, and win Williams did. Paul Lozano also won. Not only did his suffering end, but he gave his parents in death what he was unable to give them in life: financial security.

Meyer, the perfect choice for Williams, was the instrument of those victories. He pursued his quarry with a certain intelligence and shrewdness. The results of the case seem to bear out that he was a superb tactician, because he managed to force a settlement without risking a judgment on the merits of his case. By blitzing the willing houses of information—TV and newspapers—and applying sudden, unexpected pressure on the skittish medical board, Meyer was able to make the determinants of his case not the careful deliberation of a complex legal issue, but the glare of unwanted publicity. And publicity is the lifeblood that circulates in the veins of the media.

Meyer's reward for his good work is more publicity (of the sought-after kind), interviews from admiring reporters who seek expert opinion about medical malpractice law, and, presumably, a growing legal practice. In the context of an adversary system that records winners and losers, profit and loss, Meyer is not only blameless but praiseworthy.

The press is equally "blameless." The First Amendment guarantees its right to print what it sees fit. The rhythm of news gathering and publication militates strongly against adequate representation of complex issues. Reporters must write "history on the run." There is no time to delve into the whirl of details and concepts requiring months of painstaking research on a breaking story whose deadline is only moments away.

In the early days of the story, several female reporters at the *Globe* did raise the issue of sexual backlash. Was a woman being

treated differently from a man? They asked why male psychotherapists accused of sexual misconduct hadn't been given
equally prolonged front-page exposure? The *Globe*'s ombuds-
man, Gordon McKibben, wrote, "[I]t is inconceivable that coverage would have been any less if genders were reversed in this
tragic case, given the serious charges and access to relevant medical records." Metro editor Bradlee defended the coverage for
several reasons. This was a "Man Bites Dog Story." In other
words, news focuses on the unusual. No female physician had
ever been publicly accused of sexually exploiting a male patient.
Also, there was abundant evidence in her own handwriting,
which seemed to support the allegations. Finally, a patient had
died. No deaths had resulted in the recently reported cases involving sexual abuse of female patients by male therapists. Bradlee agreed that the first few days of coverage in large measure
reflected the Lozanos' sensational allegations, but then, "We
leaned over backward to make sure her [side of the story] was
reported."

Despite many phone calls and letters to the newspaper, the
Globe waited nineteen days after the initial news broke, an
unusual delay in a controversial story, to run the first "letter to
the editor." A remarkably astute, but anonymous, letter was sent
to editor-in-chief Jack Driscoll on April 14. It could not be
published because it was unsigned:

> I am writing to express the conviction that
> human decency, if there is any left at the
> *Globe* . . . call(s) for you to publicly apologize
> at length . . . for your misconduct in reporting of
> the Lozano/Bean-Bayog case . . . The human
> cost of your behavior is incalculable.
>
> I am repelled by your sensationalized report-
> ing and your relentless, strident attack on Dr.
> Bean-Bayog's character and competence. She
> is right to characterize the voyeuristic, vindictive
> hounding nature of the attention the case has
> received as the continuing "rape" of her repu-
> tation . . .

For example, why did you have no front-page (or even back-page) continuous daily coverage of the story involving Frederick (J.) Duhl, the Boston psychiatrist recently named in the *New York Times* as (allegedly) having sexually abused the poet Anne Sexton (who committed suicide in 1974)?[1] For another example, why did you not give major coverage to Harold Goldberg, the Boston psychiatrist who recently lost his license for having (allegedly) sexually abused a client. For still more examples, why did the cases of client abuse made against local therapist Sheldon Zigelbaum, Edward Daniels, and Richard Ingrasci[2] cause not much more than a few ripples at the *Globe*? Where were the half-page photo spreads of them? Why does only Dr. Bean-Bayog rate this tabloid treatment? . . .

You have served not the public's need or right to know, but only our taste for blood and scandal—the basest desires to pry, be titillated, and see the powerful and successful brought down.

---

1. DR. DUHL WAS SEXTON'S PSYCHOTHERAPIST IN THE LATE 1960S. HE ALLEGEDLY HAD SEX WITH HER IN THERAPY. AT THE SAME TIME, HE BILLED HER FOR THERAPY AS WELL. A PSYCHIATRIST WHO KNEW OF THE PURPORTED AFFAIR DID NOT DENOUNCE DUHL TO THE STATE MEDICAL BOARD, BECAUSE "I DIDN'T WANT TO RUIN (HIS) CAREER." IN A BRIEF INTERVIEW WITH THE *NEW YORK TIMES* IN 1990, DUHL, WHO STILL PRACTICES FAMILY THERAPY IN BOSTON, SAID, "I AM NOT GOING TO COMMENT. YOU ARE DEALING WITH AN EXPLOSIVE SUBJECT: BASICALLY ANY DOCTOR WHO HAS AN AFFAIR WITH A PATIENT LOSES HIS LICENSE IN MASSACHUSETTS." NO ONE KNOWS, EXCEPT DUHL, WHETHER HE HAD ACTUALLY PERFORMED SEXUAL ACTS WITH SEXTON, AND IF SO, WHETHER THESE ACTS CONTRIBUED TO HER SUICIDE IN 1974. WHEN I ASKED A TOP OFFICIAL AT THE MEDICAL BOARD ABOUT IT, HE SAID THE BOARD DID LOOK INTO THE ALLEGATIONS BUT COULD NOT PROSECUTE THE CASE, BECAUSE DUHL DENIED THE CHARGES, THE PATIENT WAS DEAD, AND THIS WAS THE ONLY ALLEGATION OF SEXUAL MISCONDUCT AGAINST HIM, A DESCRIPTION ALMOST IDENTICAL TO THAT OF BEAN-BAYOG.
2. BECAUSE PSYCHOTHERAPISTS NEED NOT BE LICENSED IN MASSACHUSETTS, SOME PSYCHIATRISTS WHO HAVE LOST THEIR MEDICAL LICENSES CONTINUE TO PRACTICE PSYCHOTHERAPY, INCLUDING ZIGELBAUM AND DANIELS. DR. GOLDBERG IS CURRENTLY LICENSED AND PRACTICING IN HAWAII.

You had it in your power not to deal with the
abuse theme by becoming abusive. Instead
you became an abuser and victimizer. Sadly,
your performance in reporting this case seems
to confirm just how mean our society has
become . . .

For many months, perhaps because I was feeling guilty about
my involvement in the initial coverage of the story, I wanted to
believe that Bean-Bayog's gender was narrowly relevant only
because female psychotherapists rarely, if ever, sexually abuse
male patients.[3] What's more, the story did have all the riveting
elements: lurid sadomasochistic sex, perversion at Harvard, class
and race exploitation, psychiatry and suicide. But after spending
so long studying this story, I began to doubt it. One of the
thickest documents in my extensive Bean-Bayog library was the
400-plus-page tome of news stories on the subject. Would we
have written so prolifically if Bean-Bayog had been a man? Or if
her alleged victim had been a woman?

Our culture's mythology, literature and popular entertain-
ments are filled with Eves, Sirens, and Delilahs who use their
powerful and mysterious sexual powers to weaken further the
already weak, naive men and lead them to their destruction. In
a society still dominated by men and, more importantly in this
case, masculine perceptions of the world, Bean-Bayog as destructive seducer provided a too seductive image for the press to
ignore. It should be remembered also that, except for Amy
Stromsten, all the medical and legal accusers were men. Certainly, all the professional actors who had any real power—the
psychiatrists: Drs. Gault, Pope, Strasburger (Meyer's expert wit-

---

3. A 1990 SURVEY OF 10,000 FAMILY PRACTITIONERS, INTERNISTS, OBSTETRICIAN-GYN-
CECOLOGISTS, AND SURGEONS (BUT NOT PSYCHIATRISTS), CONDUCTED BY THE UNI-
VERSITY OF CALIFORNIA AT SAN FRANCISCO, FOUND THAT OF THE 1,891 PHYSICIANS
(19 PERCENT) WHO RESPONDED ANONYMOUSLY, 164 MEN AND 12 WOMEN ADMIT-
TED TO HAVING SEXUAL RELATIONS WITH PATIENTS. HENCE, NEARLY 7 PERCENT WERE
FEMALE PHYSICIANS. THE SURVEY DID NOT DETERMINE, HOWEVER, THE GENDER OF
THE PATIENTS SEXUALLY ABUSED BY THEIR FEMALE PHYSICIANS.

ness), and McHugh;[4] and the lawyers: Blau, O'Hare, Meyer, Connolly, Tierney, Fleming, Waring, and Fabiano—were all men. In the climate of extreme sensitivity about the number of men who abuse women, the opportunity to turn the tables on a woman also provided special animus against the accused.

Finally, an interesting aspect of this story involves the kinds of stories that it produced. The dominant story is the one I have been trying to outline: the bad, seductive mother contaminates the innocent boy. There is another story that has run alongside this one, however. This story narrates the fate of a working-class boy from a Hispanic family, who came to Harvard on scholarship only to be abused and driven to suicide by a powerful member of a powerful elite institution. Even worse, the institution and its minions conspired to hush up the case until Lozano's sister and a lawyer with no Harvard connections caused justice to be done. In a way, this story is even more scurrilous than the first, because it uses race and class as ploys to construct a melodramatic cautionary tale, while retaining the scandal of the mother-boy plot. It also masks a far more interesting aspect of the case than any supposed class discrimination. The reality is that Bean-Bayog was far from a powerful member of the Harvard establishment. She was merely one of approximately 9,000 physicians nominally connected to the medical school as an "assistant clinical professor."[5] The divisions within this institution are severe and endemic. Bean-Bayog was attacked primarily by Harvard-trained doctors, who for their own reasons, wished to demonstrate that the group to which she belonged lacked the serious scientific rigor of biological psychiatry. It is true, of

4. A FEMALE PSYCHIATRIST AND COLLEAGUE OF BEAN-BAYOG'S AT CAMBRIDGE HOSPITAL TOLD ME THAT PSYCHIATRY IS THE ONE AREA OF MEDICINE IN WHICH MALE PSYCHIATRISTS FEEL THE MOST THREATENED BY THEIR FEMALE COUNTERPARTS, BECAUSE OF THE BELIEF THAT FEMALES HAVE A MORE NATURAL INTUITION AND EMPATHY AND THEREFORE MAKE BETTER PSYCHOTHERAPISTS. IN FACT, MALE PSYCHIATRISTS ARE USED TO PERCEIVING WOMEN AS DEPENDENTS BECAUSE THE MAJORITY OF THEIR CLIENTS ARE WOMEN.
5. AT THE TIME THE CHARGES WERE LEVELED AGAINST BEAN-BAYOG, SHE WAS A PART-TIME, UNSALARIED FACULTY MEMBER.

course, that talk therapy is more an art than a science, that the uncertainties of human behavior and emotion cannot be wholly accounted for by any psychodynamic theory, and that the predictive or curative power of psychoanalysis and its heirs are far from perfect. It is also true that standards of practice in psychotherapy are notoriously difficult to define, sexual transgression being one act that seems to count as a definite abuse.

The trouble is that biological psychiatry is an infant science. Drug therapies have worked wonders for some who are afflicted with major mental illnesses, especially depression and manic-depressive illness. Much drug treatment is still not much better than a trial-and-error process. Drugs sometimes "manage" mental illness, but the streets and hospitals are full of people who, for one reason or another, have found no wonders in drug therapy. At the present time, psychotropic drugs can count only as crude remedies for many serious mental illnesses. The astonishing lack of insight into Paul Lozano's behavior exhibited by Gault and Pope do not necessarily follow from the fact that they practiced somatic therapies rather than long-term close and intricate talk therapy, but their testimony does not increase one's confidence in their acumen. McHugh dismissed whole areas of psychotherapy with a wave of his medical expertise, but he, a Harvard-trained physician himself, has apparently spent little time on the therapeutic turf of those he dismisses. McHugh's "eleven violations" shows no evidence that he recognizes the difference between condemning a way of doing psychotherapy practiced by great numbers of therapists and the particular activities of one, Dr. Margaret Bean-Bayog. As a result, those "eleven violations" reads very much like a tract against certain accredited psychotherapeutic practices forced to do service as a description of a departure from "standards." He uses his role as expert witness to promulgate theories he had developed, but presents them as established fact. Moreover, he uses a legal forum where the judges are incompetent to make that distinction. At least Jack Fabiano seemed entirely unschooled in understanding the implications of McHugh's views.

Beneath the stories of the seductive mother and her boy, or the upper-class shrink and the abused Hispanic "genius," lies a more hidden narrative, hidden because it involves professional differences within a supposedly monolithic institution that protects its own. In fact, the institution known as Harvard University is a collection of jealousies, rivalries, intrigue, and degrees of exclusion. Members of the psychiatric profession, in particular, are in conflict much more than they are in harmony. Bean-Bayog got caught in the crossfire of professional and sexual politics every bit as much as she was wounded by Drew Meyer's body blows. If there is a cautionary tale in all of this, it is too general to be of much use within the constraints of moral fables.

The medical and civil issues never saw their way to a legal and legally contested resolution. Even if they had, I doubt that the serious human problems they represent for psychiatric medicine would have received much help. I also doubt that, given the rebuttals carefully prepared by Michael Blau, Bean-Bayog could not have been found guilty of more than minor, if any, infractions. Of course, the medical board was under intense pressure to find her guilty or else face more unwelcome political pressure. The same is true of Drew Meyer's civil case. There is always a chance a jury will find against a doctor, especially if the plaintiffs can elicit sympathy. Meyer's tactics, though, seemed geared to push through to a settlement without trial. So, Bean-Bayog may have had a strong defense, but once she came up against the public pressure from an excited and provocative media and the crushing economic burden of trying to defend herself, she knew the battle was over. She knew she could not win.

EPILOGUE

When the bankrupted Marcos Lozano fled Upper Sandusky in November 1979, he left behind a few loose ends. In 1978, he sold a house on Edgewood Drive for $32,000 to Roger and Judith Sears under an arrangement called a "land installment contract." Essentially, the seller holds title to the property until the mortgage is paid off, then delivers the title "free and clear of all liens and encumbrances." After making a $3,000 downpayment and promising to pay the loan across twenty years at 8 percent per annum, the Searses moved in. In September 1985, they decided to discharge the remaining balance and sent Marcos a certified check for about $23,000. In return they asked for what he had promised: a clean deed. Unfortunately, Marcos couldn't deliver it, because the Edgewood Drive property had become heavily encumbered by state and federal tax liens. The Searses hired attorney Richard Grafmillan, who also serves as the Wyandot County prosecutor. He filed a lawsuit against Marcos Lozano. Grafmillan mentioned that he occasionally used to work with Pilar Williams when she was a home investigator for Children's Services.

"Mr. Lozano did not use the money [he received from the Searses] to pay off the liens. He just put it in his pocket and ignored the subsequent lawsuit," Grafmillan said.

Infuriated, the Searses had to pay off Marcos Lozano's liens and, at additional expense, decided to obtain a "foreign judgment" against Marcos in El Paso, Texas, for $63,817.21. The Lozanos were judgment-proof, however. They had no assets to attach and probably never would.

On December 16, 1992, however, a miracle occurred. The estate of Paul Lozano won a million-dollar, tax-free settlement in a lawsuit filed in faraway Boston. Initially, Marcos had been the administrator of his son's estate, but upon the advice of counsel Pilar Williams took over. On December 19, 1992, the administratrix flew to Boston to pick up the check from Drew Meyer. Williams met with Stromsten and then with Pope, both for the first time. Later, I asked Williams what was the exact amount the family had received. She told me they received between $650,000 and $700,000. Meyer got the rest.

Soon thereafter, Marcos and Epifania vacated Pilot House and moved to a leased house on Andrienne Drive in an upper middle-class neighborhood of El Paso. Williams told me the money has been "put in a trust for my parents so they'll never have to worry again." A month earlier, however, Williams had told the press that the family planned to set up the "Paul Lozano Memorial Scholarship" for worthy Mexican-American medical students, but that plan was apparently tabled.

As of January 1994, the $63,817.21 judgment had not been satisfied. Grafmillan said the Lozanos claim that Marcos's bankruptcy in 1980 wiped out the judgment. But the judgment was based on money that Marcos received more than five years after the bankruptcy.

And, as of January 1994, no tax-exempt, nonprofit corporation in the name of Paul Lozano had been established.

Bean-Bayog continues to wind down her practice, seeing only her long-term patients. As she no longer is a licensed physician, she cannot call them patients. She says she is not accepting any new "clients." Of course, she is now without malpractice insurance. As noted, psychotherapists need not be licensed.

Both she and her husband continue to have trouble sleeping. She still recoils whenever she opens her mailbox and finds a letter from a law firm. For her, television, especially the news, is an image that conjures up loathsome feelings. She admits that she winced and cringed whenever I asked her a question about the case. For the past year, I ask? Yes, she answers. She doesn't think I realize how much of a trauma victim she is. She doesn't think

I am very sensitive to what she's gone through.

Whenever I call, her son John is either crawling around in the background or sitting in her lap. She often talks to me and John in the same breath. She says sometimes she has suicidal afternoons but would never act on them. She says she is badly damaged.

For catharsis and income, she has decided to write a book, a memoir. From time to time, I think she regrets having spoken to me so extensively. She has purchased a personal computer and is learning to use it. She has already signed up with a New York literary agency but hasn't yet written a proposal to distribute to publishers. Instead, she keeps writing. She has written about 400 pages. She says she is suffering from "writer's glut." She says instead of writing a proposal, she'll just hand in the whole book. Sometimes she reads me excerpts. Some are quite moving. Her writing is full of powerful metaphors, extended imagery, psychodynamic insight, bitterness, and pain. She has become somewhat cynical. She sees many of the players in this drama as evil, yet in the next breath aptly describes their psychodynamics and forgives them. But she still bristles whenever she remembers that I once called Meyer "successful." I think she hates Drew Meyer most of all, then Pilar Williams. Lozano was too sick to blame or hate.

She decides to take a summer writing course at the Cambridge Center for Adult Education. It is literally at the beginning of my dead-end street. The title of the course is Writing from Your Own Experience.

On June 15, 1993, the first day of class, fifteen students show up and sit in chairs arranged in a circle. Her name—she has registered as Bayog, not Bean-Bayog—has not been in the news since December 1992, when the civil suit was settled. She chats with the students sitting next to her. The instructor, a former *Globe* freelancer, walks in, introduces herself and suggests that the students go around the room introducing themselves and explain why they are taking the course. One by one, they announce their names. Finally, it is her turn to speak. She clears her throat and says buoyantly: "Hi! My name is Margaret Bean-Bayog." She sees the faces all around her suddenly change expression. She starts to speak and bursts into tears.

DOCUMENTARY SOURCES

The documentary sources listed below, which are referenced in the end notes, are available to the public at only one location: The Massachusetts Board of Registration in Medicine, Ten West Street, Boston, MA 02111. A Freedom-of-Information-Act request is required.

I. Plaintiff's Offer of Proof (The 24 sections appear exactly as follows):
Introduction
1. (Process Notes) Office Records of (sic) Paul Lozano of Margaret Bean-Bayog, M.D.—July 1986—June 1990
2. Flashcards created by Margaret Bean-Bayog, M.D. for Paul Lozano to be used in conjunction with therapy
3. Children's books and children's stories authored by Margaret Bean-Bayog, M.D., which were read and given to Paul Lozano as part of therapy;
4. Letters and cards sent to Paul Lozano by Margaret Bean-Bayog, M.D.
5. Letters and cards sent to Margaret Bean-Bayog, M.D. from Paul Lozano
6. Articles on sadomasochistic sexual torture instruments, incest and sexual abuse of children, transference and substance abused (sic) discussed by Margaret Bean-Bayog, M.D. during therapy sessions with Paul Lozano
7. Sexual Fantasies authored by Margaret Bean-Bayog, M.D. read and discussed by her with Paul Lozano during therapy sessions
8. McLean Hospital (#1) Inpatient Admission of Paul Lozano— 9/24/86—11/19/86
9. McLean Hospital (#2) Inpatient Admission of Paul Lozano— 5/3/87—6/22/87
10. Faulkner Hospital (#1) Inpatient Admission of Paul Lozano— 6/22/87—7/28/87
11. Faulkner Hospital (#2) Inpatient Admission of Paul Lozano— 3/15/90—4/19/90
12. Faulkner Hospital (#3) Inpatient Admission of Paul Lozano— 4/26/90—5/02/90
13. Faulkner Hospital (#4) Inpatient Admission of Paul Lozano— 5/02/90—7/20/90
14. Consult Note of Thomas Gutheil, M.D. dated 4/09/90
15. Human Resource Institute, Outpatient Records of Paul Lozano— 5/02/90—5/08/90
16. Massachusetts Mental Health (Center), Outpatient Records of Paul Lozano —6/90—10/90
17. Malden Hospital, Inpatient Admission of Paul Lozano—9/25/90— 9/28/90

18. Massachusetts General Hospital, Outpatient Records of Paul Lozano—9/24/90—4/02/91
19. Carney Hospital, Inpatient Admission of Paul Lozano—Discharge Summary—10/05/90—11/21/90
20. Newton Wellesley Hospital, Inpatient Admission of Paul Lozano— Discharge Summary and Physicians' Notes—10/19/90—11/21/90;
21. Letter of William Barry Gault, M.D. dated 1/11/91
22. Death Certificate and Autopsy Report of Paul Lozano
23. Affidavit of Pilar Lozano Williams regarding the sexual conduct and contact of Margaret Bean-Bayog, M.D. with Paul Lozano during the course of his therapeutic treatment.
24. American Psychiatric Association Ethical Guidelines
25. Expert report of Larry H. Strasburger, M.D., a psychiatrist and expert in the field, presenting an analysis of the care rendered by the defendant, Margaret Bean-Bayog, M.D. and attached curriculum vitae.

II. Depositions

1. Margaret Bean-Bayog, M.D. on February 26, 1992; June 12, 1992; June 15, 1992; and June 16, 1992; in Boston, MA
2. Maria Pilar Williams on July 7, 1992 in El Paso, TX
3. Harrison G. Pope, Jr., M.D. on May 11, 1992 in Boston, MA
4. William Gault, M.D. on July 16, 1992 in Boston, MA
5. Frances R. Frankenburg, M.D. on May 11, 1992 in Boston, MA
6. Thomas W. Watkins, M.D. on June 23, 1992 in Columbus, OH
7. Gerald Adler, M.D. on June 18, 1992 in Boston, MA
8. Leonard Lai, M.D. on May 27, 1992 in Boston, MA
9. Jose A. Saporta, Jr., M.D. on June 24, 1992 in Boston, MA
10. Michael Lew, M.D. (sic) on June 26, 1992 in Boston MA
11. Thomas G. Gutheil, M.D. on September 12, 1992 and September 14, 1992 in Boston, MA
12. Dan H. Buie, Jr., M.D. on June 22, 1992 in Boston, MA
13. Kathryn B. Kogan, M.D. (sic) on May 20, 1992 in Boston, MA
14. Irene Fox Briggin on September 11, 1992 in Boston, MA
15. Christi L. Clark on May 14, 1992 in Boston, MA
16. Rita Falk, M.S.W. on August 25, 1992 in Boston, MA
17. Carol S. Birnbaum, M.D. on August 27, 1992 in Boston, MA
18. Nancy Butters on August 28, 1992 in Boston, MA
19. Susan Witkie, M.D. on June 9, 1992 in Boston, MA
20. Marguerite Ryan on August 28, 1992 in Boston, MA
21. Elizabeth A. Spargo, R.N. on May 22, 1992 in Boston, MA
22. Thomas Thompson on May 20, 1992 in Boston, MA

III. Records of the Massachusetts Board of Registration in Medicine: docket #91–041 (partial list):

A. Respondent's Evidentiary Submission
B. Appendix to Evidentiary Submission
C. Agreed Statement of Facts, Conclusions of Law and Jointly Recommended Sanction
D. Internal letters, including
    1. original letters of complaint by Gault and Becker
    2. letter notifying Bean-Bayog of complaint against her
    3. Blau's 5 June 1991 nine-page memorandum summarizing her defense
    4. letters in the failed negotiation for settlement
    5. Bean-Bayog's resignation letters
E. Interviews with board witnesses, including
    1. Amy Stromsten: on tape and later in memo
    2. John Collins, M.D. (name changed/privacy)
    3. Pilar Williams
    4. Abel Lozano
    5. Victor Gonzalez, M.D.
F. Articles by Paul R. McHugh, M.D.
G. Affidavits and letters of support for Bean-Bayog
H. Anonymous 14 April 1992 *Boston Globe* letter-to-editor
I. Paul Lozano's high school (Upper Sandusky and Coronado), college (West Point and U. of Texas at El Paso), and medical school records
J. Articles by Bean-Bayog
K. Data on Bean-Bayog, including
    1. Billing records for Paul Lozano
    2. Medical license renewals
    3. Conviction for operating under the influence
    4. 1989 car accident
    5. Tape of Bean-Bayog reading children's stories and flash cards to Lozano and three messages left on her answering machine
    6. Six color photographs taken by Lozano of Bean-Bayog in her office
    7. Additional materials given to Bean-Bayog by Lozano
        a. cartoons
        b. letter to Melissa King (name changed/privacy)
        c. birthday cards
        d. canceled checks for payment for therapy
        e. essay by Lozano on his professional ambitions

IV. Records of the Middlesex Superior Court: #91–06306

V. National and local print and TV news stories

END NOTES

CHAPTER 2

18: [M]anipulat[ed] him into a dangerous: Intro Offer Proof p2

18: fn: interviews/lawyers

19: Dr. Bean-Bayog employed an inappropriate: Intro Offer Proof p3

19: restraints Mr. Lozano was placed: Intro Offer of Proof p12

20: there are numerous references: Intro Offer Proof p13

20: sexual feelings on both sides very much: Intro Offer Proof p13

20: being pulled apart by her . . . slowly: Intro Offer Proof p14

20: only one of them . . . could survive: Intro to Offer Proof p17

20: sustained an irretrievable loss of: Intro Offer Proof p18

21: [P]ressing my clitoris into your mouth: Offer Proof, Section 7; Settlement Agreement

24: We should note that Paul's depression: McL Hosp#1 H-7

25: We should note that in a family meeting: McL Hosp#2, I-3,5

26: Prior to his death, my brother told: Williams affidavit, Offer Proof, Section 23

26: Based on the information which I have: Dr. Larry H. Strasburger's expert opinion, Offer Proof, Section 25

27: innumerable needle marks are noted: Lozano's autopsy, Offer Proof, Section 22

CHAPTER 3

33: "Margaret, how many other patients did you: WCVB-TV5 18Spt92

33: There weren't any "rumors or rumors: *Herald* 5Apr92

33: "an inspiring lecturer" "highest: *NYTimes* 1Apr92

33: "This is a lady who is known for being: *Herald* 1Apr92

34: "and could be heard sobbing:" *Herald* 31Mar92

CHAPTER 4

36: substandard care . . . during the course of: med board docs

36 fn1: medical board records

39: formally requesting that copies of his: In large part because of this case, in December 1993, Gov. William Weld signed a law restricting patients' access to their psychiatric records.

37–40: [Blau's statement and press release]: med board docs

40: It does appear that the publicity: [See Dr. Alan A. Stone's comments in December 1992 and his review of *You Must Be Dreaming* in *Psychiatric Times* April 1993; Dr. Jules Masserman's response to Stone's review in *Psychiatric Times* October 1993]

CHAPTER 5

43: Holland . . . had launched her initial: med brd docs

43: "confirm allegations and provide:" med brd docs

43: "sufficient reason to pursue investigation: med brd docs

43: "In any action or other civil judicial:" med brd docs

43: Holland also began reviewing Lozano's: med brd docs

43: She contacted three local psychiatrists: med board docs

45 fn: Massachusetts Medical Malpractice Joint Underwriting Association brochures.

CHAPTER 7

56 fn: In 1963, graduates of Radcliffe College: interviews / Harvard officials

59: Bean-Bayog was pulled over and arrested: med board docs

CHAPTER 8

61: Having just crossed the Rio Grande: McL Hosp#1 H-15

61: Their jalopy had expired in East Sigglington: Proc Nts A70

61: [Williams's version]: Letter to authors from Williams

61: Wyandot Mem Hospital on Route 4: P.L.'s birth certificate

61: 85% rural . . . of German descent: interviews/county officials

62: Lozanos . . . one of two Hispanic families: Flknr Hosp#1 J-75

62: only black family . . . has since moved on: interviews/ residents

62: his father, a former union activist: interview/Williams

62: [Parent's ages from bankruptcy docs in Wyandot courthouse.]

62: [Epifania] never learned to speak English . . . [Paul] refused to speak Spanish to his mother: McL Hosp#1 p17; Williams depo p190; Process Nts A-60; Carney Hosp S-1

62: [Ages of siblings are from sundry med and court rcrds]

62: [Epifania] was a 'gift,' " said Williams: *Herald* 1Apr93

62: 435 N. 4th Street: Wyandot County records

62: across . . . backyard to . . . school: interview/school officials.

62: Janice Schmidt and Mary Steiner: Proc Nts A-66 and schl records.

62: "[Paul] was an intelligent boy . . . : interview/Schmidt

63: Schmidt had . . . other memories: interviews/confidential sources

63: always felt like a misfit: McL Hosp#2 I-2

63: curly hair . . . adopted . . . never felt . . . attached: Proc Nts A-17

63: [Pilar] feels . . . much of his difficulty: McL Hosp#2 I-81

64: Brian Getz . . . "somewhat emotional": *Herald* 1Apr92

64: Debra Amos . . . "short fuse": *Globe* 12Apr92

64: Nelson Dilley . . . no hint of abuse: *Herald* 1Apr92

64: "Because I respected Paul Lozano: Steiner to authors

64 fn: Getz . . . "crazy": Process Notes A-391

64: "Paul did not stand out": phone interview with authors

65: he skipped kindergarten: *Globe* 12Apr92

65: 3 or 4 . . . read English . . . Dr. Seuss: Pilar depo, p162–3; *LATimes* 8Apr92; *Globe* 12Apr92

65: mail order a Mercedes Benz: Pilar depo p190; *NYTimes* 12Apr92

65: reading directions on . . . St. Joseph's: interview/Williams.

65: The aspirin my sister glossed over it: Process Notes A-126

65: [childhood suicide attempts]: Process Notes A-11,14; McL Hosp#1 H-6, 72; McL Hosp#2 I-2; Flknr Hosp#2 K-3, 122; *Globe* 30Mar92

66: Lozano claimed . . . parents took him to psychotherapist: interview with Bean-Bayog; Watkins depo p54–5

66: would put a few aspirin in his pocket: *Herald* 7Apr92, 12Apr92

66: "Perfect Attendance" at . . . high school: authors photographed a copy of the certificate

66: he was identified as the intelligent: Frankenburg depo p57

66: Frankenburg . . . believed . . . suicide attempts: Frankenburg depo p53

66: . . . helping . . . older siblings . . . homework: Process Notes A-17 *Globe* 12Apr92

66: suffered from boy-genius syndrome: *Herald* 1Apr92

66 fn: In the admission note: Human Resource Institute O-2

67: nerd . . . weird . . . eccentric: interviews by authors with Williams; Process Notes A-42; McL Hosp#1 H-6; *Herald* 1Apr92; *NYTimes* 12Apr92

67: [burdened by family expectations]: McL Hosp#2 I-6,64; Frankenburg depo p57

67: teased, mocked, ridiculed . . . locked in closet: Pro Nts A-17; McL Hosp#1 H-6,47; McL Hosp#2 I-13.

67: this was only the 'tip of the iceberg': McL Hosp#1 H-45

67: Paul acknowledged . . . difficulties began long before: Flknr Hosp#4 M-48,50.

67: his parents beat him and yelled: Process Notes A-392,449

67: [F]uming for hours/days: Process Notes A-53

67: When he was little . . . mice in our house: Process Notes A-53

68: imaginary friends: Process Notes A-704

68: he states he . . . heard voices since . . . very young: Flknr Hosp#4 M-44

69: You told me I had serious problems: Process Notes A-237

69: carried . . . card around . . . for two years: Process Notes A-196

69: problems could be cured in three months: interview/Bean-Bayog

69: only aspect of Lozano that was at peace: interview/Bean-Bayog; Flknr Hosp#4 M-45

69: command hallucinations: Lai's depo p36,72

69: regression therapy: *Herald* 28Mar92; WCVB-TV5 1Apr92

69: most heinous crime in all of this: *Herald* 28Mar92

70: in a deposition, she flatly denied it: Williams depo p164

70: not uncommon for young children to invent "friends": interviews/psychiatrists

70: Paul's preoccupied sealed over: Flknr Hosp#4 M-83

70: sealed over: Flknr Hosp#4 M-44

70: This morning his mother who "sees things in dreams and visions: Process Notes A-135

71: felt guilty that he did not quit school: Proc Nts A-74

71: dream of buying . . . parents a house: Proc Nts A-141,858

71: Harvard Medical School application . . . father . . . "manager": medical board records

71: stable, likable guy . . . very quiet, good-: *Herald* 1Apr92

71: release of my USMA academic records: medical board records

72: didn't . . . give us any permission to contact the family, which is unusual: Frankenburg depo p64; also see Malden Hosp P-22 -- "patient does not want family contacted"

72: govern what they would be told: McL Hosp#2 I-72

72: he was embarrassed at his family having: McL Hosp#2 I-76

72: Lozano's need to conceal and control . . . information to family: McL Hosp#1 H16,94,102–3

72: Lozano . . . refused to give [Bean-Bayog] permission to contact: Process Notes A-120, Bean-Bayog interview

72: more suicidal when he visited home: Bean-Bayog interview

72: witnessed his mother sexually abusing her grandchildren: Process Notes A-449, *Washington Post* 17Apr92

72: Russian roulette with his father's gun: Flknr Hosp#4 M-113

72: He . . . feared . . . family would strip him of: Proc Nts A-120.

72: [Patient] feels possessive of me: Process Notes A-120

73: Lozano . . . replicating his childhood: Process Notes A-93

73: [T]he patient . . . to have succeeded in exactly: McL Hosp#2 I-68

74: I have had a relationship . . . an incestuous: Adler depo p40–1

74: remembered . . . sexually abused by . . . mother: Lai depo p51

75: Can I suck my thumb? I get too excited: Proc Nts A-722–3

75: [He was] able to remember her stimulating: Proc Nts A-923–5

76: My father would make dirty jokes: Process Notes A-925

76: Retrieved memories of hating to have his hair shampooed: Process Notes A-943.

77: [I] reviewed . . . [the] severe nature of his son's illness . . . including . . . sexual abuse . . . father said he was relieved to know what the problem was: Flknr Hosp#4 M-59–60.

77: Patient . . . rigid during meeting with father: Flknr Hosp#4 M-60

77: A. I recall my father visiting my brother at the hospital: Williams depo p180

77: Q. Just so I understand, your father didn't tell you: Williams depo p181

78: No, no, no, 'it's not drugs or alcohol: *Globe* 12Apl92

78: Paul met with . . . Cheryl Izen . . . to discuss news that brother Abel: Flknr Hosp#4 M-71

78 fn: "primary therapist": Flknr Hosp#4 M-6

79: These people . . . always upbeat . . . to be a full conspiracy: Watkins depo p22

79: Paul stated he had not appreciated how much he missed: Flknr Hosp#4 M-83

79: Abel came to Boston in May 1990 to visit: med brd rcrds

79 fn: only remembers . . . Pilar, Paul, and: Watkins depo p14

81: Patient's brother Abel called from North Carolina: Flknr Hosp#4 M-91

81: utterly without a basis in reality: Gault's letter to O'Hare in Offer of Proof, Section 21; *LATimes* 8Apr92

82: [Williams] opened the meeting . . . she went on to say: McL Hosp#2 I-75

CHAPTER 9

83: Pilar . . . town belle . . . movie star: interviews/residents

83: [Pilar] felt more like my mother. [It's a] good thing she was there: Process Notes A-237

83: "nothing in common: Williams letter to author.

83: In March 1969 . . . Williams's sweetheart impregnated: birth certificates and interviews

83: quiet, well liked, and willing to marry her: not-for-attribution interview with city official and classmate.

84: occupation "case worker" . . . "teacher": the child's birth certificate

84: vacant lot . . . for $2,500: county rcrds and interviews

86: "the kind of boy . . . other kids model after: *El Paso Herald-Post* 25Apr92

86: [Lozano's high-school accomplishments in Upper San-dusky]: Upper Sandusky high school records

86: [Outside high-school accomplishments]: certificates and awards in Williams's possession shown to authors

86: "room and board, medical . . . monthly pay": West Point records

86: 1978–79 student council president was Pam Williams: also confirmed by high-school principal.

86: "who stuck a few local people financially": interviews/ local residents

87: [In] my culture . . . [it's] more important to please: Process Notes A-115

87: Before I didn't kill [my]self for . . . parents: Proc Nts A-21

87: When Dad took us to El Paso . . . other brothers: Proc Nts A-124

87: [Lozano's high-school records in El Paso]: Coronado High School records

87: [Lozano's] not even in the . . . yearbook: *El Paso Herald-Post* 25Apr92

87: Lozano did befriend . . . Castellanos: *NYTimes* 12apr92

87: thirty-two days after their . . . graduation: Coronado High School and West Point records

88: [I] kicked [my]self . . . went to West Point: Proc Nts A-173

88: attention to detail . . . when speaking in a: West Pnt rcrds

88: I hated it, really hated it . . . When I was: Proc Notes A-6

88: [They were] good at making beds: Proc Notes A-485

88: On 2 November, 1981 I contacted Mrs. Williams: West Point rcrds

89: I left feeling a failure . . . my mother [was] crying: Proc Notes A-21,68

89: materials handler at Farah Slacks: Harvard Med Schl application

89: [My mother] reminded me I was a factory worker: Proc Nts A-21

89: West Texas Higher Education Authority . . . $9,500: med
    board records

89: During the last year I have worked as a volunteer for 5 hours:
    med brd rcrds

90: very quiet and a very good student: *NYTimes* 12Apr92

90: She was 27; Lozano was 21: marriage certificate

90: when [Paul] transferred to U. Texas: McL Hosp#1 H-48, 15

91: [O]ne of [my] sister called her: Process Notes A-4

91: married by gospel minister David J.: El Paso court rcrds

91: I found it extremely curious that he would: *El Paso Herald-
    Post* 25Apr92

91: Lozano expressed bitterness over his family's pressure: McL
    Hosp#1 H-7,15,16,48; McL Hosp#2 I-66;

91: Why do I feel this desolation?: Process Notes A-320–1

92: the marriage was a ruse to help Halperin get into Harvard:
    Herald 1Apr92, 5Apr92; *NYTimes* 12Apr92; Williams depo
    p197–203

92: applications . . . October 17, 1983: med schl rcrds

92: February 15, 1984 . . . marriage annulled: El Paso court rcrds

93: Dear Paul: Remember there are many people who care: *Her-
    ald* 5Apr92; photographed by authors at Williams's home

93: In 1988, Halperin graduated from U. of Texas at Houston
    Medical School: phone interview with Texas med brd

93: Boston City Hospital for four-year residency: state med rcrds
    and interviews with hospital personnel.

94: "I loved him. I loved him": interview with hospital personnel

94: Halperin moved to another New England state where: Free-
    dom of Information Act; nearby state med brd rcrds; inter-
    views

94: [His] sister introduces him to . . . nurse . . . to cocaine: Pro-
    cess Notes A-921.

95: Well, the one thing that I remember . . . there was a young
    woman . . . nurse . . . and this nurse and cocaine were sort of
    linked up: Gault depo p196

95: This is a difficult letter to write: confidential source

95 fn: six years older . . . blue eyes . . . 190 pounds: Dept of
    Public Safety in Austin, Texas.

96: recovering from surgery: Williams depo p210

96: [Paul] told me . . . discovered some prescription medications: Williams depo p212–213

CHAPTER 10

98: This statement enraged Stromsten: *El Paso Herald-Post* 2Apr92

102: Levy . . . launching a lawsuit against Stromsten: med brd docs

102: "the first two weeks of January 1991:" taped interview

102: "mysteriously lost.": *Harvard Crimson* 4Apr92

102: board . . . acknowledged . . . her letter: *Herald* 5Apr92, 6Apr92

102: [T]o her knowledge, Mr. Lozano's problem was: *NYTimes* 2Apr92

103: If Lozano was sexually abused as a child: *LATimes* 8Apr92

103: Stromsten . . . suspects . . . covering up: *Harvard Crimson* 3Apr92

103: Paul was scapegoated in the family and appears to have suffered emotional abuse: McL Hosp#1 H-16

104: When he told his parents . . . very upset: McL Hosp#2 I-65

104: I met with Victor Gonzalez: McL Hosp#1 H-47

105: My impression was . . . some family trouble there: *Herald* 7Apr92

105: Major affective disorder, depressed, without melancholia, and without psychotic features, probably: McL Hosp#1 H-4

105: A social worker who filed an affidavit in court last week: *Globe* 9Apr92

105: After that, the mystery witness dropped from sight: interview/Stromsten

CHAPTER 12

111: Didn't want to come . . . [I was] married and annulled. . . . Embarrassed. No one knows: Process Notes A-1-4

112: [He] saw me two years ago. "[I've been] thinking about treatment since: Process Notes A-5

112: he sued the driver and won a $55,000 out of court settlement: Appendix to Respondent's Evidentiary Submission, Section 4.

112: when his apartment was burglarized . . . retaliation for his filing a false insurance claim: interview/Bean-Bayog

112: reached his limit, been drunk a lot . . . to get anesthetized: Process Notes: A-6,7

112: his job was to kill with lethal injection: Proc Nts A-9

112: Another bad habit. Stuffed animals. Very: Proc Nts A-9

113: Shame. Wish to be a puppy: Process Notes A-11

113: Each time [a suicidal desire] came: Process Notes A-13

113: Previous suicide attempts untreated: Process Notes A-15

114: If I go running in park, woods, if: Proc Nts A-18

114: Lite Salt (KCL) and was contemplating: Proc Nts A-23,25,31

114: It doesn't matter if it's sterile if: Proc Nts A-31

114: reading veterinary journals learning how to painlessly kill large animals: Proc Nts A-31

114: Don't expect to live to my dad's age: Proc Nts A-30–31

115: like it was all hilarious, horrible things, went to bathroom and roared: Process Notes A-16,17

115: half [my] brain splattered . . . wallpaper: Proc Nts: A-49

115: Skulls break in very characteristic places: Proc Nts A-31

115: Furious. Feel[s] good to say, 'Fuck you: Proc Nts A-21–25

115: diagnosed with a major recurrent: McL Hosp#1 H-4

116: urinary retention: McL Hosp#1 H-35

116: prognosis was only fair and Frankenburg . . . urged him to put off his psychiatric rotation: McL Hosp#1 H-4

116: I agree to reimburse Dr. Margaret Bean-Bayog: Appendix to Respondent's Evidentiary Submission, Section 7

117: six checks . . . $ 1,535. And in July 1989 . . . a $9,000 check . . . outstanding balance was . . . $25,692: med brd rcrds

117: [He] mention[ed] having sexual feelings outside office: Process Notes A-38

117: a list of instructions, reminding him not: Proc Nts A-38

117: Patient made the blanket in my office into a transitional object: Process Notes A-40

117: makes me feel sick to my stomach: Process Notes A-42

118: Patient may be telling Dr. Pope I told him to discontinue drugs: Process Notes A-45

118: Patient came in . . . with a bag of intravenous equipment and drugs: Process Notes A-45

118: Still [had] substantial suicidal impulses and thoughts: Process Notes A-47

119: Describing his reaction to my first weekend away when he shot up trilafon: Process Notes A-53

119: went on vacation, Lozano felt abandoned and rejected, in creasing his suicidal: Flknr Hosp#1 J-26,34,73,123,124; Flknr Hosp#2 K-59,61,67,69,73,76,102; Flknr Hosp#3 L-16,31; Flknr Hosp#4 M-62,76,112,113,115,126,128,139, 143,149; *Washington Post* 17Apr92

119: 12:30 am. Patient called slightly drunk . . . from the 13th floor: Process Notes A-80

120: his confinement in four-point restraints: Proc Nts A-80

120: informed his family . . . of his prior admission . . . allowed them to visit: Process Notes A-112,114; McL Hosp#1 H-16, 28,40,65; McL Hosp#2 I-64,71,71

120: Frankenburg raised . . . issue of her possible overinvolve ment: Proc Nts A-93

120: What do they know? . . . They may have a point: Proc Nts A-84

120: Drs. Dan H. Buie, Jr. and Gerald Adler: Process Nts A-93

120: Dr. Shervert Frazier: Process Notes A-147

121: Frankenburg refused to discuss with Lozano why he wanted to feel like a 3-year old: interview/Bean-Bayog

121: Met with Dr. Frankenburg who was concerned I was over involved: Process Notes A-91–93

123: "dumping": Lozano's niece, Coral Grossman in *Globe* 1Apr92

123: couldn't tell if his Mom was also his: Proc Nts A-66

123: [Psychological Damage Associated with Extreme Eroticism in Young Children]: Process Notes A-95–99

124: Article given to patient: Process Notes A-95

125: they were her own very private way of dealing with a power-ful countertransference, and learning from it: [For discussion of countertransference with borderline and sexual abused patients, see the following: "An Overview of Countertransference with Borderline Patients" by Glen O. Gabbard, M.D. in *Journal of Psychotherapy Practice and Research*, Winter 1993; "The Concept of Boundaries in Clinical Practice: Theoretical and Risk-Management Dimen sions" by Thomas G. Gutheil, M.D. and Glen O. Gabbard, M.D. in *American Journal of Psychiatry*, February 1993; "Psychotherapists Who Transgress Sexual Boundaries With Patients" by Glen O. Gabbard, M.D. in the *Bulletin of the Menninger Clinic*, October 1992; and "Sexual Misconduct by Female Therapists: The Love Cure Fantasy" by Glen O. Gabbard, M.D. in *The Psychodynamic Letter*, June 1991.]

125: Just gets bent over all the time. Gets fucked: Proc Nts A-145–6

125: lying, covering up sexual abuse: Process Notes A-132

125: May 26 family meeting: [Dr. Frankenburg's version] McL Hosp#2 I-2,3,75; [Lozano's version] Process Notes A-123 31; [nurse's version] McL Hosp#2 I-75

125: Williams emphatically denied that her brother had been abused in any way: McL Hosp#2 I-75

126: Intense reaction to split between hospital staff buying his family version: Process Notes A-123–26

126: I am doing better with my parents. Before I'd call and lie . . . Now . . . don't call: [This is not found in the version submitted by Meyer, but found in Bean-Bayog's original version, which I saw in Blau's office.]

126: I guess you lie. I do. I've gotten into the habit of lying: Process Notes A-458

126: falsified research data, shoplifted, stolen books from the Countway Medical Library (which has elaborate security), had done "a little breaking and entering" while on vacation in Texas, drove drunk without insurance or registration, and thought about running a child prostitution ring: Process Notes A-397,670,671,755,817,827; interview/Bean-Bayog

126 fn: Bean-Bayog omitted her 1984 drunk driving conviction from her 1986 and 1987 . . . license renewals: med brd rcrds

127: Note on P.L.'s Suicide Risk: Process Notes A-275–86

127: Go ahead. Break your ass trying to get me better. I'll watch a while: Process Notes A-198

CHAPTER 13

128: his prognosis as "extremely guarded: McL Hosp#2 I-6

128: on a brief pass for ice cream: McL Hosp#2 I-242

128: escape status: McL Hosp#2 I-140

128: refused a toxic screen: McL Hosp#2 I-242

129: second time in a week that McLean had placed Lozano on escape status: McL Hosp#2 I-135

129: [I] can speculate what happened with your mother: Process Notes A-237

129: give up on the boy. Please keep hugging: Proc Nts A-248

129: I was really angry with you: Process Notes A-297

129: described wanting to put me in restraints: Proc Nts A-297

130: Maybe what's happening now . . . what happened . . . when . . . little: Proc Nts A-298–9

130: I'm glad I talked to you about this: Proc Nts A-305–6

130: When you were talking . . . boy wasn't real: Proc Nts A-291

131: review use of transitional objects to comfort: Proc Nts A-328

131: Reviewed safety . . . he can feel anything and talk about the feelings but [we must] keep boy safe: Process Notes A-332

132: He brought Pound Puppy to show me: Process Notes A-343

132: strange countertransference reaction: Process Notes A-360

133: Only three year olds get to play: Process Notes A-374–5

134: [I] shared mother-child incest fantasy: Proc Nts A-375

134: Don't wanna talk to you: Process Notes A-376

134: Acting aroused. "I'm having a day dream: Proc Nts A-398

135: spent [the Labor Day] weekend with: Proc Nts A-405–6

136: I had a specific fantasy about you: Proc Nts A-409–10

136: sexual feelings on both sides are much: Intro Offer Proof p13

136: sexual feelings on both sides are common: Proc Nts A-410

136: the seventeen letters she had written in advance: Offer of Proof; Settlement Agreement

137: P[aul] L[ozano], Keep yourself safe: Process Notes A-415

137: I'm just *worthless*: Process Nts A-420

137: I get so angry at self. I hate it: Proc Nts A-436–7

138: stands on the lawn just outside a: authors' visit

138: didn't want to talk to you about: Process Notes A-449–50

139: I did something else. I took the folder: Proc Nts A-573

140: [I'm] angry at Dr. Frankenburg: Process Notes A-574–5

141: threatening to shoot McLean staff: Process Nts A-611–15

142: he instructed McLean to forward them: McL Hosp#2 I-156

142: More storm about reading the discharge: Proc Nts A-621–4

144: I guess I'm not a very nice person: Proc Nts A-506–7

144: two cartoons: med brd rcrds

144 fn: Relieved. Gave back fantasy: Process Notes A-948

145: Seeing you wakes . . . internal longings: Proc Nts A-636–39

145: grabbed his "blanket" and became more: Proc Nts A-639

146: Notice I get really angry about: Process Notes A-641–2

146: *very* suicidal, ...finally cajoled: Proc Nts A-652–54

147: [I feel] guilty about hurting you: Proc Nts A-658–9

147: [We] read flashcard set. [We] read: Process Notes A-663

147: [We] made . . . flashcards about distortions: Proc Nts A-663

148: I think you're my mom. Right: tape in med brd rcrds

148: Do I love you? Yes, absolutely: tape in med brd rcrds

148: back-up arrangements at the Faulkner: Proc Nts A-661–2

149: scheduled two phone conversations: Proc Nts A-674–5

149: met for the first time after her: interview/Bean-Bayog

149: Can I suck my thumb? I get too excited: Proc Nts A-722–3

149: [I] want to really *have* sex with you: Proc Nts A-850–1

150: he wanted to kill Collins: interview/Bean-Bayog

150: I feel compelled to inform you: Process Notes A-877–80

151: persuaded her patient not to mail: interview/Bean-Bayog
151: other scientists who collaborated: med brd rcrds
151: [I] saw Pope. The other guy knew: Process Notes A-856–63
152: left [him] in parking lot at McLean: Process Notes A-900
152: left the grounds and took a bus: interview/Bean-Bayog
152: [He had] angry, rape fantasy, locking: Proc Nts A-895
153: More elaboration of [his] confusion: Proc Nts A-919–20

CHAPTER 14

156: Lozano suffered a breakdown after: Flknr Hosp#2 K-8
157: Since his discharge from his first admission: Flknr Hosp#2
K-106–10.
158: BEAN-BAYOG'S NOTES CONVEY . . . FANTASIES:
Globe 5Apr92
160: [I] talked with patient's sister: McL Hosp#2 I-81
160: "Another thing we take great exception to: *Herald* 1Apr92
161: Bean-Bayog had insisted Lozano join impaired: Proc Nts
A-960,968,971,976; Flknr Hosp#2 K-64–5.
161: pounded on her doors and windows: Process Notes A-966
161: to more than $25,000: med board docs
161: a four-month maternity leave: Human Resource Ctr Inst
O-2; Process Notes A-976; Flknr Hosp#4 M-56; *Herald*
8Apr92; *Washington Post* 17Apr92
162: two Hollywood production companies: *Herald* 2Apr92,
7Apr92, 17Apr92, 23Apr92, 5May92
162: "What you're getting now in the press: *Globe*12Apr92

CHAPTER 16

175: "not a very high-priority case . . . ": speech before Massachusetts Continuing Law Education forum, 10Feb93
176: September 1990 . . . $52,000-a-year: interview
176 fn: "devote a significant portion of its:" Task Force doc,
January 1992, p9
177 fn: "explore whether expertise and time:" Task Force doc,
January 1992, p13

178: received requests for credentials from scores: interview Michelle Haynes

178: "[It's] one of the things that has:" *Herald* 14Spt92

179: have her read her sexual fantasies: confidential interviews

CHAPTER 17

181: As of today I am resigning my license: med brd rcrds

185: This is to respectfully request that: med brd rcrds

190: What [Bean-Bayog] asked for: *Globe* and *Herald* 19Spt92

191: to provide for an orderly transition of: med brd rcrds

191 fn: Bean-Bayog received a letter from her insurer terminating: interview/Bean-Bayog

192: It appears that Margaret Bean-Bayog has: *Globe* 19Spt92

CHAPTER 18

194: matter was handed over to Richard Waring: med brd rcrds

194: had graduated college from Johns Hopkins: *Martindale-Hubbell Law Directory*, 1986, Vol. 3, p1831b

194: Waring decided to call his alma: interview/Fleming

194: Fabiano . . . was free to hire his own expert: interview/Fabiano

195 fn: If discussions with Blau and Mone lead: med brd rcrds

200 fn: The institute expressed its continued: institute brochure

201: who had been paid about $11,000 in public: med brd rcds

202: For [McHugh] to discuss psychotherapy: interview/Gutheil

202 fn: Understanding the brain—that is: *Baltimore Sun* 1Aug91

204 fn: To treat for repressed memories: *Psychiatric Times* August 1993

206: The responsibility of a public prosecutor differs: Andrew Kaufman's *Problems in Professional Responsibility*, 1976, Code of Professional Responsibility, Canon 7, p675

CHAPTER 19

210: indicates that the patient-physician: Intro Offer Proof p14

210: Being pulled apart, by me, slowly: Process Notes A-195

211: Patient (Paul) made the blanket in: Intro Offer Proof p9

211: However, the actual citation, reads: Process Notes: A-40

211: [He was] calmed, much comforted by: Process Notes A-71

212: Had family meeting today including: Flknr Hosp#1 J-37

213: In the Malden Hospital admission: Intro Offer Proof p17

213: In this relationship there were a number: Malden Hosp Q-4

214: apparent to Dr. Frances Frankenburg:Intro Offer Proof p10

215: discussed at length with the therapist: McL Hosp#2 I-3

215: The patient shouldn't lose you, for good: McL Hosp#2 I-3

216: However, he and Dr. Bean-Bayog are: McL Hosp#2 I-7

216: a very administrative one: Frankenburg depo p48

216: Lozano's health insurance picked up some: med brd rcrds

216: Bean-Bayog reported that she talked Lozano: Proc Nts A-68

217: Lozano told Bean-Bayog that if she had: Proc Notes A-68

217: her brother told her he had never called Bean-Bayog from: In an official medical board memorandum, Fabiano wrote, "[Williams] says that . . . Paul gave a quite different version of the May 3 13th floor episode. He told Pilar that he had three beers before he called Bean-Bayog. He said that at that time they were physically involved. He was upset because Bean-Bayog would no longer see him. He called her to urge her to meet him. They met, and she told him that she wanted to take him to McLean 'to check him out.' There never was, according to Pilar, any suicide threat. When Paul arrived at McLean, he became fearful that Bean-Bayog was going to commit him. He tried to flee and was restrained."

217: This 'overinvolvement' was noted: Intro Offer Proof p11

217 fn: In the 13th floor rooms, there are radiators: med brd rcrds

218: Psychopharmacological evaluation: McL Hosp#2 I-15

218: Dr. Bean-Bayog employed an inappropriate course of treatment: Intro Offer of Proof p7

218 fn: This is not the only case in which Meyer's ethics have been questioned: [See article by Mark Jerkowitz in *Boston Phoenix* 1May92; also see Ilona Laszlo Higgins M.D.

vs Andrew C. Meyer, Jr., et al. in US District Court for District of Hawaii, civil #90–00679 DAE]

CHAPTER 20

220: Stromsten said she had called: *Harvard Crimson* 4Apr92

221: If she knew about sexual misconduct: *Harvard Crimson* 4Apr92

221: "the first two weeks of January 1991,": med brd rcrds, taped interview/Stromsten on April 8, 1992 with Richard Waring and Barbara Cullen

221: [In January 1991,] I called the National: same interview

221: [Stromsten] said that the people at: Pope depo p47–48

222: the far tip of Gloucester: med brd taped interview/Stromsten

222: "not to my knowledge" had he ever met: Pope depo p8

222: had no evidence of [Bean-Bayog's] overinvolvement: med brd rcrds, confidential "work product," not available to public

222: I called Michael Lew afterwards: med brd rcrds, 8Apr92 taped interview/Stromsten

223: told me that Paul had committed suicide and: Lew depo p15

223: I told her at the time that, basically, I: Lew depo p16

223: "verify" ... "was clearly sexually abused: Stromsten's April 1, 1992 affidavit

223: Adler had no idea that Paul Lozano was the patient: Adler depo p42; interview/Bean-Bayog

224: You know, I really have to talk with you: Adler depo p40–1

224: Blau cited this anecdote as an independent: interview/Blau

224: left a message on Adler's answering: Adler depo 32–3

224: Out of compassion, Adler gave Lozano a passing: Adler depo 45

224: Adler expressed a formulation: Adler p73–6

224: that his therapist or former therapist: Adler depo p75

225: Stromsten induced Pilar Williams, a woman: Interview/Pilar

225: Tom O'Hare ... asked Lozano how he had: Interview/O'Hare

225 fn: We will never know [whether they had sex]: O'Hare's
   interview in *Psychiatric News* 5Feb93, p6–7
226: used to be the in-house counsel at McLean: interview/
   O'Hare
226: a lawsuit for malpractice and wrongful death was pending
   against his wife: Norfolk County Superior Court records
226: Pope . . . ministered to Lozano at least: Pope depo p20–2,39
226: My memory is that I wrote a note: Pope depo p38
226: I made it clear that I was available should: Pope depo p18
226: I do not specifically remember such questions: Pope depo
   p18
227: April of 1988, a year after his second McLean's: Pope depo
   p31
227: I confess that Paul and I had visions: Pope depo p32–3
228: when I got a call from Amy Stromsten in: Pope depo p47
228: The psychopharmacologist is Dr. Pope: Flknr Hosp#1
   J-36
228: Dr. Osser suggested . . . start lithium: Flknr Hosp#1 J-40
228: Discharged to home today. Follow up: Flknr Hosp#1 J-43
229: Re: Lithium. Dr. Pope plans to: Process Nts A-339
229: Pope's name is mentioned seven more times: A-339
   (28Jul87), A-345 (4Aug87), A-812 (9Mar88), A-830
   (22Mar88), A-837 (28Mar88), A-838 (30Mar88), A-839
   (31Mar88), A-843 (2Apr88)
229: Patient used Dr. Pope for psychopharmac: Proc Nts A-228
230: People from [the] Southwest like horses: Proc Notes A-863
230: Pope's daughter does indeed have a white pony: interview/
   local equestrian
230: Wants to stop desipramine. Decreases: Process Nts A-953
231: Off desipramine 24 hours. Getting drunk: Proc Nts A-957
231: referred by Dr. Skip Pope at McLean: Mass. Mental Health
   Center P-37
231: I do not believe that I ever formally: Pope depo p17
232: I hardly knew her. She remembered me: Pope depo p49
232: One more time. She followed my suggestion: Pope depo p49
232 fn: In 1982 . . . Meyer moved . . . to a magnificent: Middlesex Registry of Deeds; Concord Assessing Dept

232 fn: The mansion's most striking: confidential sources
233: [Stromsten] said that she had talked to: Pope depo p49–50
233: who is notorious for working at a: confidential sources
233: had died with unpaid bills to credit card: med brd rcrds
233: "Polara": McL Hosp#1 H-16; McL Hosp#2 I-26–7
233: which contain the home address of Marcos: McL Hosp#2 I-18
234: Williams told Fabiano that Stromsten called her about: med brd rcrds, Williams interviewed by Fabiano on 10Aug92

CHAPTER 25

285: warned . . . O'Hare in her February 4, 1991 letter: Med brd rcds
285: has always stopped himself or called: Flknr Hosp#4 M-12
285: burial by the Martin Funeral home: Lozano's death certif
285: spoken by father Ricardo Rodriquez: interviews at church
286: possible that his son had taken: El Paso police report
286: In her July 1992 deposition, when asked: Williams depo p169
286: risk taker. He liked to toy with death: Flknr Hosp#2 K-32; interview/Bean-Bayog
286: he could simply turn off the air: Process Nts A-18
287: My M.D. would stand for Monster Doc: Process Notes A717; interviews/Bean-Bayog
287: He reports . . . injecting . . . ketamine: Flknr Hosp#2 K-34,120
287: he felt terrible shame about: Process Notes 106
288: leaving a suicide note: Process Notes A-75
288: a note [was] found on [Lozano's] bed: El Paso police report
288: "me' . . . "neurotic nag" . . . "take care of yourself": these are visible in the police photographs
288: "skin popping,": Dr. Stan Kessler, medical examiner
288: Innumerable needle marks are: Lozano's autopsy report
288: also needle marks on Lozano's feet: El Paso police report
288: "Fresh" means . . . if: Dr. Stan Kessler, medical examiner
288: Lidocaine . . . adulterate: Stan Kessler, medical examiner

289: Otolaryngologists and ophthalmologists: Dr. Chafetz et al

289: Cocaine can kill in high: Stan Kessler, medical examiner

289 fn: often reported . . . that many: Kessler, medical examiner

289 fn: Marks are scars . . . tuberculin-: Kessler, med examiner

290: April 1 letter from Dr. Kevin T. Allen: Police photos

290: family's claim that he was not a habitual: *Globe* 1Apr92, 5Apr92; *Herald* 2Apr92;

290: the third year of medical school is particularly stressful: "Increased clinical responsibility may evoke feelings centered on caretaking, sexuality and aggression that cannot be contained by an as yet fragile emerging profes sional identification," wrote Dr. Michael H. Sacks in the American Journal of Psychiatry.

290: A number of studies . . . third year of medical school . . . activate . . . dormant psychological problems: *Globe* 11Apr92

290: Bean-Bayog . . . if he had stuck to: interview/Bean-Bayog

290 fn: *NYTimes*: "surely one of the major detectives since Chandler's Philip Marlowe.": stated on book cover

290 fn: Dr. Collins . . . believed Lozano was: med brd rcrds

291: Even Williams acknowledged . . . decline: interview/Williams

291: Dr. Gerald Adler . . . gave Lozano a passing: med brd rcrds

291: After discussing the termination of therapy, on and off, for seven months, Bean-Bayog finally ended therapy: Process Notes A-959,960,968,974,985,986; Flknr Hosp#2 K-43,49, 50,63,64,65,70,73,90; Flknr Hosp#4 M-59,60,61,66, 82,-115,125,187;

292: We've done an incredible piece of work: Offer Proof; Settlement agreement

292: I love you. I loved working with you. I want you to stay alive and get well: Offer Proof; Settlement agreement

292: Lozano did not bond with his: Malden Hosp Q-3,8

292: He was also seen on an out-patient basis at: Offer Proof

292: In his final Boston-area hospitalization . . . bond: Newton Wellesley Hosp T-3; Williams depo p236,243,252

293: [Lozano] floated in an out . . . psychosis: Saporta depo p58

293: When deeply depressed patients ... their risk of suicide may increase: Dr. Chafetz and other psychiatrists

293: fails, the choice would be ECT or fluox: McL Hosp#1 H-35

293: To feel well, I would do whatever the: McL Hosp#1 H-90

294: whenever he was home on vacation, his agony and thoughts of suicide: Process Notes A-40,45; interviews/Bean-Bayog

294: admitted to the psychiatric ward of the Sun Valley: Med brd rcrds -- Appendix Respondents Evidentiary Submission

294: was taking two powerful drugs: *Herald* 6Apr92

294: hearing on the complaint against: O'Hare/interview

294: Mr. Lozano has been my patient since October 19: med brd rcrds

295: terrified of failing upcoming boards: Saporta depo p48

295: Dr. Marquez told me Paul said he was going: *Herald* 1Apr92

295: this patient ... wanted to shoot himself with a gun: Sun Valley med rcrds in Appendix Respondent's Evidentiary Sub

296: [Patient states [that he] got anxious: Sun Valley medical rcrds in Appendix to Respondent's Evidentiary Submission.

297: Paul ever threaten suicide? A. Never: Williams depo p168 71

298: Paul ... called his sister to tell her of:McL Hosp#2 I-210

298: [I] met with patient ... to discuss the: McL Hosp#2 I-72

299: "My sister called yesterday ... I guess: Process Nts A-181

299: [The] social worker from McLean: Proc Nts A-232–3

300: her brother was released into: Sun Valley Med rcrds

300: Williams stated that he was taken to: Williams depo p179

300: Lozano resided in a room about a hundred feet from his parents' unit: Lozano lived in unit #15 according to police photographs and author's personal visit to site.

301: that half way through her depo: Williams depo p70–71

302: Paul sounded revved up: Gault depo p195

302: sounded manic, with pressured speech: Gault depo p114–5

303: I was worried about his condition: Gault depo p116–7

303: The next day it was Williams who called Gault to report that her brother: Gault depo p117; interview/Williams

303: The night before Lozano died, he dined on: *Herald* 1Apr92

303: Lozano had paged Gault all day. Finally: Gault depo p116
303: Lozano took a shower . . . spritzed: *Herald* 27Mar92, 29Mar92
303: He then associated [his suicide] to his: Proc Notes A-49
304: Near the body, the police found a blood-:police photos
304: knock at the door at 9 P.M: police report
304: Marcos discovered his son's body: police report
304: put on his best clothes and injected: *Herald* 27Mar92
304: He had everything (needle, injection: *Herald* 1Apr92
305: family claimed to have found a baby: *People* 20Apr92
305: Large quantities of Lithium and Haldol: autopsy report
305: near the maximum of their suggested: *Herald* 6Apr92
305: irreversible brain damage and: Kessler, medical examiner.
305: However, This is impossible to: Kessler, medical examiner
306: two-day exam in Boston, from 8 A.M. to 5.m: interview/ National Board of Medical Examiners in Philadelphia, PA
306: a gift from my son. I feel at peace now: interview/ Williams
306 fn: the exam, which was given again in September, 1991: interview/National Board of Medical Examiners in Philadelphia, PA

CHAPTER 26

307: I didn't want to see my mom hurt: Process Notes A-125
308: Exposure of Mr. Lozano to the psychiatric material: Appendix Respondent's Evidentiary Submission, Section 18

CHAPTER 27

310: In June 1984, she was stopped and arrested: Med brd rcrds
310: In 1984, she had just gotten married for the first at the age of 41: marriage certificate; interview/Bean-Bayog
310: with several bottles of "California: interview/Bean Bayog
310: her blood alcohol was 1.9, she wasn't: interview/Bean Bayog
310: failure to drive in the right-hand lane: med brd rcrds
311: The medical board had included this minor: med brd rcrds

311: Meyer had advanced the theory: interview/Meyer
312: In the early afternoon of June 5, 1989: med brd rcrds; interview/Dwelling
312: I show you a picture and ask you: Bean-Bayog depo p100–6
314: Would you consider the demeanor as portrayed in that photograph appropriate: Bean-Bayog depo p233
314: Also expressed some terrible sadness: Proc Nts A-576
315: "Restless," "Morning," "Cookies," "Fishing," "Pie," and "Shots.": Offer of Proof; Settlement Agreement
315: This drives me *nuts*: Offer Proof; Settlement Agreement
316 fn: At the 37th Annual Meeting of the American Academy of Psychoanalysis in San Francisco: *Psychiatric Times* Jul93
318: Only three year olds get to play like: Proc Nts A-374–5
320: I'd touch you everywhere, running my: Proc Nts A-623
320: Then, at last, not caring, you: Offer Proof; Settle Agreement

CHAPTER 28

326: it is inconceivable that coverage would: *Globe* 13Apr92
326: Bradlee defended the coverage for: interview/Bradlee
326: We leaned over backward to make sure her: *Globe* 13Apr92
326: I am writing to express the conviction: med brd rcrds
327 fn: [See *Anne Sexton* by Diane Wood Middlebook, 1991, Houghton Mifflin Co.]
327 fn: I didn't want to ruin [his] career: *NYTimes* 15Jul91
327 fn: I am not going to comment: *NYTimes* 15Jul91
327 fn: some psychiatrists . . . lost their: WHDH-TV7 11&12Feb93
327 fn: Dr. Goldberg is currently: Hawaii: confidential source
328 fn: A 1990 survey of 10,000: *Psychiatric Times* Oct92
329: one of approximately 9,000 physicians: *Washington Post* 17Apr92
329 fn: At the time the charges were leveled against Bean Bayog: *Harvard Crimson* 4Apr92; interview/Bean-Bayog

EPILOGUE

333: In 1978, he sold a house on Edgewood Drive for $32,000 to Roger and Judith Sears: Wyandot County court records

333: In September 1985, they decided to discharge the remaining: Wyandot Country court records; interview/Grafmillan

333: obtain a "foreign judgment": El Paso court rcrds

334: moved to a leased house on Andrienne: forwarding address through Freedom of Info Act by El Paso post office

334: in an upper middle-class neighborhood of El: interview/ Sgt. Bill Pfeil, public info officer, El Paso police dept

334: As of January 1994, the $63,817.21: interview/Grafmillan

334: as of January 1994, no tax-exempt: interview/Eduardo Mercado, spokesman Exempt Organizations IRS, Dallas, TX

335: registered as Bayog, not Bean-Bayog: confidential source

335: [The former *Globe* freelancer was Mopsy Strange Kennedy]